13TH GRADE

Real World 101

Always be learning

DANIEL G. HOFSTEIN

ISBN 978-1-7322375-1-3

CSTINSC, Las Vegas, NV

Edited by a CreateSpace team (an Amazon affiliate),
Melissa Carmean, and Daquan Jackson

Email danoventuresllc@gmail.com for any and all questions.

To you, the reader. I hope this helps.

Contents

Part Five: Miscellaneous

Part Six: Conclusion

Acknowledgments

Many talk, but few are up for the call to action.
Thank you.

I HAVE LEANED ON MANY people throughout the creation of this book. Each chapter was vetted by professionals to ensure that the information contained therein was not taken out of context and was not missing an incredibly important aspect (as well as for general accuracy and understanding).

Being the first to join a movement, stand up for someone, or help with a project takes far more courage than being the last to do so. It is easy to help others when doing so is popular (or you may receive a financial reward, fame, or otherwise). The following are just some of the people who I consider to have stood up for me and helped a no-name author on his first book:

CHAPTER 2: MONEY
Benjamin Epstein, marketing and finance professional
Siddarth Jain, finance professional
Aaron Sigal, finance professional

CHAPTER 3: COLLEGE (OR NOT COLLEGE)
Rebecca Troianos, high school career counselor

CHAPTER 4: JOBS
Anonymous, recruiter
Ashley Cottrell, recruiter

Chapter 5: Credit and Large Purchases

Tyler Gregory, credit specialist

Robert Torch, real estate agent

Chapter 6: Taxes

Cort Arlint, certified public accountant

Chapter 7: Economics

Raul Izquierdo, credit risk and analysis professional

Chapter 8: Sex

Jonah Zachary Lavitt, dating and intimacy coach

Chapter 9: Parenting

Shanee Moas, family and marriage therapist

Chapter 10: Generational Differences and Similarities

Sumer Azam, anthropology and religion major

Chapter 11: Laws

Anonymous, attorney

Derron Woodfork, criminal defense attorney

Chapter 12: The Bill of Rights Applied

Anonymous, attorney

Derron Woodfork, criminal defense attorney

Chapter 13: Last Will and Testament

Anonymous, attorney

Derron Woodfork, criminal defense attorney

Chapter 14: Politics

Andy Bookman, political professional and registered voter

Bryan Griffin, political professional and registered voter

Jeffrey Kelman, political activist and registered voter

Courtney Kravitz, nonprofit fundraiser, political activist, and registered voter

Vincent Rennie, registered voter

Johanna Zarur, French law student

CHAPTER 15: DRUGS

Kayti Ellis, former drug rehab center employee (intern), human services (counseling education) major, and addiction treatment minor

Sanna Malick, former synthetic organic chemistry researcher

Joshua Schorr, emergency medicine medical doctor

Paige Shaffer, epidemiologist for The Bureau of Substance Abuse Services

CHAPTER 16: HEALTH

Robyn Ward, occupational therapist

CHAPTER 17: RELIGION

Sumer Azam, anthropology and religion major

Tzvi Bronchtain, rabbi

NONSPECIFIC CONTRIBUTORS

Joshua Fisher, entrepreneur

Samuel Gensburg, product designer

Charles Goetz, professor and entrepreneur

Rebecca Hofstein Grady, psychology major

Victoria Hofstein, my mother

Scott Hollander, entrepreneur and lawyer

Morgan Kolber, medical biller

Naomi Lewis, political professional

Joseph Martin, entrepreneur

And MANY more

Thank you to Luisa Benson, my middle school English teacher, who has helped from before the manuscript was a manuscript and for coming up with the subtitle Real World 101. Thank you to Michael Lubelfeld, my middle school vice-principal, for your advice on creating a book and for coming up with the name 13th Grade.

Lastly, thank you to all the people I came in contact with throughout this journey who helped by adding thoughts and ideas of their own.

Part One: Introduction

*Much in life is simple, but that
doesn't mean it's easy*

Chapter 1

Introduction

THE FOLLOWING QUIRKS APPEAR WITHIN this book:

1. TL; DR sections begin every chapter. They highlight the most important aspects of the chapter. They're not all inclusive and aren't a summary. They are meant to be read prior to the rest of the chapter. TL; DR literally translates to "too long; didn't read."

2. {Search.} Please verify everything on your own. Sometimes, a specific search phrase is suggested. Rather than listing one specific resource, I ask you to verify and find the information for yourself. The words that follow the word *search* are meant to help you navigate what to search. Other reasons for it are the following:

   a) If information changes over time, it allows for updates.

   b) If a search can answer a question easily, I probably shouldn't write about it.

   c) If you are interested, you have the option to seek out more information.

3. Contributions from Alvin Chester. Alvin Chester is my late grandfather. Most of his writings are from around the early 1990s. Agree, disagree, whatever. The idea is to inspire your continued thought on the subject, but his contributions are not a necessary piece of this book. Feel free to read them now, skip them, or read them at a later date. His philosophy book, *you, You, YOU are the Philosopher,* is

included at the end of this book. It is meant to be read at any time (before, during, or after reading the rest of this book).

4.   The chapters on economics, generational differences and similarities, politics, health, and religion have been significantly reduced. Upon writing this book, I went off on a few tangents, and these are (some of) those tangents. I may write another book with these topics (and others), but because these did not seem to be "the absolute most important" aspects to know, I initially wanted to eliminate them from this book. Because that next book may never be written, I decided to include them in this heavily reduced format.

▲ ▲ ▲

TL; DR:

If you agree that you will not use anything you read here to justify your actions and will not hold the author or any other entity involved in the publication of this book liable for the information herein, you may keep reading.

In most parts of the United States, at the age of eighteen, you are legally responsible for your own decisions and actions, no matter what your parents, teachers, preachers, or anyone else may tell you. Your actions are a result of your choices, and any consequences that may follow those actions and choices are your responsibility as the person who made them. Once you turn eighteen, the US government says you must take responsibility for your actions.[1]

But are we ready, at age eighteen, to assume responsibility for our actions? Let's take a look at some of the things you may not have been taught over the course of your schooling. In high school, were you taught the proper way to file your taxes? Were you taught how to invest? Were you taught (realistically) what effects drugs and alcohol can have on you? Did you receive sexual education? Were you taught about the benefits and drawbacks of being compliant with the law?

This book seeks to bridge the knowledge gap that many people face after graduating from high school and aims to bring more equity to all. When you turn eighteen, you are a new adult with all of the responsibility of a fifty-year-old.

Common sense is simple and easy to understand, but it often needs to be learned. I am attempting to provide unbiased information by presenting many ideologies simultaneously and seeking the opinions of relevant experts where their additions are valuable. However, the following should be noted:

> An expert doesn't so much argue the various sides of an issue as plant his flag firmly on one side. That's because an expert whose argument reeks of restraint or nuance often doesn't get much attention.
>
> —STEPHEN DUBNER AND STEVEN LEVITT, *FREAKONOMICS*

Hopefully, you'll gain an understanding of various subjects and be better equipped to make knowledgeable decisions yourself.

The goal of this book is to have you come away thinking in more complex ways about various topics while maintaining the awareness that we are all different and ultimately coming to the understanding that choice is our greatest power.

End of TL; DR.

> If I can in any way contribute to the diversion or improvement of the country in which I live, I shall leave it with the secret satisfaction of thinking that I have not lived in vain.
>
> —JOSEPH ADDISON, EARLY EIGHTEENTH-CENTURY
> ENGLISH POET AND POLITICIAN

Question everything. Always ask why something happens or why a person is behaving in a certain manner. Why? Because it prompts you to analyze the motivations of others and to better understand their intentions. If we understand, we can better evaluate.

> Wise Men learn by others' harms; Fools by their own.
>
> —BENJAMIN FRANKLIN, FOUNDING FATHER AND BUSINESSMAN

Why have I written this book? Because I could have used it, and I believe it will help others. One of my best friends pushed me, eleven years ago (after I complained to him about the many problems in our world), with a simple sentence: "The point is, Daniel, I want to know what you're going to do about these thoughts that you're having."

It's not who you are underneath; it's what you do that defines you.

—RACHEL DAWES, BATMAN BEGINS

What makes me special in writing this? Honestly, not much. I am writing it and have a lot of varied experience. But this book is not about me or filled with anecdotes from my life.

While I am not rich, I have done fairly well and have a current net worth of about $250,000 (at age thirty-one). Over the years, I have participated in many non-revenue-generating activities for the greater good of society, including donating blood, organizing volunteers, serving food to the elderly and poor, helping friends with finances, assisting small-business entrepreneurs, and generally trying to be a positive influence on society.

I was taught a lot about finances growing up but little about the law or drugs. When I was eighteen, I had saved nearly $40,000 from working at an accounting firm, playing poker in underground casinos, investing in the stock market, and dabbling in other small businesses. By the time I was nineteen, that $40,000 had dwindled to $5,000, I had been arrested on felony (albeit not that serious) drug charges, and I had failed every college class I attempted.

I spent five years working as a casino employee, eventually becoming a casino-pit supervisor. I completed an undergraduate degree in gaming management from the University of Nevada, Las Vegas in 2010. I invented and sold a casino game (which won Best New Table Game of the Year in 2014). I worked in real estate for five years total (2008–12 and 2016–17). I invested in an axe-throwing business, with a return of over four times what I put into it shortly thereafter. In 2015, I graduated from Emory University's Goizueta Business School's master of business administration program (for which the average first-year compensation in 2015 was $136,908)[2] and, instead of taking a traditional job, chose to pursue my own entrepreneurial ventures (which include helping others start theirs) and to write this book.

This book is far from perfect. Some information may already be outdated. I am hoping to explain why things work the way they do to allow you to better make your own decisions. Sometimes there is straightforward, practical advice. Additionally, I have done my best not to advertise for any company, but sometimes it can't be avoided, like how Warren Buffett recommends purchasing VOO (Note: VOO is the ticker symbol to purchase on the stock market) or another low-cost exchange-traded fund for the average investor—more on this in chapter 2.

> I don't need to watch you practice. If you cheat, you won't win.
>
> —ANONYMOUS, (OVERHEARD AT THE GYM)

You don't need to physically witness people working out in the gym to know that they work out often and eat well-balanced diets; their physiques speak for themselves. The same goes with this book. If you only read the TL; DRs, you'll get something out of it but not much.

If your wrestling coach instructs you to practice a certain technique and you choose not to practice it, you'll probably have a harder time winning the match. If you don't do your homework, you'll be less educated and less capable of applying what you've learned in the real world. If you don't save money, it should come as no surprise when you struggle financially.

There is a balance to most things in life. We often sacrifice our short term (present selves) in order to gain for the long term (future selves) or vice versa, indulging in our short-term pleasures to the detriment of our long-term futures.

Much research on this topic {search: delayed gratification research} has shown that more successful people engage in delayed gratification and are more satisfied (happier) with their lives. It is because they engage in short-term pain for long-term gain. Of course, there must be balance. Saving for retirement is an excellent example of this.

Every dollar you save and invest properly for forty years should be worth approximately fifteen times what it was (after accounting for inflation). This means that if you save $10,000 today, your future self will have $150,000.

(See "Chapter 2: Money" for sources and further details.) However, if all I have is $10,000, I cannot save it all as I must spend money to live (and hopefully be happier because of spending that money) today.

We shouldn't deprive ourselves of everything pleasurable in the short term by always focusing on the long term. If we don't live for now, when are we actually living? There are other risks to saving, like death. However, taking control of our finances with our futures in mind will allow us a greater level of freedom and stress reduction in the long term. Balance here means that rather than taking a $1,500 vacation today, take a $1,400 vacation, save (and invest) the $100, and take another $1,500 vacation in forty years.

The knowledge in this commonsense book is (hopefully) simple to understand. However, it's not always easy. Many of us know how and what to do, but we still don't do it. For instance, I know how to be healthier.

If it tastes good, spit it out.

—JACK LaLANNE, GODFATHER OF FITNESS

Eat more vegetables and fewer processed foods, and move more. It's simple, but it isn't easy.

I know how to save for retirement: be conservative in spending, and pay my future self-first. So I know how to get six-pack abs and how to be a millionaire. I also then know that I choose not to have six-pack abs and to delay retirement or live a more modest lifestyle later. These are simple in concept but difficult in practice.

Much of life is this way, and this book attempts to provide simple solutions to what most would call the commonsense aspects of life…but that doesn't mean it will be easy. The goal of this book is to bridge the gap of knowledge of how and what to do, creating a more equal opportunity for all. It's up to you to actualize the knowledge, and that can be hard. Each of us has the ability to rationalize almost anything, including eating that chip, buying that bag, seeing that performance, exercising tomorrow, and so on.

I realize that we're not all born equal. Some of us are smarter, some are faster, some are born rich, some are stronger, and some have diseases— all of which can impede or strengthen progress in many aspects of life. We are all unique. Our experiences are also unique. Look up and understand the word *sonder*, which in short means that we all find our personal lives fascinating and that we all feel that we are extraordinarily unique {search: sonder}.

Tell Your Friends! YOU ARE UNIQUE (just like everyone else)

—SAMUEL GENSBURG, PRODUCT DESIGNER

Every man feels that his experience is unlike that of anybody else and therefore he should write it down. He finds also that everybody else has thought and felt on some points precisely as he has done, and therefore should write it down.

—MARK TWAIN, NINETEENTH-CENTURY WRITER

We are all completely unique and incredibly similar at the same time. We will never be fully equal, but we should all do our personal best. Hopefully our outcomes are mostly determined by us.

This book isn't about what should be and tries to take as few stances as possible. Rather, it aims to discuss what is. For better or worse, we live in this reality. Ever think you were given poor luck in life? Henry Ford had no education.[3] Helen Keller went blind and deaf at eighteen months of age and was still a productive and intelligent member of society.[4] Stephen Hawking became a quadriplegic midway through his life.[5] A janitor amassed a multimillion-dollar fortune.[6] People with rare and life-threatening diseases achieve great things all the time. We can find endless examples of those who have risen above what appeared to be their lots in life.

> If it is to be, it is up to me.
>
> —WILLIAM H. JOHNSEN, FREAK-SHOW ARTIST

Circumstances do not make you; *you make you*.

Every eighteen-year-old (or any person at any age) everywhere should have equal opportunities in life. This book aims for you to recognize that this is a goal and not a fact. It is an ideal that we strive toward.

> If you look for perfection, you'll never be content.
>
> —LEO TOLSTOY, *ANNA KARENINA*

I don't believe that we're all equal. In fact, you're unique, just like everyone else. In the end, I aim for equal opportunity, not for equal outcomes.

The information contained herein won't pertain to everybody, and each of us may have extenuating circumstances that may make some aspects of our lives harder (or easier) than others. I realize this, but I *will not be making caveats* for everything—or even for most things. Most people are able to exercise and eat healthily. Most people make excuses. Most people can rationalize nearly anything to themselves.

> So convenient a thing it is to be a reasonable creature, since it enables one to find or make a reason for everything one has a mind to.
>
> —BENJAMIN FRANKLIN, FOUNDING FATHER AND BUSINESSMAN

I will not be addressing extenuating circumstances such as medical and psychological conditions in the health and drugs chapters, large inheritances and homelessness in the money chapter, and so on, and this may upset some people. There are vast resources available for specific situations; use them.

This book is meant to address much of the *Anna Karenina* principle for life. The *Anna Karenina* principle describes an endeavor in which a deficiency in any one of a number of factors dooms it to failure. Consequently, a successful endeavor (subject to this principle) is one where every possible deficiency has been avoided.[7]

WHY ISN'T THIS TAUGHT IN SCHOOL?

Schools cannot teach everything. Since the times of ancient Greece and even earlier, it has been literally impossible for anyone to learn everything. We can debate all day about what topics are most important to teach our youth, but we will likely have disagreements.

How are schools incentivized?

"According to the National Center for Education Statistics, state and local funding accounts for approximately 93 percent of education expenditures. What's the source of these funds? In most states, it's sales and income taxes (both corporate and personal). But on a local level, these funds usually come from property taxes, which are set by the school board, local officials or citizens. It's this system that causes the most dramatic differences between states, and even within districts. Depending on the property wealth of a community, its schools might boast gleaming buildings and equipment, or they might be dilapidated—struggling with the burden of outdated equipment and unpaid bills."[8]

The funding issue relates to economics and incentives. Economics is fairly simple in this regard. Imagine you are a parent who wants the best for your children. You may move to the best possible school district that you can afford. This increases the demand in that area, pushing home prices up, increasing local property taxes and thus funding for education. This cycle continues so that nearly everyone with school-aged children moves to the areas where they can find the best education for their children.

What makes a school "good"? In general, high school–graduation rates, college-acceptance rates, standardized-test scores, and low incidence of crime. Schools, then, do not care as much about providing classes that teach things like life skills, rather aiming to adopt programs that enable their students to get good test scores and go on to college.

Is it a teacher's (and school's) purpose to teach what should be known or how to learn or something else entirely? I have often heard teachers state that they teach children to think for themselves rather than teaching them what to think. There is also contention associated with teaching many of the more controversial aspects of life (drugs, sex, laws, etc.), which discourages and limits some aspects of teaching. (Even English and math classes have controversy over what books and how far along to teach.)

At one point, the answer to two plus two was difficult for all of us. Later, we learn more difficult, seemingly obscure mathematical concepts like the Pythagorean Theorem. "When will I ever use this?" is a common question. While not 100 percent the same, I have heard it related to people lifting weights in a gym. They don't lift weights in order to lift weights (usually); they lift them for the functional purpose of being stronger, healthier, and better looking. Similarly, people learning complex mathematical equations are able to use their brains in a stronger capacity to figure out other, unrelated, complex problems due to their "brain training."

The original thought was that this book would be crowd sourced. When I finished the rough draft, I sent chapters to industry experts and professionals for their review. It was difficult for me to find professionals outside of my personal network who were willing to help a no-name writer. *Thank you, everyone who did help!*

If I write another version of this book, it will (hopefully) be more crowd sourced and from a more diverse group of people. Ideally, professionals will chime in by sending love e-mails, adding to arguments, adding opposing views, adding research, and so on. *I welcome this!* (Contact me at danoventuresllc@gmail.com.)

Question everything and come to your own conclusions after learning various viewpoints. I aim to encourage your own thinking and to influence it as little as possible. Alvin Chester's book, *you, You, YOU are the Philosopher*, says this within the first few sentences: "My aim is to encourage your own thinking, not to influence it."

I'm sure he realized that everything we do influences others, which is why he kept his book as short as possible to demonstrate the necessary points he wished to get across. I hope to emulate that philosophy of conciseness and little influence.

This book is meant to teach common sense. The problem with common sense is that it is different for everyone. Hopefully you already have much of it (common sense).

If you come across a chapter that you are knowledgeable about, skip or skim it (the choice is yours, after all), but the reinforcement of ideas (and hopefully contrasting ideas) may also help. The Alvin Chester contributions that often appear at the end of chapters mainly serve to further stimulate your own thoughts and are not necessary to be read.

Nothing in this book is so profound that you will be ruined without it. Life has gone on for a long time. We'll all be OK. The goal is that all people in this world (this book is tailored to the United States) will have equal opportunities, and what outcome they produce is up to them. If they are unaware of an aspect, then nearly no matter how hard they try, there's a chance they'll go nowhere. For instance, if I don't know how to exercise properly, I may end up doing more damage than good to myself (either through the use of drugs, poor diet, poor form, hereditary disease, or something else). This book is meant to teach the basics in a simplified and easy-to-understand format. I encourage you to do your own research, get expert advice, and continue to learn after you finish this book. Ultimately, it's up to you. Choice is your greatest power in this life. Use it wisely.

Very little in the long run just happens naturally.

—ZE FRANK, "ARE YOU HUMAN?" (TED 2014)

▲ ▲ ▲

Alvin Chester:

To: PROFESSIONAL EDUCATORS, AN OPEN LETTER:

> Should schools teach moral/ethical values?
> No
>
> Can schools help student acquire moral/ethical values?
> Yes

Among the many responsibilities being foisted upon our school systems (by a society that has not learned to accept its own responsibilities) is that of instilling into the students a set of moral/ethical values.

Fortunately, this society, which has been steadily losing its own values and reneging on its responsibilities, is at least still aware that there should be values…and hopes that their children can acquire some.

If they can't learn them at home with the families serving as role models…let's give them to the schools to teach.

Firstly, I do not believe the schools are institutions that TEACH. That is one of the major errors made when considering what schools are and what they should do. The purpose of schools is to PROVIDE A PLACE, THE OPPORTUNITY, and ASSISTANCE TO LEARN.

I FIND NO FAULT WITH OUR SCHOOL SYSTEMS. Our schools can be less fully equipped, have less qualified teachers, and still be places of great learning.

What are missing…are STUDENTS WHO WANT TO LEARN. I went to school in classrooms of forty-five students…with teachers whose only qualifications were two years at what was then called (I believe) "Normal School" and a willingness to be somewhat underpaid.

My generation LEARNED. WHY? Because WE WANTED TO. We were Depression Era children, and our parents told us that the only way we could achieve anything was to BECOME EDUCATED. We received that information in our homes.

Today, families seem unable, or unwilling, to instill that into their children. Many families feel we live in a society that does not offer opportunities for their children even if they do become educated. So the schools are asked to do the impossible. I have great sympathy for professional "educators." Our society's potential future seems to be tied to our schools' success at fulfilling a task they should not be called upon to do.

But society is apparently unwilling or unable to adjust to a system that provides significant opportunities for all and, in that manner, instilling into children the desire to learn, the values of learning, and the fruits thereof.

So the SCHOOLS HAVE THE JOB.

Despite the fact that I do not believe the schools can accomplish the task being put to them, there are some things that might be done to assist.

One of these is to help children DEVELOP moral/ethical values.

Here I shall present to you an idea which I believe can be added to any curriculum at very little cost (including the cost of time) and which helps children to DEVELOP THEIR OWN SYSTEMS OF MORAL/ETHICAL VALUES. Cultivating one's own value system seeds those values more strongly within the inner person and makes for a lasting effect.

I shall give you a brief history of that which preceded this idea.

In the army (1946) and in basic training camp, I found in a nearby army unit a friend of mine from college. We would take whatever free moments we could find and talk and take walks together around the camp. We discussed many things.

At one point, I broke into our conversation, stating that what we had determined was that our belief (about whatever it was we were discussing at the time) was not consistent with what we had agreed to during a previous discussion about a different topic. We couldn't properly BELIEVE BOTH THINGS AT THE SAME TIME. We reviewed both thought processes and adapted them to find new beliefs that were consonant with each other.

This became a regular feature of our conversations.

In due time (many years beyond 1946), after maintaining that idea of trying to never be self-contradictory, I developed what I called a PERSONAL PHILOSOPHY. I wrote a short book (never published) about how to develop and maintain a personal philosophy.

In short, it involves scrutinizing one's immediate and unconsidered responses regarding a variety of themes and then subjecting these "values" to careful examination to avoid anomalies of consistency. The necessary adjustments are then made. The result is a coherent, cohesive person who has inner consonance and a set of compatible values. These values, thus true to the individual, become one's PERSONAL PHILOSOPHY.

These "considered" value decisions, giving importance to the effect on others as well as oneself, recognizing that what you allow for yourself as proper behavior must also be allowed to others, WILL ALWAYS BE POSITIVE SOCIETAL VALUES.

Now, back to SCHOOLS.

This kind of discussion, which works for adults, CAN ALSO BE VALID FOR LESS DEVELOPED MINDS…and will, in effect, hasten their maturation.

There are things which can be discussed at ALL LEVELS of growth, even with quite young children.

First graders can discuss whether it is right or wrong to hit another person…to lie…to take things that do not belong to them but are the property of others…and so on and so on.

There are many, many experiences all people have (even though these will be dissimilar for different ages and groups) that force them to set values for…and those can be discussed.

In every case, it is important to both discuss the right and wrong of the current subject (what I will allow myself to do must also be allowable to others) and also whether the result is consistent with previous decisions.

It would be INAPPROPRIATE to insist that every child come to the same conclusion. The purpose of this is to help people to think with validity by requiring a consistency of thought process. (In the end, they will all be very close. However, that will be because there will be a concordance of belief and not due to an insistence on agreement.)

The teacher (moderator/coordinator) should also be able to explain (at the various levels) that there are such things as group values, which may be different from our own…and that there may be problems (and benefits) if we deviate from those group values in our own behavior.

Thus, without talking about establishing a value system, we can begin to organize the thought patterns of children so that they will establish their own. They will learn to compare all new thoughts against the "test" of previously accepted values.

There will come times when the NEW THOUGHT will force the change of a previous one…maybe a number of previous ones.

But the resultant ability of the student to confront values (either new ones of his own or ones encountered from outside sources) and determine their validity for infusion into one's own value system shall be greatly enhanced.

I sincerely believe that this will make for better people, more prepared to brave their futures.

(My essay on "GOALS," how to select and utilize them as a method of achieving success, also provides assistance in preparing for the future. However, it must follow what we are now discussing, and I only mention it for eventual consideration.)

How does the TEACHER participate in this?

The teacher must be more than a discussion leader. Because the children will come forth with "values" (from whatever sources) that are emotionally oriented and not consistent with rational thought processes, the teacher must be responsible for keeping logical thought as the basis for the dialogues.

The teacher must also avoid entering into discussions regarding matters (such as religion) in which a "learned belief" is the basis for the contention.

Here is another example of how a teacher can help. An interesting tract that may come up is the student's knowledge that one of their beliefs is based on a legal right. The teacher may desire to advise the student that just because there is a legal right…it does not make the thought (or action) "right" or correct.

It is also imperative that the teacher emphasize that what is determined in the class is personal to each child and that no matter how strongly one individual (or group of individuals) believes in something, it is not proper to demand that others hold the same convictions.

I believe that this idea can be developed into one class period per week (for each class) and can continue all through the grades.

As we get into the classes wherein the students are capable of expressing thought on paper, it might become advisable for each student to maintain a notebook so the student can easily refer to previous thought expressions.

I do not have any opinions about how to choose the teacher(s). However, it might be a good idea for all teachers (not only those chosen to lead the classes) to work this regimen with their own thoughts, so we don't end up with students more cohesive than teachers.

I would also recommend the continuation of this into the high schools as more and more new ideas and experiences eventuate until (and even beyond) maturity.

The above is, basically, the idea…the program.

I am submitting this to you because I believe it will work…and, if it does, then I will have made some contribution to society.

Part Two: Money

*Money cannot buy happiness, but a lack of money
can sure bring unhappiness*

Chapter 2

Money

TL; DR:

MONEY IS THE MEANS OF trade in our society. Money is basically stored work and has value because others recognize that it has value as stored work. There are many ways to earn and to grow money. The most common ways to earn money are either to work for someone else or to open your own business. The most common way to grow money is through investing rather than working. You invest your money, hoping that more money than you've put in comes back at a later date. "Let your money work for you" comes from this ideology of investing.

Investing is risky and does not always return a favorable outcome. Businesses close for a multitude of reasons. However, money generally decreases in value due to inflation.[1] Inflation poses a risk to keeping a lot of stored work not working.

If you save $10,000 by the time you are twenty-five years old and retire at the age of sixty-five, your $10,000 will have the value (meaning post inflation) of approximately $149,000 (based on a 10 percent annual rate of return and 3 percent annual inflation [1 + 10 percent − 3 percent] ^ 40 = 14.9) and a nominal (looks like pre inflation) value of $453,000 ([1 + 10 percent] ^ 40 = 45.3).[2] This means that if you forego one thing (nights out, sushi meals, vacations, etc.), you will be able to afford 14.9 times that many (nights out, sushi meals, vacations, etc.) when you retire. Spoil your future self: save and invest today. Of course, you may die today…so don't save *everything* for tomorrow.

In 1757, Benjamin Franklin wrote *The Way to Wealth*, a copy of which is included at the end of part two. Though printed centuries ago, the principles apply today. Franklin's advice is as follows:

1. Industry—always be employed.

2. Care—trust few, and take care of your own finances as much as possible.

3. Frugality—beware of small expenses, for "a small leak will sink a great ship."

4. Knowledge—"They that will not be counseled, cannot be helped."

This is how Warren Buffett recommends you invest: Open a stock brokerage account with Vanguard and purchase ticker symbol VOO {search: what is a ticker symbol} or another low-cost US broad market exchange-traded fund. Stay invested, and place more money into this each month. Do not sell based on fear, other emotions, or what other people are saying. Sell slowly when you need the money—hopefully after forty years, during retirement.

End of TL; DR.

Ideally, you began working and saving money as early in your life as possible. When I work, rather than being paid with what I have physically produced—like a piece of pottery, food, or entertainment—I am paid with money. I can then trade this money with a willing party for something else I desire. However, I cannot store the work forever and expect it to always retain the same value.

Stored work usually loses value over time; this is known as inflation. There is no single reason on which economists agree regarding why inflation occurs, but it is basically due to new and more efficient technologies (my output of creating a typewriter thirty years ago was useful at the time but is practically useless today) and continuously striving to charge consumers an optimum price (supply/demand).[3] If you decided to live as people did two hundred years ago, your needs would cost much less, and you would need to work much less, but you would also be giving up many of our modern luxuries, such as softer linens, air conditioning, hot water, Internet, and so on.

Imagine that we did not have money. Rather, everything we do is a favor for someone, and we expect the favor to be returned. If I do a favor for you now and expect something immediately, this is simple; I do this so that you do that. What if I come to you and say, "I did something ten years ago for you, so now I want something from you today"? Most likely, that favor I did ten years ago will have been long forgotten or is remembered differently by both parties. If we did not explicitly state what the returned favor would be and when, it would be difficult to measure the value the favor has today.

When I have stored work, I don't know what favor I will be asking for in the future. The same concept occurs with money. I made money years ago and want to spend it today. If I kept the money in a bank or underneath my mattress, it would likely have less value today. When you store work, it is best if you let that stored work actually work for you.

In today's society, there are many ways to earn money. You don't have to choose the "right" or "perfect path" to earning money, but choosing a path and earning money is paramount. There are many ways to become wealthy. Much of wealth depends on your personal goals.

There are always reasons to spend money: a nicer car, clothing, nights out, a fancier house, expensive dinners, massages, new gizmos, vacations, charity, and so on. The list is limitless, and some of those listed items may be worthwhile for you and not for others. This is OK. The practice of saving may be easy for some and difficult for others. Spending less than you earn is a simple concept, although the practice can be hard. I urge you to only think of yourself in terms of what you need (and want) and to not care what your neighbor has or does with his or her money.

Many say, "We have always made do with what we have and always will." This is usually a self-fulfilling prophecy from those without much money. If you never worry about saving, live paycheck-to-paycheck, and believe, "I'll be OK," you're probably right. You will be "OK." But you will likely be stuck responding to your circumstances rather than creating them. If your motto in life is "Live for today because tomorrow is never guaranteed," you are correct. Eventually we will all die. But when we are alive, being "good" with money generally makes life more enjoyable.

This chapter is not about how to earn more money. This chapter is about what to do with the money you earn.

When you save enough money to be able to invest, your money begins going to work for you. There are seemingly an endless number of investments you can make. (At age twenty-nine, I invested $20,000 in a friend's axe-throwing business. When I was thirty, he sold it, and I received $92,000 over the course of the next year. It amazes me how many people are astounded that I was able to have $20,000 in savings available for an investment when I was twenty-nine.)

Many investments are good, many are bad, and all contain some form of risk. Possibly the most common and easiest way to invest is the public equity stock market—that is, purchasing part of a business on a regulated stock exchange. The average return (growth plus payouts) of businesses in the Dow Jones Industrial Average Thirty from 1917 to 2017 is slightly under 7 percent after inflation {search: Average Dow Jones Return}. The Standard & Poor 500 (S&P 500), five hundred of the largest companies in the United States, is similar (upon my own calculations, from 1913 to 2017 it returned 6.9 percent yearly) (Note: purchasing VOO is a purchase of this S&P 500 index, owning a part of all 500 companies at once). This means that, on average, you will double your money's value approximately every ten years.

> Interest is the birth of money from money.
>
> —ARISTOTLE, ANCIENT GREEK PHILOSOPHER

Compound interest means reinvesting the money that your money made. My $1.00 investment earns $.07 in a year, for a total of $1.07. In my second year, the $1.07 investment earns $.075. In my fortieth year, my compounded investment earns over $1.04 every year. By saving $1.00 for forty years, I can withdraw over $1.00 for the rest of my life. After forty years of compound interest, my $1.00 investment will be worth about $14.90. The $14.90 will then, on average, make over $1.00 per year.

> Money makes money. And the money that money makes, makes money.

—BENJAMIN FRANKLIN, FOUNDING FATHER AND BUSINESSMAN

An investment of $450 per month will yield, forty years later, over $2,000,000, on average, or over $1,000,000 post inflation, and will have only cost a little over $200,000.

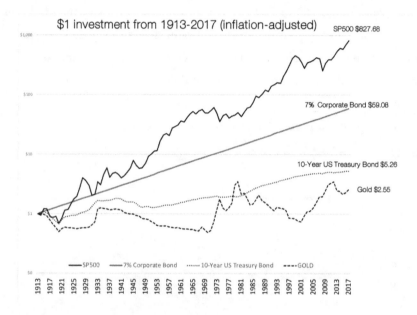

S&P500 $827.68. Corporate Bond $59.08. US T-Bond $5. Gold $2.55

Save a dollar when you are twenty-five for when you are sixty-five, and that dollar will have a value of about 14.9 times what it was when you were twenty-five. Wait until you are seventy-five, and it is worth nearly 30 times. When you're eighty-five, it would be worth nearly 60 times what it once was. The flaw in this logic is that you may die, and you can't take it with you (and the 7 percent number is an average from the past and does not guarantee future outcomes). You may also live, and what has happened in the past is most likely to happen in the future; it would probably be nice to have your stored work do so well for you.

I created these graphs (pages 23 and 24) utilizing data from the Consumer

Price Index (CPI, which measures inflation), S&P 500 (large US stocks), ten-year US treasury bonds (commonly known as the safest investment, or "risk-free"), and historical gold prices.[4] The 7 percent corporate bond is fabricated and a slightly high estimate, as 6.42 percent is the historical average from 1984 to the present day.[5] (The graph does not use historical corporate bond data, so the 7 percent is a somewhat straight line and not volatile, but it should be more erratic like the rest.) The graphs show how much a single dollar grew from 1913 to 2017 based on different investments. Had you kept the dollar under your mattress, CPI rates that the average item would cost twenty-five times as much after this time period, meaning that one dollar was once able to purchase twenty-five dollars' worth of goods but now may only purchase one dollar's worth of goods. Investing in stocks would have allowed you to purchase 828 times as many goods (rather than 1/25 of a good, a difference of 20,458X).

S&P500 $20,458. Corporate Bond $1,137. US T-Bond $130. Gold $63. CPI $25

Why are stocks worth so much more than everything else? They create output. Gold is a decent store of value but has only slightly outpaced CPI. When the world goes to rubbish, the theory is that everyone will still recognize gold as stored work. Investing in corporate bonds is investing in companies' ability to repay debt (which is less risky than investing in what they produce because if they do not repay their debts, bondholders will close the company and seize the assets).

When you invest in US treasury bonds, you are investing in the US government repaying its debts (commonly known as "risk-free"). When you leave your money under your mattress or in an account that bears very little interest, you leave yourself susceptible to inflation.

This chapter will cover the following concepts in the following order:

- What is the proper order for building wealth?

- What is investing?

- How do you invest?

- What are scams?

▲ ▲ ▲

What Is the Proper Order for Building Wealth?

1. Build (and stick to) a budget.

2. Build an emergency fund.

3. Save and invest in employer-sponsored matching funds.

4. Pay down high-interest debts.

5. Contribute to an individual retirement account (IRA).

6. Save more for retirement.

7. Save for other goals.

This "proper order" is meant to grow your net worth in a balanced way that reduces risk.[6] If all goes well in your financial life, every year you will have more money than the last.

1) Build (and Stick to) a Budget

> It's funny how people making $60k happen to spend $59.9k. And people making $40k happen to spend $39.99k.And people making $20k happen to spend $19.99k. Everyone

is just one paycheck away from the street. But why can't the person making $60k just spend the same amount as the person making $40k?

—WILLIAMWALLACE ON REDDIT.COM

A budget is a list of all of your expected earnings and expenses within a given time frame. Begin with a yearly budget for big-ticket items like savings and vacations, and build those into your monthly budget. The following is a sample budget plan for a single person with no dependents, who lives in a leased dwelling and makes $48,000 per year.

YEARLY BUDGET

Yearly Earnings

Salary	$48,000.00
Bonus	$0.00
Commissions	$0.00
Dividends	$0.00
Interest	$0.00
Gifts	$0.00
Other	$0.00
TOTAL	$48,000.00

Yearly Expenses

Taxes (federal)	$5,178.00
Taxes (state)	$480.00
Rent and utilities	$14,000.00 (maximum)
Car (payments + insurance + gas + repairs + other)	$4,200.00 (maximum)
Savings and investments	$9,600.00 (minimum)
Other/remaining	$14,542.00
TOTAL	$48,000.00

Monthly Budget

Monthly Earnings

Salary	$4,000.00
TOTAL	$4,000.00

Monthly Expenses

Taxes (federal)	$431.50
Taxes (state)	$40.00
Rent and utilities	$1166.67
Car (all inclusive)	$350.00
Savings (see the rest of this chapter for how to properly save and invest)	$800.00
Food	$300.00
Entertainment	$200.00
Vacation fund	$200.00
Charity	$400.00
Health insurance	$100.00
Other/remaining	$11.83
TOTAL	$4,000.00

Siddharth Jain, a finance professional wrote (in review of this chapter):

"For people like me, knowing how much you typically spend on such things every month and tracking your spending intra-month is a big challenge.

There are apps that link to your bank account and automatically categorize all your expenditures into categories like food, entertainment, grocery, transport, bills, and so on.

I use these and find it immensely useful to make and track my budget."

Maybe the easiest way to save for the long term is to do so when you get raises and bonuses. First, get comfortable living on whatever you currently earn. Then, when you receive a salary increase, spend half on yourself (improving your current life) and put half in savings (improving your future life). The half you spend on yourself may be split into anything on your budget (even savings if you want to spoil your future self even more), but most people will likely choose better or more vacations, an upgrade in living situations, a new car, entertainment, other splurges, and so on. This applies whether you are eighteen and single or forty with a family. Bonuses can be dealt with in a similar manner.

As with everything, it is completely up to you. Save for your future, and be content with what you have. If you aren't content, ensure that it's not because you are looking at others and wanting what they have but that it's what you personally need to be content.

> Don't save what is left after spending, but spend what is left after saving.
>
> —WARREN BUFFETT, INVESTOR/CEO OF BERKSHIRE HATHAWAY

Pay yourself first. Your budget will include many items, but if you aren't helping your future self-first, your future self may never be able to control life. The percentage that you pay yourself is usually recommended to be 10 percent of your income, but I believe that is low. Ideally, save 20 percent or more.

After paying your future self, much of your budget comes down to personal preference. There are many outside tools to help you budget {search: build a budget}. In general, budgeting is simply a matter of evaluating your personal preferences. Kevin Clark of the *Wall Street Journal* wrote a great article, "Why the Redskins Players Are So Frugal" (https://www.wsj.com/articles/why-the-redskins-players-are-so-frugal-1452014607), which discusses an NFL team filled with multimillionaires who live frugally. It is a great example of people who are aware that their large paychecks will not last forever.

Many athletes, lottery winners, and others who make a lot of money in a short period of time, lose it (often declaring bankruptcy) because they become accustomed to spending large amounts of money and have trouble scaling back. Once you are accustomed to a lifestyle, it is hard to pull back.

"I lived like ____, and I can do it again" is easier said than done.

The order in which your savings should be invested is illuminated here:

2) BUILD AN EMERGENCY FUND

An emergency fund should always be available to you. It acts as a safety net for when life happens. Common knowledge states that a safety net should include three to six months' worth of living expenses as a guideline. If you work in an industry where jobs are hard to come by or you would not be willing to accept a job at a lower pay, you may need a longer time frame for an emergency fund. If you have a rich family or other safety nets that would help you out when times get tough, then you may need less. There are many risks that would necessitate an emergency fund, but figure out what your personal safety net should consist of and cater to that.

3) SAVE AND INVEST IN EMPLOYER-SPONSORED MATCHING FUNDS

Employers often offer incentives besides regular paychecks to those who work for them, like health insurance, meals, retirement savings plans, and so on. Retirement savings plans are often 401(k)s (the most common), 403(b) s, SIMPLE (Savings Incentive Match Plan for Employees) IRAs, and SEP (Simplified Employee Pension) IRAs. Each plan is slightly different, but many of them work as follows.

The employer will match every dollar that employees contribute to their employer-sponsored retirement accounts—up to 5 percent of the employees' pay per pay period. For example, if you earned $100 a week and contributed $3 to a 401(k), your employer would also contribute $3, so you would have a total of $6 in your account. If you contributed $5, your employer would also contribute $5, for $10 in total. If you contributed $10, your employer would still only contribute $5 (the maximum in this scenario being 5 percent of $100, or $5), for $15 total. In these scenarios, it is optimal for you to contribute the maximum amount that your employer will match and no more because these types of retirement plans often have other fees associated with them, making them less appealing than other forms of investment.

At the beginning of this chapter, we discussed how every dollar saved turns into $14.90. With employer-matched contributions, that amount is doubled (so every dollar turns into $29.80). For these reasons, we invest in these types of plans before paying down debts.

Other aspects of these plans include the following:

A) The money is not easily withdrawn.

Until you reach what the government considers early retirement age (fifty-nine and a half years old), the money cannot be withdrawn without incurring a penalty. The penalty is usually 10 percent.

B) Employer plans usually have a vesting period.

A vesting period means that any amount the employer contributes is not 100 percent yours until you have remained at the company long enough, encouraging you to stay. Companies generally want to invest in their employees and keep them around. Even if you are not fully vested and leave, it is almost always still worthwhile to invest (and you never know; you may end up staying longer than you thought).

A typical vesting schedule is 20 percent per year so that after five years, the employer-contributed amount is fully vested. Using the above example (where you earned $100/week and contributed $5, while your employer matched with $5), after one year (without accounting for investment growth—only the match), each $5 you contributed would be worth $6. After two years, that $5 would be worth $7; after three years, $8; after four years, $9; after five years, $10; and then it would stay at $10 for the remainder of time.

C) Money is invested by management professionals.

This is both a drawback and a benefit. The drawback is that these management professionals do not allow you as much flexibility, and they take a fee for their services. The benefit is that your money is managed by professionals.

D) Tax advantages.

In order to incentivize retirement savings, the government gives tax breaks for contributions into these types of accounts.

4) Pay Down High-Interest Debts

> Compound interest is the eighth wonder of the world. He who
> understands it, earns it…he who doesn't…pays it.
>
> —Albert Einstein, theoretical physicist

Debt is when you have borrowed stored work and have not paid it back. When you borrow stored work, it is often valued higher than you would like it to be. When we borrow on a credit card, the credit card company often says, "Pay us back within thirty days, and the money is free to borrow. If you do not pay us back within thirty days, we will charge you a lot for it."

The idea of "good debt" comes from the notion that if I borrow at a rate of 2 percent and grow that money at a rate of 5 percent, I will make 3 percent. This can be good logic and can work very well. However, it is incredibly difficult to consistently earn large returns. People who issue debt know this. They lend to you because they believe it is in their best interest to do so—not yours.

If your debt is financed at greater than a 5 percent rate, it is almost always better to pay off your debt. This is because that 5 percent is a guarantee, while everything else is speculative. When I pay off the debt, I keep that 5 percent, guaranteed.

Lastly, debt sucks. When you have debt, compound interest works against you. Getting your money to work for you (through compounding growth) is the most important aspect of this chapter, and when you are in debt, other people's money is working against you in a similar way. There is rarely a time where there is "good" debt—though this is a hotly debated topic.

Dave Ramsey, a personal finance specialist, wrote about the following six reasons people stay in debt on his website at http://www.daveramsey.com/blog/6-reasons-people-stay-in-debt?et_cid=2718702&et_rid=0&linkid=: (some items here have been shortened)

    a)   "They want to keep up appearances.

          This is the dreaded "keeping up with the Joneses" mentality. But little do you know, the Joneses have a leased BMW, an underwater mortgage, and an unwelcome visitor named Sallie Mae living in their basement. The Joneses are the most broke people in your neighborhood. And if you're trying to follow their example, you'll be following them into bankruptcy.

b) They are unwilling to sacrifice.

How can you possibly give up eating out three nights a week? Or what would your life look like without cable? If you're in debt, something in your lifestyle has to change. It's about priorities. Here's the question: What are you willing to temporarily give up?

c) They fear change.

Debt can be comfortable. If you've always used a credit card, and if you always had car loans, then you know what to expect. We can promise that you have a lot more to fear if you stay in debt, rather than if you make this change in your life.

d) They're addicted to stuff.

e) They don't know how.

All you need is a plan.

f) They're lazy.

These people know what to do. Maybe they sorta, kinda want to get out of debt. You know that you're ruining your future—but you still go into debt anyway."

Siddharth Jain, a finance professional wrote (in review of this chapter):

"More often than not, people in debt know very well what they need to do to get out of it. But it's their habits and cognitive biases that render them unable to change.

Here are some interesting biases that may be in play. (Sometimes just knowing how the human brain works and is impacted by these biases can help people control their behavior.)

a) Lake Wobegon Effect: People often overestimate their ability (e.g., to manage a debt) over others. So when they read about the bad effects of too much debt, they think, "That's not going to happen to me. I'm better."

b) Status quo bias: contrary to classical economic theory that we are all rational utility maximizers, all humans have a tendency to keep things as they are.

c) Restraint bias: tendency to overestimate one's ability to show restraint. (This is why you often need rules of thumb to guide you around bad habits.)

d) Hyperbolic discounting: people tend to make choices today that their future self would not have made. (In economic speak, they discount future happiness much more than a rational maximizer would)."

5) Contribute to an Individual Retirement Account (IRA)

An IRA is another type of government tax-advantaged account. The problem with IRAs is that, like 401(k)s, you will be penalized if you access your money before the age of fifty-nine and a half, and the investments you are allowed to make are restricted (though you can easily invest in the stock market through an IRA). However, the benefits of tax advantages (and, for many, the mental block of "I cannot spend this money without a severe penalty") outweigh the detriment of inaccessibility.

6) Save More for Retirement

Once you have contributed fully to your IRA, go back and contribute more to your 401(k) and other tax-advantaged accounts.

7) Save for Other Goals

These goals can include purchasing a home, starting/investing in a small business, and so on. The idea of other goals is that you are flexible with their use when opportunities arise. The choice is yours, but having these available funds makes life easier and more easily controlled by you.

WHAT IS INVESTING?

*Investing is an activity in which consumption today is foregone
in an attempt to allow greater consumption at a later date.*

—WARREN BUFFETT, INVESTOR/CEO OF BERKSHIRE HATHAWAY

Investing is taking stored work (money) and entrusting it to a person or entity in the hopes that it becomes worth more when you redeem it. Investing can have other definitions, depending on how it is used, like investing in sweat equity, where you contribute time rather than money.

Example: I take $1, and I invest it in my brother, who says he has a great idea for a lemonade stand. He needs $5 to start. I invest $1, 20 percent of the startup needed, and he agrees to give me 20 percent of the profit. If he profits $20 with his stand, I get 20 percent of that ($4), which is a 300 percent return!

However, your brother may say that he is investing both money ($4 of the $5) *and* time (managing everything), so for your $1 investment, he will only give you 10 percent. You agree, and in the same scenario, your $1 would double to $2, a 100 percent return, and your brother would earn $14 on his $4 investment.

If another person or entity can turn your $1 into $3 within ten years, it would be an amazing investment (historically speaking). If the person or entity can do the same ($1 into $3) within one hundred years, it would be too long a time frame relative to the gain (historically speaking). Percentage gain matters, and time matters; one without the other is nearly meaningless.

Most people would consider 10 percent yearly gains good. Warren Buffett, probably the greatest investor in the modern era, has recognized yearly gains of 22 percent, on average, for fifty years with his company, Berkshire Hathaway. From 1965 to 2015, this 22 percent annual growth amounts to a 1,826,163 percent gain (not a calculation error).[7] Had you invested with Warren Buffett in 1965, every dollar you invested would be worth $18,261 dollars in 2015 (not adjusted for inflation). Warren Buffett is one of those people we would have liked to have invested our money with, not because he was superior at working, like our brother and the lemonade stand, but because he was superior at finding others like our brother, superior at working and producing, and investing in them.

One thing to keep in mind about investing is that many businesses would not be able to start without many people working in them. If I want to open a hair salon, I may need $50,000 to do so. There is rent, equipment, and so on. If my friend had $50,000 to invest, we might work out a deal together. I would be better off utilizing my friend's $50,000, and without both of us (their stored work, my current work), we would not be able to open up our new hair salon.

Without that stored work (money), many businesses would not come to fruition. However, investing is risky. Many businesses fail no matter how much work is put into them. That work ultimately becomes worth nothing. Your investment can easily turn into nothing. Invest wisely.

Common stores of work are gold and/or precious metals, real estate and physical assets, and investments in businesses. Each method has its own benefits and detriments. Financial advisors recommend owning a lot of dissimilar investments, a method that is known as diversification.

> Don't put all your eggs in one basket.
>
> —MIGUEL CERVANTES, SIXTEENTH-CENTURY SPANISH WRITER

Diversification is meant to bring greater returns with less risk. For instance, if you invest everything in a single company, and someone in the company commits fraud, you may lose everything. Even without fraud, a competing company, a new invention, or an economic stall may bring losses.

How do you value an investment?

> Everything is worth what its purchaser will pay for it.
>
> —PUBLILIUS SYRUS, FIRST-CENTURY BCE LATIN WRITER

The following are the most common ways to determine the present value of an investment:

1. Synergy value (or value-based pricing)—How much does the purchaser gain from the investment?

2. Replacement/reproduction cost—how much would it cost to build this myself?

3. Competitive market pricing—How much do similar investments sell for?

4. Discounted cash flow—what are the future earnings (cash flow) of the investment (discounted to the present, based on time and risk)?

How Do You Invest?

> The stock market is a device for transferring money from the impatient to the patient.
>
> —Warren Buffett, investor/CEO of Berkshire Hathaway

Thirty years ago, the cost of a stock trade could be $60 plus 1 percent of the trade. Today, many brokerages offer trades for free. The higher the fees, the more money you need to invest to offset those fees. In order to invest today, you will need to open a stock brokerage account with a reputable company {search: open a stock brokerage account}.

> It is not about timing the market. It is about time in the market.
>
> —Unknown

Smart-sounding reasons to sell stocks during a period in which the market went up 100x after inflation

Recession, Korean War, Red Scare, Sputnik, Recession, Recession, Rising interest rates, Bay of Pigs, Cuban Missile crisis, Kennedy assassinated, Rising interest rates, Civil Rights

movement, RFK/MLK killed, North Korea seizes Navy ship, Vietnam War, Recession, OPEC embargo, Oil prices, Nixon resigns, Recession, Inflation, Double-digit interest rates, Recession, Beirut embassy bombing, U.S. bombs Libya, Market falls 22% in one day, Soviet Union collapses, S&L crisis, Recession, Iraq war, Housing slump, LA riots, World Trade Center bombing, Interest rates surge, Oklahoma City bombing, Government shutdown, Olympic bombing, Asia financial crisis, Russia defaults, LTCM collapse, Y2K, Recession, 9/11 London/Madrid bombing, Oil prices surge, Bank crisis, Housing bust, Recession, Europe debt crisis, Deficits, Slow growth.

It's easy to look back and say, "I knew it," but it's very difficult to do so in the moment. Almost no one can, as shown in the graph above by Morgan Housel.[8]

> The typical investor definitely has a positive ROI but below that of the market. It's like grilling a piece of meat: the less you fuck with it, the better it is. Every time an investor makes a move, he has the opportunity to fuck it up. The typical investor causes more harm than good for each move he makes. But moving it around is the only way to get above average. So, in an effort to make a perfect steak, one steak turns out better than average, and nine turn out worse. But everybody is convinced they're the grill master, so they keep fucking up their steaks.
>
> —5DaysSober on Reddit.com

How does Warren Buffett recommend people invest? He recommends investing in US broad-market exchange-traded funds (ETFs) or similar mutual funds—not one that is actively managed by professionals. A US broad-market ETF invests in many companies in the United States, and those companies often do business in other countries. This allows you to invest in a large number of companies, giving you great diversification. The focus is on US equities, but many companies also have finance teams that deal in commodities, bonds, and other forms of investment, and many companies operate outside of the United States, giving you international exposure. The diversification within a US broad-market ETF is great and nearly perfect for an average investor (anywhere from $100 to $10 million).

If you choose your own ETFs (like a health-care ETF, an international

ETF, etc.), choose those with low fees—an expense ratio less than 0.1 percent per year is ideal.

Warren Buffett made a $1 million bet with an asset-management-and-advisory fund in 2008.[9] He wagered that an investment in a low-cost S&P 500 fund would be better over a ten-year period than what the professional management company could provide. The professional management company chose five different hedge funds to invest in (as a way of diversifying the hedge fund). In 2017, at the end of their ten-year bet, the low-cost S&P 500 fund finished up 99 percent, and the management company finished up 24 percent.

Investing in commodities and currencies (oil, gold, euros, Bitcoin, trading cards, artwork, Beanie Babies, etc.) is difficult because the asset itself does not produce anything and is more speculative, whereas a business produces to increase its value. Business: input metal, output chair. Artwork: Hold artwork and hope that others will pay more for it later. If you were to take that piece of art and rent it to a museum, then it would be a better investment.

Lastly, Warren Buffett recommends investing in businesses that have been producing for a long time. A business that will produce "in the future" (and make money later) is a guess. A business that only recently started making money is ripe for disruption (further improvements) and competition. A company that has been making money for ten or more years makes money now, produces now, is working, and is more stable.

What Are Scams?

A fool and his money are soon parted.

—Thomas Tusser, sixteenth-century poet, farmer, and businessman

Some people steal. There are many reasons they may steal. Sometimes stealing is thrilling. Sometimes people need the money. Sometimes it is just easy. Sometimes they feel that they are stealing from the rich so it's no big deal. Some poor people steal. Some rich people steal. And some from every social class steal. Some people lie when they're caught and explain how it would not be in their best interests to steal in order to "prove" why it couldn't have been them. Others, no matter what is happening in their lives, would never steal. Logic is often not present when someone chooses to steal, but there usually is plenty of deceit.

> The loveliest trick of the Devil is to persuade you that he does not exist!
>
> —Charles Baudelaire, *The Generous Gambler*

Most people are not trying to scam you; however, it does help to understand how everyone makes money. A literal scam is someone trying to steal your money and giving you nothing in return. This rarely happens with your knowledge. However, there is likely a well-known company that is currently scamming investors (like Enron in the early 2000s).

Be wary of anyone asking for up-front investment for anything. Franchises can be wonderful, but the reason a company offers franchises is to reduce its own risk—the franchisee takes on the risk. As the old adage states, "If it seems too good to be true, it probably is."

Multilevel marketing (MLM), direct marketing (DM), network marketing (NM):

These programs often get people to invest in up-front merchandise. Many lose money, though some of these companies are legitimate and simply exploring alternative marketing methods by cutting out intermediaries. I am sure that some are good, but many present themselves as a new, easy way to get rich (and help friends). If it were easy, everyone would do it, and then no one would get rich from it anymore.

People often confuse MLM, DM, and NM with illegal pyramid schemes. To begin with, most organizations—businesses, family trees, and so on—are formed like a pyramid. In the normal course of business, the money earned comes from consumers. An illegal pyramid scheme is one in which the money earned comes from within the company. The illegal company earns money by charging employees rather than consumers. If employees earn money through sales, then they are acting like commissioned salespeople. Usually, commissioned salespeople do not need to pay for their goods up front. An illegal pyramid scheme is where the people (salespeople) "working" within the company are not actually working—rather, they are funding the company by purchasing the products (and therefore are the end consumers). For a business to operate, the purchases must come from outside the company, not from within.

People usually keep "gold rushes" to themselves. If people let you in on a "secret," they are likely making more money and/or reducing their risk by telling you about it than pursuing it themselves.

> The most people making money during a gold rush are selling picks and shovels.
>
> —MARK TWAIN, NINETEENTH-CENTURY WRITER

If a person cannot explain how you will make money or how he or she is making money (possibly in a Ponzi scheme) or needs to get another person to explain it, the person is likely selling "fool's gold"—something that looks like it is worth a lot but is in fact nearly worthless.

The only way you can get scammed is when you contribute time or money to a venture.

CASINOS AND THE LOTTERY

Casinos and the lottery are wonderful for entertainment but little else.

The following is the idea of how a casino game operates: If I were to offer you a coin flip, with a fifty-fifty chance of a win, how much would you wager? If a casino offered this, it would be amazing. Instead, the casino takes the coin, shaves down one side, and then says, "Let's play!" The casino chooses which side, and it always chooses the side with the higher likelihood of winning. This is not illegal—this is known. The games are purposely rigged in the casino's favor, or else the casino could not operate. After shaving the coin, a result is not guaranteed, only more or less likely. If you win, it's great for the casino because it shows people they can win and, therefore, keeps them coming back.

An interviewer asked Steve Wynn, a casino owner, "You have never known, in your entire life, a gambler who comes here and wins big and walks away?"

Steve Wynn answered, "Never."

Lottery tickets are similar to casinos but with much worse odds. Lotteries make money off poor odds and taxes on winnings. The poor odds on lotteries, before tax implications, are around 20 percent advantage, meaning for every dollar wagered on the lottery, you should expect to receive $0.80 back. (Casino odds vary widely, but many games, like blackjack, are at around a 2 percent casino advantage: wager $1.00 and receive $0.98 back.) The additional taxes on large lottery winnings are about 40 percent. In turn, this often makes every dollar invested in the lottery worth about $0.40. Losing $100 each month on the lottery, or $1,200 a year, often keeps people poor. Over the course of forty years, investing $1,200 a year at 10 percent growth would be $585,422. That is $3.29 a day.

If you play these games, ensure that it's for pure entertainment—and that you are ready to lose.

> My issue with the scratch-off games is that when I was a kid, never having actually seen them around in my house or anything, I assumed they were actual games, where like how [we] played them mattered. That there were like choices in scratching stuff off that determined the payout. Then as an adult when I actually saw them, I realized oh wait, they just have a fixed value; you don't need to scratch anything off; the gas-station employee can just scan them and determine the result.

> Well, okay, that would just be a little disillusioning to learn, not really enough to get into a state of real dislike with scratch-off games, just a state of meh. But the fact that they're designed in this sort of disingenuous way of being like a game, of dressing themselves up like a game, and artificially giving people a sense of near-win when in reality there's nothing significant in matching three but not four of the widgets needed to get 1,000,000 dollars, you didn't almost get that money. Basically the techniques used to design these things are all based around trying to fool people's sense of how close

they got, and fire off endorphins, and generally be good and addicting. But it's not even like designing World of Warcraft; at least there you're getting people addicted to something that is a game. And the government is actively promoting it and profiting from it.

People say the lottery is a tax on stupidity, but that's not quite even a half-truth; it's like a third truth. Between all the work being done very clearly designing toward addiction, and the fact that the people who are most likely to turn to the lottery regularly, the people who have the most emotional investment in getting the relatively small amounts of money, and most desperate for the dream of getting a large amount of money are pretty often the people who have the least amount of money. Where people who have comfortable lives will occasionally play, but are harder to hook, they don't get as much emotional highs and lows from it. And when the state takes revenue from the lottery to add to its funds, what that boils down to is that what the lottery really is, is a tax on poor people. I think that's shitty.

—CROSSEDSTAVES ON REDDIT.COM

There are many things in life that cost little, like $3.29 a day, that, if invested, add up to a lot.

In *you, You, YOU are the Philosopher*, Alvin Chester writes, "There are those who say it is valueless to save only a little bit at a time; unless one can put away large sums, life will not be changed. They, therefore, never save, because they never have 'a lot' to save. Yet, there are many who understand that each penny grows on top of every other one, and pennies do add up to dollars and more."

LIFE INSURANCE

Life insurance salespeople often receive 30 to 90 percent of a person's first-year investment as their commission, and then 3 to 10 percent of all subsequent years (and this is just the money the salesperson is receiving!). Life insurance is unnecessary until you have someone you would like to take care of financially after you die. If you purchase life insurance before you have a beneficiary, your money might have been better invested elsewhere. However, life insurance is another form of diversification and a way to keep your money out of reach. If you are terrible with money, every time you put money into an account that you won't have access to for a long time may be beneficial for you. In most cases, a person should opt for term life insurance (no cash value, not an asset to you) when he or she is interested in life insurance, but whole life and universal life provide some sort of cash value/asset for you (though these are still not recommended).

MANAGEMENT FEES

Managers will claim they are better with your money than you are.

A management fee of 1 percent per year means that your single dollar, which used to turn into $15 over a forty-year period (after inflation), is now turning into $10, which amounts to 33 percent less. Quick, approximate math is $(1 + 7 \text{ percent} - 1 \text{ percent}) \wedge 40 = 10$.

With a yearly 2 percent fee, $15 becomes $6.67 (55 percent less).

At a fee of 3 percent, $15 becomes $4.43 (70 percent less).

However, many of us are susceptible to listening to what our emotions dictate rather than our logic. When everyone is talking about a stock, it is usually very high, and when everyone is scared, it is low, which leads to "selling low, and buying high"—the opposite of what we would like to do, which is buying low and selling high.

> Be greedy when others are fearful and fearful when others are greedy.
>
> —WARREN BUFFETT, INVESTOR/CEO OF BERKSHIRE HATHAWAY

This is extremely difficult. Managers are especially helpful in ensuring that you don't sell low and buy high, encouraging you to "stay the course," regardless of emotions and market sentiment.

LENDING MONEY TO FRIENDS

The first time someone asks for money from you, it is usually the hardest (on them). When you ask for your money back, that person may feel like paying you back is a "favor" to you. The next time that person needs money, asking becomes easier. The next time, it's even easier, and so on, until you have reached the point where you will no longer lend the money, and the person becomes upset with you for not lending them money!

> Give a man a fish, feed him for a day. Teach a man to fish, feed him for a lifetime.
>
> —MAHATMA GANDHI, LEADER OF THE
> INDIAN INDEPENDENCE MOVEMENT

It may be better to help people get their lives in order, set them up with jobs, and so on, rather than lend them money, which may push them even further into debt. Seek to help friends rather than give them money that they may (continue to) squander.

LUCK

My father used to tell a story about a stockbroker who cold-called one hundred people.

The stockbroker tells the first fifty people that X stock is sure to go up and the last fifty that it is sure to go down. The stockbroker says, "I would like to help you with this investment." No one invests, but he tells them all, "I will call you back in three months. Maybe then you will trust me."

Three months later, he only calls the fifty he was right about. Of these fifty, he tells the first twenty-five that Y stock is sure to go up, and the last twenty-five that it is sure to go down. He says, "I would like to help you with this investment." Some of them will invest, and others will still need to gain more trust in him.

Three months later, he calls those who he was right with. Eventually, he has trusting customers. While this example is illegal, many people engage in similar behaviors, eventually building up trust. It is up to you to determine the scammers and the lucky ones from the people who actually know.

It is very difficult to know who to trust, and using past experiences is your best bet. Remember that just because some artwork is worth millions of dollars and was once nearly worthless does not mean that you should buy nearly worthless artwork today, hoping it will appreciate in value.

CONCLUSION

A short play: A man asks a woman out via online dating, and they meet at a coffee shop.

Man: Thank you for joining me.

Woman: Thank you for inviting me, but to be honest, it's been a long day, and when you said drinks, I was expecting to meet at a bar. *Chuckles.* But this is great, too!

Man: I don't drink. Do you?

Woman: Yes.

Man: How often?

Woman: Usually about one to two drinks per day.

Man: How much do they cost?

Woman: Ten dollars each.

Man: And how long have you been doing this for?

Woman: Twenty years or so.

Man: So for each day of the last twenty years, you have spent, let's say, fifteen dollars per day on alcohol?

Woman: That sounds about right.

Man: Do you realize that over the last twenty years, you've spent, before accounting for inflation, over $100,000, and if you had invested that money in the stock market, it would be worth nearly a quarter of a million dollars after adjusting for inflation.

Woman: Sure.

Man: You could buy a beach house in a foreign country with that money!

Woman: And you don't drink?

Man: No!

Woman: Where's your beach house?

Man: [speechless]

Woman: I choose how I spend *my money* and don't rely on anyone else. I usually spend my time after work sipping drinks with persons who judge less and worry about themselves more. Not that it is any of your business, but for the past twenty years or so, I have fully funded my IRA, mostly fully funded a 401(k), nearly have my home paid off, and helped a friend start her business, of which I am now a partial owner. I have what I want monetarily. You should go work on what you want, which appears to a beach house. I want a good man, so I am dating...but I do not think we would work out. I am going to meet some friends now. Good luck and good night.

Man: [speechless]

We all choose how we spend our money. Do not ridicule others for the way they choose to spend their time or money, for we are all different. Pay attention to your own money. If you do pay attention to others, do so to ensure that they have enough.

▲ ▲ ▲

Alvin Chester:

MORE

If more is what you want,unhappiness is your lot
If more is what you need,how much is "more"?

Some people just want MORE. It doesn't make any difference what they may have...they want MORE. The one who earns $20,000 a year wants $30,000. The same one who now makes $30,000 wants $50,000. Then $100,000 and $500,000. And on and on and on. There is no end to MORE. There is no end to wanting.

At which point will that person find happiness? NEVER. Because the goal was not to find that income that will provide happiness; the goal was MORE.

There are those who need MORE. NEED…not WANT. There is a level of NOT HAVING where happiness is beyond reach. It is very difficult to find happiness when the totality of living is concentrated on survival.

The problem is how to determine where happiness is.

I believe that happiness is not something that you achieve from without (outside of yourself). Happiness is internal. From within each person is the decision made.

The fastest path to happiness is…HAPPINESS NOW. Can you find ways to be happy now, today…with what you have? Try it. Do it. You don't have to give up the desire for additional happiness.

If you can be happy now with what you have, consider that you might be even happier if you aspired to and achieved extra.

When you get to the point where you can save a little each week… WOW. Look, I'm happy with what I have, and I am not spending everything I have. If I want to I can have more. That, my friends, is HAPPINESS.

Being happy does not mean that one should cease aspiring for and working toward something extra. But now we are looking toward EXTRA HAPPINESS…not basic happiness.

I think my point really is…to look for the earliest happiness that you can attain. Don't put it off. You might be surprised to find that you are happy right now.

And you might get to a level of attainment wherein you say, "I don't need anything more than what I have. I can curtail some of the aspirations I had and seek additional happiness while still spending some of the time working toward my ambitions for more.

Chapter 3

College (or Not College)

TL; DR:

At eighteen years of age, you are fully responsible for yourself. If you choose to drop all your friends and family, you are well within your right to do so. However, they are well within their rights to drop you too.

What would you like out of life? If you still have no idea, that's OK. However, depending on what you do choose to do, different opportunities will arise. Time is one of the few resources you cannot get back.

You are the only one who can choose your path. Many people may influence you, but only you will live it. The decision whether to attend college should be just that: a decision. Take a year off and travel? Great. Take ten years off and travel? Also great. You do you…just don't expect to suddenly become a major partner in a firm in the eleventh year because "you're a natural."

For a detailed look at a college cost/benefit analysis, see the Khan Academy website (https://www.khanacademy.org/college-careers-more/college-admissions/get-started/importance-of-college/a/financial-costs-and-benefits-of-college) or {search: cost-benefit analysis of college}.

End of TL; DR.

The Find Law website explains parents' legal obligations to their children as the following:

"While parents have the right to make important decisions about their children's lives, they also have certain legal duties. Parents are legally required to support their minor children. Supporting your kids includes providing food, clothing, shelter, and basic care. Failing to provide for your kids can lead to neglect or abuse charges in most states.

Parental obligations typically end when a child reaches the age of majority, which is 18 years old in most states. However, you may wish to check your state's legal ages laws to see if they vary from this standard. Parents who have children with disabilities may have their parental obligations last beyond the age of majority. There are also certain circumstances in which such obligations can be terminated prematurely.

For cultural reasons, many parents choose to continue to support their children after the age of majority, such as while the child attends college. The federal government expects parents to contribute to their children's education and calculates financial aid based on parental income. Federal financial aid doesn't consider a parent who doesn't want to pay for college, even if the student no longer lives at home, to be a sufficient reason to consider the student independent."[1]

Before you turn eighteen, someone is supposed to provide for you. After that, you are incredibly lucky if someone still provides such things for you. (Note: even under the age of eighteen, people are lucky to have this sort of support.) When you are legally considered an adult, you have options about what you will do and when you will do it, as well as with whom, and such options include nearly anything you can imagine:

1. **Convince whoever you are currently living with to let you continue to live there in the same way as you did before you became an adult.**

2. **Travel.** There are many ways you can travel for almost nothing, monetarily speaking {search: travel for free}.

3. **Work.** Find a job. Hopefully, you have already been working for some time now and have saved money before turning eighteen. It is not easy to support yourself on minimum-wage entry-level jobs.

4. **Join a cause.** You can work, volunteer, travel, and more through various causes: military, Peace Corps, AmeriCorps, and more. Many of these causes and services will also help you significantly when you are applying for college or your next job or whatever it is you may want to do.

5. **Learn a trade.** Apprenticeships provide people who know what they want to do, at least in the immediate future, with a succinct, achievable goal.

6. **Start a business.** However, you will need that business to be profitable. Starting a business is easy while becoming profitable—especially for the time you've sunk into the business—is much more difficult. The nice thing about starting a business is your age doesn't matter. The market will determine who is successful. If you provide sufficient value to others, then you will be valued (and earn that value in money).

7. **Go to college.** College can be nearly every one of the previous options combined. You can join causes on campus, study abroad, get a job, and more. Not having a path (major) can hurt your long-term goals because the sooner you know what you want to do, the better. Starting a business and applying everything you learn in your various classes, from psychology to marketing, can help to grow a business tremendously. If you want to join the military, you can begin training while you're in school and then join the military at a higher level upon graduation.[2]

8. **Invent your own option.** You're a free person. This includes literally anything you can think of.

However...most people have no clue what they want to do when they enter college. Ask a few adults what they wanted to do when they were your age and how they ended up where they are in life. Most will probably say something like, "I sort of fell into it."

Obligations can change things immensely. If you feel obligated to take care of someone else (like a child, parent, or sibling), you may not have the chance to continue exploring what you would like to do...but realize that taking care of that person is 100 percent your choice.

Having a direction helps people immensely.[3] For a long time, knowledge has been too abundant for one person to learn everything. This was true in ancient Rome in 2500 BCE and is still true today. When you know what you want to do, you can dedicate your entire life to pursuing that singular goal. From a young age, I knew I wanted to be a pit boss in Las Vegas. I attended the University of Nevada, Las Vegas, majored in gaming management, became a casino dealer one month after turning twenty-one (the legal age at which one can be a dealer in Las Vegas), and became a pit boss at the newest casino in Las Vegas when I graduated. I was twenty-three and on top of the world.

At twenty-six, I changed my mind. I figured out that I didn't want to be in that career forever (and went back to school for a master's in business administration), but I had learned how important and helpful it was to have a goal in mind and to align my life (work, education, etc.) toward achieving that goal. Having that direction was a great part of my success and a contributor to it (and forever I will have a great fallback option—working as a casino dealer or supervisor).

Many statistics show that those with a college degree, on average, earn more money, are happier, and are incarcerated less often, among many other "positive" statistics {search: college and happiness}. (Note: a similar search {search: college and depression} can turn up results about how college attendance and excessive loans can cause depression, although it seems that the depression in such studies is widely experienced during school rather than after.) We can never be certain whether those who went to college would have made just as much money, experienced the same levels of happiness, and so on, without their college degrees. College is not necessary but, statistically speaking, is very helpful.

Napoleon Hill observed and wrote in 1937, "Knowledge has no value except that which can be gained from its application toward some worthy end. This is one reason why college degrees are not valued more highly. They represent nothing but miscellaneous knowledge."[4]

To go to college or not to go to college—that is a question many people face. The question is not whether you should get an education. The real question is *how* you should get an education.

I have never let my schooling interfere with my education.

—MARK TWAIN, NINETEENTH-CENTURY WRITER

As early as one hundred years ago, an expert professor could send students a curated, simple, succinct class to learn at their own convenience.[5] There should be no excuse for an unwillingness to attain knowledge.

I value a college education for a multitude of reasons, but I probably shouldn't have attended when I was eighteen. Attending college is a daily choice. There's no one bugging you to wake up in the morning or to get anything done. Everything is up to you. (Note: this can be the case when you turn eighteen without college, but college adds the additional funding pressure.)

Colleges teach a myriad of subjects designed to stimulate your thinking in more than one focused subject.[6] Elements of psychology are important in nearly every aspect of life, as are sociology, writing, communication, and more. Many schools purposely do not teach "to the job" but, rather, believe that they enlarge students' brains to think in more complex ways. Adapting the brain to the specifics of the job is up to an individual once he or she acquires the job (similar to how lifting weights alone will not make you better at athletic activities but will usually make you improve more quickly when you do begin to practice). The ways in which we apply these skills seem to be always changing, so it may be for the best that we learn the reasons why they work (education), rather than the details on how to apply them (training).

Some of the downsides to attending college are that you can be riddled with debt and that jobs are rarely guaranteed. The following is a comparison of the year 1967 to the year 2017.

1967 Expenses	Item	2017 Expenses
$275[7]	Yearly tuition (public, average)	$9,650[8]
$751[9]	Room and board (average)	$10,440[10]
$2750[11]	New car (average)	$31,400[12]
$14,250[13]	New home (average)	$365,000[14]
$7,200[15]	Income (median)	$61,000[16] (estimate)

The cost of college tuition has gone up more dramatically than almost anything else. Tuition once cost about 4 percent of the average American's yearly income, and now it costs approximately 16 percent (a 300 percent increase). Room and board was 10 percent; now it's 17 percent (a 70 percent increase). A new car was 38 percent, and now it's 51 percent (a 34 increase). A new home was 195 percent and is now 598 percent (a 207 percent increase).

A few caveats: (1) some attribute the drastic rise in tuition to government assistance and recognize that the poorer a household, the more help is given, so that only the wealthiest pay the full price. (2) Most items cost less today (rather than more). This includes small-ticket items like clothing and food, where our choices are also more plentiful than ever, and technology, which makes our lives easier. (3) I used average prices for past and current prices of a new home rather than median prices (which were approximately $22,000 in 1967 and $320,000 in 2017). Unfortunately, I believe that methods have differed slightly over the years and that the median price, which would be a better indicator, is less accurate. No single source has all this information, and I attempted to find sources that agreed with other sources. This other source would have shown a dramatic increase in price, but it was a 75 percent increase rather than the more dramatic 207 percent that we saw. Statistics, sources, and facts matter. As always, please verify for yourself.

MEDIAN SALARY BASED ON EDUCATION

(ages twenty-five and older, 2016)[17]

Educational Attainment	Median Salary
Less than ninth grade	$27,100
Some high school	$30,647
High school or GED	$37,391
Some college (no degree)	$42,310
Associate's degree	$46,276
Bachelor's degree	$61,970
Master's degree	$75,317
Professional degree	$106,434
Doctoral degree	$101,674

If making money is your only goal, it may seem obvious that you should stay in school for as long as possible. However, that isn't always the case. Depending on how long your education takes (a PhD often takes an additional six years after an undergraduate degree), there is the lost earnings opportunity cost of those years. If in every one of those six years you earned $0, went $20,000 into debt, and forewent saving $10,000 per year, you would have a net deficit of $30,000 each year. Over six years, you would have $180,000 less than when you would graduate. Additionally, that $180,000 can grow (see "Chapter 2: Money"), and there are many other factors that keep it from being such a simple algebraic problem.

The cost of college is often a large concern. Maybe your family can help you, but maybe not (and let your parents know that the government expects the family to help). Free Education for Federal Student Aid (FAFSA) is government student loans. {Search: FAFSA}. Getting a part-time job can also help you in college—and if it is in your desired profession, such a job could give you a head start at graduation.

Do the following to decrease the costs of your degree:

1. **Apply for grants** {search: grants for college}.

    Grants generally don't need to be repaid, but you must qualify for them.

2. **Attend a community college** (at least for the first couple of years). Check with the college you desire to attend before taking classes to ensure that your credits will transfer properly. Community colleges (two-year schools) are usually about one-third of the price of traditional colleges (four-year schools).[18]

3. **Go to college in state instead of out of state.** Out-of-state tuition is often as much or more than a private institution.[19]

4. **Pass your classes.**

5. **Use the library's textbooks or share with a classmate.** Textbooks, while often required, are not always used. Forming a study group and sharing with friends can keep your costs down and keep everyone on track.

6. **Graduate on time or early.** Each semester adds on large costs, both in tuition and living expenses. Living expenses often cost just as much or more than tuition.

7. **Take summer classes.** Summer classes are often available at a reduced price.

8. {Search: How to lower the costs of college}.

You'll find new tips to lowering your costs every day. Read through a few articles and find what will best suit you based on your situation.

One of the worst financial decisions you can make is to start college too early. When you are eighteen and broke, failing classes can easily leave you worse than broke: in debt. (Note: a student loan is one of the few debts that cannot be erased through bankruptcy.) The nice thing about life is that no matter when you begin applying yourself, other people will likely recognize it (if it is sincere).

Your efforts also compound on each other, much like investments do. When you begin applying yourself (or transfer careers, begin a new relationship, etc.), you start mostly anew. Your past is less relevant, and people tend to care about what you are currently doing. Experience goes a long way, but starting over too many times can hurt your long-term goals. Some people are naturally gifted, while others must work at it. Almost no matter what you put your heart and mind to, you will excel at it. If you are incredibly gifted but never apply those gifts or slack off, you will be eerily similar to the most common people in the world.

Nothing is more common than unsuccessful men with talent.

–CALVIN COOLIDGE, THIRTIETH US PRESIDENT (1923–1929)

Chapter 4

Jobs

TL; DR:

You can't build a reputation on what you are going to do.

—Henry Ford, founder of the Ford Motor Company

Work is the act of fulfilling someone else's want or need in exchange for money:

1. When looking for a job, showing up in person after sending your résumé is best. Making a human, face-to-face connection will help show that you are serious about the job.

2. Before quitting a job, have another source of revenue lined up. It's easier to find a job (and you are a more desirable applicant) when you already have one.

3. Leave your job on good terms. Bad behavior makes rounds fast, and you never know if or when you will work with these people again.

4. You may attempt to negotiate your salary, but it is best to do so only once you have received an offer.

5. When preparing a résumé, writing a cover letter, interviewing, and so on, research the company and tailor everything to that company. Hiring managers can usually tell which résumés are generic and which are tailored, which shows a strong work ethic and a more competent

applicant. Typos am easily noticed by others but are often difficult for the righter to detect. Have a trusted friend review everything.

6. Be 100 percent truthful, but tell your best truth. If you are caught lying, it can ruin relationships within and even outside of the immediate job.

7. Do your absolute best work before you are hired? Many think that presenting a potential employer with your average self is more honest, but the company has no way of knowing the truthfulness of your presentation. Imagine that you are being interviewed at a similar time as another applicant. You display your average self, and the other applicant presents his or her best version and gets the job after performing only slightly better than you did. The fake person (in your eyes) benefits at the expense of both you and the company. There may be times throughout your employment where you make a presentation, research, and practice for it. Your interview is a reasonable way for the employer to see how well you perform when trying hard and are under pressure. Additionally, if you do not prepare, you will likely come off as unprepared and not serious about wanting the job.

8. Culture matters. You will have much higher success if the way in which you work and interact with people matches how the company works and interacts with people.

9. Your employer can fire you for exercising free speech, although the government cannot hold you criminally liable for it (usually).

10. If you have a thirty-year general direction mapped out for yourself, it will make life easier. If you cannot decide on the direction for thirty years, try to decide on twenty. If not twenty, ten. If not ten, five. If not five, two. If not two years, six months. If you do not know where you'd like to be in six months, find some way of paying the bills and grow your skill set. If you fail to plan for six months, chances are you still won't know what you want to do, and you will be older but without any new skills. That looks bad and makes you less employable than your younger self.

Ideally, you will have a long-term goal that is attained through many short-term goals. Being honest, addressing issues as they arise (rather than behind someone's back), making continuous improvement, and keeping open communications with both past and present colleagues are the best ways to get ahead. If you do not have a long-term goal, then at least ensure that you are building your long-term prospects in some way.

Know that personal activities may disqualify you from jobs. Companies may choose not to hire you based on your social media profiles, drug use, or other personal choice. As an example, some companies restrict (cigarette) smokers from becoming employed due to the increased insurance costs (which the company reasons is similar to giving that employee a large, unwarranted raise, something a personal friend who is a head-hunter/recruiter related to me).

Last, know your rights as an employee. Look up your rights as a paid versus unpaid intern, wage and overtime laws, hazardous-condition safety requirements, and anything else that may be relevant to your employment to ensure your safety and the company's compliance. (Note: it appears that many companies take advantage of low-wage earners through wage theft {search: wage theft}.)

End of TL; DR.

> If we are industrious we shall never starve; for, as Poor Richard says, at the working man's house hunger looks in, but dares not enter...Work while it is called today, for you know not how much you may be hindered tomorrow, which makes Poor Richard say, one today is worth two tomorrows.
>
> —BENJAMIN FRANKLIN, FOUNDING FATHER AND BUSINESSMAN

What is the difference between a career and a job? Direction.

Hopefully we all find some joy in our work. Hopefully, we contribute in some way to the betterment of society or make things happen that wouldn't have been possible without us. There seems to be nothing more common than brilliant individuals who lead ordinary lives.

The number of job possibilities must be in the millions. Many of us grow up thinking there are five to ten jobs in the world: doctors, lawyers, firefighters, teachers, garbage collectors, restaurant staff, marketers, farmers, and maybe a few others. Chances are that if you can imagine a job, it exists. It is someone's job to test roller coasters, finance roller coasters, determine the feasibility of adding a roller coaster to a theme park, purchase the land for the roller coasters, make the graphics to be put on the roller coasters, paint the roller coasters, help people strap into the roller coasters, operate the roller coasters, sell snacks before and after the roller-coaster rides, and so on. If you are interested in a profession, reach out to people in that profession and ask how they came to do what they do! Most people enjoy speaking with others who are interested in them and their work.

How Do You Get a Job?

1. Find businesses that are hiring (or at which you would really like to work). If a business isn't hiring or if you don't succeed in securing employment with a desired company, that's OK. You'll gain experience in conversing and, if done properly, at least gain a potential opportunity for future employment.

2. Submit a résumé online, and then physically *show up* at the business where you would like to be employed, dressed as you would for a job interview (no jeans or tennis shoes). Yes, show up. Submitting a résumé and questionnaire online is easy (and often necessary), but physically showing up says a lot about who you are and how much you actually want the job.

3. Talk with any employee, look for the hiring manager, and tell them both your intentions. For example, say, "Hello! I'm here because I'd like a job. I've been following your business, and I really like what you do here. I would be a value-adding member of the team with my positive personality and willingness to do whatever it takes to get the job done." If the person you are speaking to responds that he or she is not the correct person to talk to, that's OK. Ask who is, ask for any advice on getting a job, and say thank you. Employers want to know that you will get along well with other employees, and having advice from someone who is already employed may help you get the job.

4. Follow up with anyone with whom you've spoken. An e-mail is usually sufficient. After an interview, a handwritten note delivered shortly after is best.

How Do You Keep a Job?

1. Show up on time. Give effort. Use energy. Be willing to change. Do extra. Maintain a positive demeanor.

2. Continue learning. If you don't continue learning, you are more easily replaced. If *your job* does not require continuing education, your job is more easily replaced.

3. Make others around you succeed. If everyone around you is successful, you will be more successful.

4. Only speak positively about people and companies when they are not with you, and only give criticism when it is appropriate to do so. Criticism is usually only appropriate when you are asked for it or when you are one-on-one with the person and always with the intent to improve the person and the work—not to belittle either.

What If No Jobs Exist?

They do. You're lying to yourself. There will always be jobs. As a race, we invent jobs. When the first farmers began farming, it created more free time for others, and they began to invent work. There will always be jobs for those who are willing to work. When the robots take all our jobs that means we will be living in excess…or are we already living in excess? Either way, there will always be people who want a masseuse twenty-four hours a day (which a robot will likely not be as good at in our lifetime) or someone to do _____ for them. We can almost always use more teachers or nearly anything service related to make others' lives easier.

Certain jobs may become more obsolete—and they will—but if you continue to learn and adapt, you will likely always be employable. All jobs change over time. They always have and always will. If farmers did not adapt to using cattle to help them till their fields, we might not have many of our common luxuries. The common thread within most jobs is staying current with technology, continuously learning, and being willing to work.

The following elements are covered in more detail:

- Résumés and cover letters

- Networking

- Interviewing

- Salary, politics, and promotions

- The next job

- Entrepreneurship

Résumés and Cover Letters

A résumé conveys data while a cover letter conveys a story. Taken together, a résumé and cover letter should show why you are perfect for the company to which you are applying. Most cover letters go barely read, but they do get read.

Almost no one should have a résumé that is longer than one page. Fill your one-page résumé, but also make it visually appealing. Keep normal margins. Tailor your résumé to the position to which you are applying.

Find sample résumés and mimic the style of one (or many) that fit your job {search: sample résumés}.

A résumé should list your most recent accomplishments first and detail your varied experience within each. Depending on the job you are applying for, you will want to tailor the amount of emphasis you place on your varying skill sets. For instance, if you are applying for a managerial role, you will likely want to highlight your managerial (or leadership) experience as well as data-driven insights within your particular role. If you are applying for a frontline employee role (cashier, server, valet, front-desk associate, etc.), you will want to highlight your people skills.

Each line on a résumé should reflect your best self and, when possible, be data driven. Most lines should emphasize a skill, accomplishment, or responsibility.

Data matters. "With a team, helped to pitch new clients with great success" is virtually meaningless. When replaced with data, it would appear as "Within a four-person team, pitched over thirty clients, resulting in an 83 percent conversion rate." The latter tells me much more about your successes, and I can more easily visualize you making relevant sales.

Education should only highlight aspects you are proud of. If you obtained a 2.3 GPA, I would not recommend adding that to your résumé. If you worked full time while obtaining your degree, highlight that.

Additional information can take on many forms. If your résumé lacks personality (which many do), it often helps to include your passions. Having one line (under 'Additional Information') that reads, "In my spare time, I enjoy cooking classes and playing the banjo," can help a recruiter make a personal connection with you by asking you about something you enjoy talking about.

You should be able to discuss every aspect and line of your résumé in great detail during an interview.

A cover letter should be in paragraph form, professionally written, with proper headings and a sign-off. The cover letter should tell the story of why you want to work with that company and showcase why the company should want to hire you. The cover letter should not be a repeat of your résumé.

NETWORKING

What is networking? It's developing professional relationships, and it can take many forms. You can meet new people and grow your network at social or business events or develop your current relationships with your friends, family, teachers, business or school colleagues, and so on. If people don't know what you would like, then it is impossible for them to help you. Most people enjoy helping others, especially professionally.

> Sometimes, idealistic people are put off the whole business of networking as something tainted by flattery and the pursuit of selfish advantage. But virtue in obscurity is rewarded only in Heaven. To succeed in this world you have to be known to people.
>
> —SONIA SOTOMAYOR, US SUPREME COURT ASSOCIATE JUSTICE

The easiest part of networking is being accessible. Keep your phone number. Keep your e-mail. Stay on social media. A line often heard is "It's not what you know but who you know." Equally, if not more, relevant is "It's not who you know but who knows you."

For many jobs, an online application and showing up is not enough. A personal recommendation is what really gets you in the door. You will still have to go through the interview process and prove yourself, but often getting to that interview stage is nearly impossible without a personal recommendation. The personal recommendation doesn't have to come from a lifelong friend, just from someone who works at the company.

INTERVIEWING

An interview is where your potential employer gets a brief impression of you. Be the best version of yourself. To some, this seems unethical because you are showcasing an unrealistic version of yourself. However, employers are aware of this.

"What is your greatest weakness?" This question is often referred to as the epitome of a terrible question in an interview. An honest person will tell an actual weakness, which makes him or her look bad and unemployable, while a dishonest person will lie. This is not a terrible question in an interview. It shows who prepared for the interview. Prepared interviewees will have a response that illuminates how they overcome their personal weaknesses but will not disguise a strength as a weakness or make them look unemployable.

> My greatest weakness is that I tend to procrastinate duties that
> I feel are boring. To help with this, I challenge myself to make
> a list every morning when I start work and first try to check off
> the things I like least. This allows me to save the tasks that I
> enjoy for later which helps me to be more productive.
>
> — FOURSEASMA ON REDDIT.COM

That type of response shows that you are aware that you have weaknesses, are honest about it, and are actively trying to mitigate it. Everyone has weaknesses. It's about trying to become better, not being a perfect person.

There are many interview questions, so being prepared for them is the key to success {search: common interview questions}. Also search for questions from the specific company you are applying to and specific questions for the same or similar jobs. Practice. Answer in front of a friend. If you are embarrassed, answer in front of a camera, and review your responses.

SALARY, POLITICS, AND PROMOTIONS

An interview is a great place to learn about a company and its culture but a terrible place to negotiate salary. When do you negotiate your salary? Only once you have been offered a job. It is inappropriate to bring up salary before you have a written offer. If you cannot get a written offer, this is a red flag.

Your salary is usually based on how much value you bring to a company. If the company bills out to others, it is not uncommon to bill a client at five times what the company pays you. Realize that the company takes on all of the risk in employing you. It gains additional taxes, often has to provide you with insurance, incurs other fees simply for being an employer, and, if you make some costly mistake, it is up to the employer to fix it. In addition, your first few weeks to months of employment usually consist of training where the company gains virtually no benefit from you—but is still paying you.

In companies where you are not billing clients for your work, there are a few ways that you may be valued (salaried):

1. Based on comparable positions. What is a similar candidate with comparable experience willing to accept for this type of position? You should be aware of this value, and it should be the lowest offer you would accept.

2. Based on value added to the company. The company will know this value better than you do. The company hires you because you add value to the company.

3. Based on your previous salary. This is a terrible way to base your new salary; your employer knows the value you will be bringing to the company, but you may not.

One of the best ways to get favorable job packages is to have competing offers. If the company is large, it may have standard packages. However, the smaller the company, the less likely that is. Additionally, are you a standard person? What makes you different from the other people the company has hired? This should give you more power in negotiations. As long as you are respectful, your employer will not be offended by negotiating your job offer.

The company may view various items at different levels of importance than you do. If you value vacation time more than a high salary, the company may be willing to give you more time off in exchange for a lower salary or a smaller/larger signing bonus rather than a higher/lower salary. If someone doesn't have the authority to change your compensation, then arrange time with a person who does have the authority before agreeing to anything.

Negotiations show that you stand up for yourself and, by extension, when the time comes, will stand up for the company. At the end of negotiations, everyone will feel better, and you will have helped to create a more positive atmosphere leading to long-term satisfaction for both you and your employer. The goal of a negotiation is mutual satisfaction, as is the goal of employment. When this is achieved, all parties walk away with a deeper respect for one another and more confidence in their decision to work with one another.

How do you get ahead within your job? Surround yourself with other high achievers. If you surround yourself with low achievers, hoping to be the exemplary person, you will likely find yourself also becoming a low achiever.

What's the easiest way to get promoted? Get your boss promoted. Always be learning, always be doing, and, if there's a lull in the work, do whatever you can to contribute to the success of others—whether they are above or below you. In short, be a team player, and try to make everyone around you look amazing. If everyone around you looks amazing, the common denominator will be you.

THE NEXT JOB

This is a touchy subject. Never burn your bridges, and always keep your network open. You never know when you'll run into a past colleague. The general rule of thumb is to give your employers a minimum notice of two weeks and to not speak with colleagues about your resignation until you have spoken with your management. Hand in a physical resignation letter two weeks before your desired last day. However, be aware that the company may let you go that same day or at some point before the two weeks. If the company asks you to stay longer than two weeks, it will be up to you and your new employer, but few will fault you for giving two weeks' notice and sticking to it. If you leave suddenly, you may be burning your bridges. Also, the world is small. If word gets out that you are a bad employee, it may hurt your future job prospects.

If you inform your current employer that you are looking for work elsewhere and would like a recommendation, this fact alone may preclude you from any promotions, even if you don't find another job.

How you go about finding your next job largely depends on the job you currently have. Many potential employers will understand this predicament and will be respectful of your current employment situation. Do what you feel is best.

ENTREPRENEURSHIP

> Ideas are easy. Execution is hard.
>
> —UNKNOWN (SAID BY NEARLY EVERY ENTREPRENEUR)

There are volumes of books for each aspect of entrepreneurship. The reason most businesses fail is lack of sales.[1] This section will barely scratch the surface of entrepreneurship. A good book that is of practical use and covers everything from marketing to setting up your business legally is *The Great Entrepreneurial Divide: The Winning Tactics of Successful Entrepreneurs and Why Everyone Else Fails*, by Charlie Goetz and Michael Axelrod.

At any age, you can build a business. No matter what age you are, the money is what talks. One of the most important aspects in starting a business is to realize that, in order to be successful, it matters less what you think and more that other people are willing to pay for what you are providing. The market will be the ultimate judge of your business. If others see value in what you do, then you will be successful. If they don't, evidenced by them not paying sufficiently for your good or service, then you will not be successful.

A lot of people believe "If I build it, they will come," unaware that, in addition to having a great product, others must find your product, and they must also believe that it is a great product. For this reason, it is prudent to test your idea as early as possible to make sure that you are building something that others actually want and are willing to pay for.

If you keep your idea a secret, no one will be able to help with it. Nondisclosure agreements are fairly useless (and should usually not be signed unless you are getting something in return for the risk). Without disclosing your idea to potential customers, it is difficult to determine what needs your customers have and how they will respond to your idea.

In every new business, there are countless hurdles before becoming profitable and likely before having a prototype. Only those who are ready to dedicate themselves and be persistent enough will make it through the gauntlet that is starting a business. Most people prefer to work on their own ideas because those are the ones they truly believe in, so failing to share your idea usually only hurts you.

If you don't have an idea but truly want to run your own business, there are online lists of hundreds of products and services people want made or done, from online writing services to massage therapists to plumbers, programmers, and more. Here is my personal idea list to hopefully spur some of your own ideas. If you like an idea on this list, go with it. If you feel the need to compensate me once you are worth a ton of money, I'll gladly accept, but it's unnecessary:

1. Individually wrapped dried fruit (mangos, apricots, figs, etc.). I believe that there is some joy in unwrapping candy, and I would like to bring a no-sugar-added alternative to candy that helps improve people's health.

2. Drugs. There is a honey that produces intoxicating (hallucinogenic) effects, but it is rarely sold in the United States. Why? I don't know. In "Chapter 15: Drugs," I discuss the drug arecoline, which comes from areca nuts, also known as betel nuts. This is one of the most commonly consumed drugs in the world, though the traditional way of consumption has been shown to cause certain cancers. It may be that if it were turned into a tea, it would have an effect similar to caf-

feine. People love drugs. Both of these ideas mainly need a marketing person behind them because they are legal in the United States. You could market these online and to physical tobacco/liquor/marijuana stores. Alternatively, you could open your own store.

3. Dishwasher-safe or washing machine-safe shoes.

4. Commando jeans (jeans purposely designed to be worn without underwear). I tried to find a market for this but was unsuccessful. People who already went commando didn't need a fancy, expensive pair of jeans, and those who did not were still disgusted by it. After creating a prototype, conducting extensive research, making a website, and paying for ads (attempting to generate a "proof of concept" through preorders), my business partner and I closed the books on this one. I listened to the market (which was screaming, *"Don't do it!"*). (Note: someone tried this in 2004 and was also unsuccessful.)

5. Flavored potato chips with actual dried ingredients. Rather than being flavored with onions, jalapenos, and so on, having real dried onions, jalapenos, and so on baked onto the potato chips.

6. Human points. Every time you do a verifiable good deed, both you and the approved company log the data, and you are given a ranked scale. Besides giving you a good estimate of how well you are contributing to others, this could be used in résumés. Rather than saying, "I volunteer by serving food to the homeless, donate blood regularly, and clean up waste in my free time," there could be a human points ranking: ninety-fourth percentile. This may be easiest if a nationally recognized charitable organization started or endorsed it.

7. Dating website. There are many ideas for dating websites, and I'm sure you can think of some yourself. A couple of ideas may be "Baggage," where you start your profile with what you think are your worst qualities or "Young Dates Old," where you can only see the profiles of those who are ten years older or younger than you.

8. Fortune cookies wrapped in bubble wrap. OK, everything wrapped in bubble wrap.

9. A social and honest website that verifies all members. Anyone may ask questions (and the questions are voted on), but only verified users may respond—and they must be experts in order to respond (rather than self-professed experts). This website will help to build trust in an increasingly digital world. While there are other sites that do something similar, I don't believe any are doing a great job of ensuring accurate information and an easy way to sort through the answered questions.

10. A *sarcasm font*. I'm not being sarcastic.

11. A cover for a shower/bathroom in order to quickly and easily turn a shower into a steam room.

12. Create an exchange-traded fund (ETF) based on the current holdings of members of Congress. Members of Congress have traditionally seen much greater returns than the market average.[2] Why not mimic them?

13. Beer-brewing company. Come to our pub, where you can hang and/or brew your own beer. During the day, host events for companies that engage in the team-building activity of brewing their own beer. Six weeks later, when the beer is ready, they come back and enjoy again. Staff members help people brew properly, and, over time, people can learn to brew better and better beer. The best beer can be promoted and sold at your pub, and the brewers could share in the profit if it is truly successful.

14. DVORAK Keyboard Company. Promote a non-QWERTY keyboard to parents of young children so that their children are better able to compete in the modern world.

15. Make joke *Saturday Night Live* items real. Some of their ideas are actually pretty wonderful, and you may have a quick and loyal audience.

16. Sell simple designs/ideas online. There are many different ways to actualize this, from starting your own website to being a part of someone else's (or multiple others). "I'm single, and wearing this T-shirt is better than any dating app. Ask me about my favorite drink (hint: its coffee)."

17. Acne-fighting shaving cream.

18. Anything utilizing block-chain technology (like a buying-and-selling ticket application).

19. Real estate bus. Every Saturday, Sunday, whatever, pick people up along your route and go home touring. Decorate your bus so that it doubles as an advertisement, and have it become known to everyone in the area that if they are looking for homes, they should hop on your bus. Even if they are not interested in purchasing a home, hopping on the bus for a day tour could be fun!

20. Ride-share convenience stores. Drivers of ride-share services want to make more money, and passengers benefit by convenience. Figure out what customers want by allowing drivers to customize their menus and sell personal goods (like umbrellas in Chicago, flats in Las Vegas, sunscreen in Miami, club host in Las Vegas, etc.). If drivers have unique products that they also manufacture, like soap or jewelry (one that does not need additional advertising/promotion), then let them first test them on their own customers. If successful, add the product to the menus of other drivers.

In time, a driver will become a millionaire, which I imagine would be a pretty positive boost for the company—empowering drivers everywhere as true entrepreneurs. I tested this idea with limited success by becoming a driver. My tips went up substantially, but I sold few high-margin products (as a driver in Las Vegas, flats for women were my bestsellers), and it was difficult to find other drivers who were willing to pay to start this.

There is another company doing something like this. (Note: the idea began as a miniature vending machine, but that proved too difficult/expensive to start.)

For all of the above ideas, check with a lawyer about the legality. Some of them have likely been tried and/or are already successful. Just because someone else is successful doesn't mean you can't do it better. There were plenty of search engines, social media sites, retail stores, and so on before the ones we have today.

Coca-Cola was not the first soda and isn't the only one either. Google was not the first search engine, and Facebook was not the first social media platform. The first to market may have an advantage, but being second or third to market with a better product—and not having to spend gobs of money to inform everyone about what you do (because past companies have already built the market)—can be a big factor in success.[3]

It can also be prudent to strike while the iron is hot. There are some businesses that it can be a good time to get involved in due to political climates, current fads, or natural disasters.

Why starting a home-repair business after a flood is a good business practice and ethical: In 2017, Houston, Texas, was hit by a large hurricane, which created a lot of demand for home-repair services. Some may say capitalizing on this disaster is unethical. However, what they are missing is that the economics of entrepreneurship and business respond well to market needs. "Needs" is the most important aspect here because without the new entrepreneurs opening their home-repair businesses, there would simply be fewer people doing home repairs, which makes demand for those services that much higher (and higher demand equals a higher price). Now, those needs will be met sooner, allowing everyone to benefit.

New businesses in renovation and other disaster-related activities will help the city return to its normal flow faster, with more people helped sooner. If a business performs shoddy work, charges too much, or otherwise does not create satisfied customers, that business will not be around very long. The market is fairly efficient at weeding out the scammers from the ones who are performing a good and ethical service. These are word-of-mouth and re-view-based businesses; without satisfied customers, the business should fail.

Realize that when you prove a market, competitors may appear—and fast. For this reason, brand name and recognition matter.

Coca-Cola wins because of its brand. Google wins because of its technology. Facebook wins because of its penetration.

Ideas are easy. Execution is difficult. If you are looking for funding for one of your ideas, please send an e-mail to me at danoventuresllc@gmail.com. I prefer to invest relatively small amounts, $10,000 to $100,000, and that you, too, will be required to put up a large portion of the capital required. (Note: I know many others who would be willing to invest in the right person and concept.) Market research, networking, working with others, marketing, and persistence are the keys to success. The idea needs to be solid, but equally (if not more) important are the timing and person behind the idea.

> If you don't build your dream, someone will hire you to help build theirs.
>
> —TONY GASKINS, MOTIVATIONAL SPEAKER

> Action is the foundational key to all success.
>
> —PABLO PICASSO, PAINTER

Everyone in this room, no doubt, has been told, "You have high potential." If in ten years, you are still "high potential"– you are not realizing your potential.

—BRIAN MITCHELL, ASSOCIATE DEAN OF EMORY UNIVERSITY'S
GOIZUETA BUSINESS SCHOOL

Our greatest weakness lies in giving up. The most certain way to succeed is always to try just one more time.

—THOMAS EDISON, ENTREPRENEUR

Laziness is when your sleep overcomes your passion, not under the influence of drugs but under the control of excuses and procrastination!

—ISRAELMORE AYIVOR, DAILY DRIVE 365

Chapter 5

Credit and Large Purchases

TL; DR:

> If you don't take good care of your credit, then your credit
> won't take good care of you.
>
> —TYLER GREGORY, CREDIT-REPAIR PROFESSIONAL

1. Why do companies lend a person money? To make a profit.

2. When do they lend a person money? After they have evaluated the
   person (often a credit score and employment status) and use of
   funds (investment purpose).

3. How much do they charge? They assess the person and use of funds
   and may offer varying amounts of credit, interest rates, and methods of
   repayment. This process is usually undertaken in order to profit (long
   term) as much as they can.

A HIGH CREDIT SCORE HELPS you borrow at a lower interest rate. A low
credit score tends to do the opposite. You may be denied entirely or offered
credit with terms that are worse. It is sometimes said that the rich get richer
while the poor get poorer. Credit scores help to prove this adage.

You can obtain a good credit score by borrowing money and paying it
back on time.

A credit score (and report) may be required in order to receive many things: loans, apartment rentals, turning on utilities, and sometimes even getting a job.

Why do you need to borrow money? In most cases, you actually don't. "Need" is a strong word.

> Conspicuous consumption: the act or practice of spending money on expensive things that are not necessary in order to impress other people.
>
> —MERRIAM-WEBSTER.COM, "CONSPICUOUS CONSUMPTION"

Large purchases are an easy way to save or spend large amounts of money. It is easy to ignore thousands of dollars on large purchase prices because they are built into a loan, only costing a fraction at a time. For most purchases, obtaining multiple quotes and pitting them against each other is the best way to obtain a lower rate. If obtaining multiple quotes, ensure that they are for the exact same or similar services. Sometimes a person or company will offer to charge less and will, in turn, deliver less.

Homes appreciate at approximately the same rate as inflation.[1] They are a great store of value and diversification, but they are not the greatest appreciating asset. When purchasing a home with a large loan, if you need to move or are unable to pay your mortgage for any reason, then it can turn into a terrible investment.

Other large-ticket items may be necessary, while others are more discretionary. Cars depreciate quickly. Vacations lose all of their tangible value almost immediately. However, most of us have a need for both cars and vacations.

End of TL; DR.

You can easily find out what is in a credit score or report {search: what makes up a credit score}. We won't spend much time discussing or explaining credit scores and reports {search: how to get a good credit score}. If you've never borrowed money, your credit score will be difficult for the credit agency to determine because you will have no record of "credit." For many, a credit card is the first step in building a credit score. The more credit you obtain, the easier it is for an outside company to determine your score.

> A credit score is a statistical number that depicts a person's creditworthiness. Lenders use a credit score to evaluate the probability that a person repays his debts. Companies generate a credit score for each person with a Social Security number using data from the person's previous credit history. A credit score is a three-digit number ranging from 300 to 850, with 850 as the highest score that a borrower can achieve. The higher the score, the more financially trustworthy a person is considered to be.
>
> —INVESTOPEDIA, "CREDIT SCORE"[2]

If you borrow money, compound interest is working against you. Borrow as little as possible, at the lowest possible interest rates you are able to find.

This chapter will cover the following topics:

- Home ownership

- Car ownership

- Vacations

When shopping, it is usually best to obtain and compare multiple offers and quotes. Ensure that when you are comparing, you are comparing items of equal value and characteristics.

As an example, here are the steps for car-tire shopping from WikiHow:[3]

1. Decide which brand of tire you want.

2. Do your homework.

3. Try not to accept the first offer.

4. Be polite.

5. Get quotes from other dealers before stepping into the store.

6. Always consider buying from an online tire store.

7. Check comparisons on reputable websites like "safercar.gov."

8. Consider carefully the lifespan of tires.

When I go to a car-tire store, I find out exactly what I need and ask for a quote. Then I continue to do research from home and call to obtain quotes from multiple tire companies. They will often ask about others' prices, and I will tell them. They will then often lower their price or match the price of one of their competitors. I continue to do this until I have found what I believe to be acceptable—which is a combination of low price, high quality, and ease of installation. This similar process may be used for many purchases, particularly those dealing with commissioned salespeople.

HOME OWNERSHIP

Home ownership, often considered the epitome of the American dream, has many factors to consider. Real estate makes a lot of people wealthy, but it also drives many people to bankruptcy. Both scenarios can often be attributed to leverage (loans/purchasing on credit).

When you purchase a home, you pay once. When you rent, your payments may rise forever. However, depending on home appreciation in your area, certain homes may never be good investments. Regardless of the specific details and where money may be better invested, a home acts as a great safety net.

Purchase a home when you are financially prepared and ready to mentally commit. Do your own research on the specific home you are seeking to ensure that it is the right home for you {search: when should I purchase a home?}. There are many transaction costs when purchasing a home, usually around 2 to 7 percent of the value, and when selling (5 to 10 percent). As stated in the TL; DR section, residential real estate typically appreciates at around the same rate as inflation. This means that the value of your home (post inflation worth) will stay roughly the same (even though the price rises).

WHY PURCHASE A HOME?

1. You only pay once (as opposed to rent, which goes up nearly every year)

2. Tax advantages on mortgages as well as property taxes

3. Good store of value (as a diversified asset and protection for your portfolio)

4. Acts as a great safety net

5. Easy to build value over time

WHY NOT PURCHASE A HOME?

1. Planning to move soon

2. Poor job stability

3. Better to invest elsewhere

4. Pressure from others as "the right" thing to do

{Search: Pros and cons of buying a home.}

There are many ways to go about finding your home. You could use a Realtor who knows a mortgage agent and home inspector and escrow company. Using a Realtor who has connections in the industry and is able to guide you through the process may make what can be a stressful endeavor much easier and smoother. On the other hand, there may be conflicts of interest. For instance, if the inspector points out a flaw in the home and the deal falls through, the Realtor may blame the inspector and not pass along future business, so the inspector may be more inclined to miss or downplay things.

Rob Torch, a Realtor, (in review of this chapter) explains:

> "You make it sound like the inspector is working for the Realtor, which is not true. I want my inspector to find all items of interest so when the buyer moves in, there are no surprises. However, I want the inspector to point out if something is major or something is minor and not to have the buyer panic on a minor matter."

If you are ready to buy a home:

DECIDE HOW MUCH YOU CAN AFFORD TO SPEND

This is done by evaluating your financial assets, your budget, and, if you need a loan for the purchase, speaking with at least the following three entities: your local bank/credit union, a mortgage company, and a mortgage broker. Remember that transaction costs are usually paid for in cash. If your down payment is 10 percent and transaction costs are 5 percent, then you need 15 percent of the home value in cash at the time of closing. Additionally, everyone involved in the process has an incentive for you to purchase a more expensive home, and everyone in the transaction (Realtor, mortgage agent, etc.) has an incentive for you to use him or her. We often look at homes and choose to buy the most expensive one that we can afford. When looking at homes, a home that costs 10 percent more will likely be a similar home with thousands of dollars in upgrades.

The government often places caps on mortgages based on a percentage of a consumer's income. If you are hitting that limit, the government is trying to protect you from potentially harming yourself by spending too much money. The governmental limit is an upper-threshold limit, and it is not recommended that any buyer use the maximum allowable amount.

To Use (or Not Use) a Realtor

The National Association of Realtors is the largest trade association in the United States. You do not have to use a real estate agent when you are searching for a home. A Realtor is a real estate agent who has taken on the additional Realtor Code of Ethics, has joined a large network, and generally has easier access to homes and information.

The most popular lie I hear in real estate is that buyer's agent's work for free. A buyer's agent is a real estate agent who helps a buyer find a home. The seller, when putting the home up for sale, usually agrees to pay a buyer's agent a percentage of the proceeds from the sale of the home. If you choose not to use an agent, you will have more negotiating power by reminding the sellers that you are representing yourself and would like to be credited the buyer's agent's percentage at closing. However, a Realtor may be able to better negotiate through more detailed understanding of the market.

A real estate agent cannot make decisions for you. An agent helps with the process, but you control the decisions. Everything in a transaction is negotiable. Standard processes may be common but are still negotiable.

Read and understand everything. You must abide by everything you sign. If you do not understand a certain clause within a contract, ask questions until you do. You can be on the hook for thousands of dollars if you don't read your contracts properly. Another danger of not reading through your paperwork is that you may later be subject to "transaction fees" and other nonsense that you *thought* you didn't agree to.

If you ever have a problem with any licensed professionals throughout the transaction, know that because they have been licensed, there is a governing board that oversees them. (This is true in more than just real estate!)

Before deciding to use a Realtor you personally know, interview multiple agents. Throughout your interview process, you will likely learn and consider much more than you expected.

SUBMITTING OFFERS

The listed price on a given home is not an agreement by the seller to sell the home for that price; it is simply the starting point for negotiations. Sometimes sellers list their homes at much higher prices than they actually expect to sell for. This strategy gives the sellers room to negotiate down to a lower price. Sellers may list their homes at lower prices than they expect to sell for, hoping to get multiple offers and pit those offers against each other. There are many ways sellers approach the list price, so view that price for what it truly is: a starting point, negotiation tactic, and nothing definitive.

NEGOTIATIONS

Everything is negotiable. Everything. Closing date, transaction costs, contingencies, leasebacks, home repairs, furniture, and so on. Everyone is different and negotiates differently. If you fall in love with a specific home, you may be willing to pay more because you've become emotionally attached to it.

Ultimately, your agent must do what you, the client, wants. This puts a lot of the negotiation pressure on you. Keep in mind that the price matters much less to the Realtor than closing the deal and making you happy {search: real estate negotiation}.

YOUR CONTRACT HAS BEEN ACCEPTED

This is an exciting time, but the fact that your bid for a home was accepted also means that you are now on a time limit, and there are many things to get done before you close. Remember when you first read that contract? Now you have a time limit to inspect the home to ensure it is up to your satisfaction, obtain the financing for the home, and more. The sooner you get everything done, the better.

Everyone who works with you on this transaction (Realtors, mortgage agents, escrow agents, etc.) has a big incentive to close the deal. Closing is when they get paid. There are usually many "outs" in real estate, but if you don't pay attention or let too much time go by, you may miss your chance to get out of the deal if something is wrong.

Closing!

The closing table will be riddled with paperwork. Plan to stay for at least a couple of hours, and read through everything. If you notice a "transaction fee" or something else you had not agreed to, dispute it, and let everyone know that you will not close until the matter is cleared up. If your agent pressures you, and you feel that you are in jeopardy of losing your deposit, do what you feel is best. Reminding the agent that you may go to the state board because you felt unduly pressured at closing may resolve the issue in short order. If everything goes well, congratulations! You have made it to home ownership.

Home Ownership 101

Stuff will break. Insects will crawl in. Property taxes will increase. Your neighbors will hopefully be fantastic. Your homeowner's association (HOA, if you have one) may give you violation notices. You own a home. Enjoy it at your leisure.

Other resources provide a lot of information that will likely be more informative than the content provided within this book. Search on your own for anything of interest and take care to get the most up-to-date information. Your neighbors are a great resource and have probably dealt with most of the issues that you now must deal with.

Buying or Leasing a Car

{Search: Is it better to buy or lease a car?}

Cars lose a lot of value the moment they are purchased (with a new car in 2016, up to 34.6 percent in the first year alone).[4] If you want to save money on a car, purchase one that is a couple of years old or, if you insist on a new car, consider purchasing last year's model.

Buying cars should usually be reserved for those who intend to own them for many years. Additionally, car purchases should be reserved for those who take proper care of their vehicles and do not place too much stress on them. The more you pamper your car, the longer it will last.

Leasing cars should be reserved for those who enjoy new cars every couple of years and those not willing to take care of their cars, either through poor maintenance or stressing the car (quick start/stops, sharp turns, fast bumps, etc.). However, it should be noted that your lessor may charge you for some damage.

What does a car mean to you? The cost-conscious consumer would be wise to consider purchasing a three- to five-year-old car and driving it until it dies and performing regular maintenance as recommended by the manufacturer. If you want a new car more often, leasing may be the right option for you. The "lease versus buy" argument mainly comes down to how long you plan to own the car and if you are buying a new one. Buying last year's model brand new can save a lot of money. The older the model, the less expensive the car will be. Use third-party reports online to decide what price is reasonably fair.

Insurance is mandatory for car ownership. Why? Because it is easy to get into an accident, and many people don't have the funds accessible to make the other party involved in the accident whole. Insurance makes certain that you can take responsibility for your actions. Additionally, like a credit report for your payment history, there is an insurance report that logs when you make a claim through your insurance company. This insurance report helps inform insurers of your likelihood to use certain types of insurance and is one factor that helps determine your rates.

VACATIONS

Go. Vacations have been shown to be good for your health. However, if you go into debt taking extravagant vacations, the added stress of the debt may be bad for your health {search: vacations and health}.

There are many ways to travel. Do your own research and figure out what is best for you. Other cultures have different laws and customs, so research those {search: ten things every traveler should know about (YOUR DESTINATION HERE)}.

Chapter 6

Taxes

TL; DR:

> In this world, nothing can be said to be certain, except death
> and taxes.
>
> —BENJAMIN FRANKLIN, FOUNDING FATHER AND BUSINESSMAN

TAXES ARE FUNDING FOR THE government and the programs that it deems necessary. Taxes exist to provide for the common welfare of citizens and have evolved to influence specific behaviors.

The government tries to incentivize many behaviors through taxes. Understanding this will help you plan for future taxation, but learning all of those incentives is nearly impossible.

> Unfortunately, most tax law is made by special interest groups
> to benefit themselves. The tax system is complex because
> everyone is trying to rig the system in their favor—so we have lots
> of different exceptions and special rules for different interest
> groups. It's not so logical, more like a big mess of compromises
> between people who have power to make the laws.
>
> —CORT ARLINT, CERTIFIED PUBLIC ACCOUNTANT

Generally, software programs for filing taxes are great (as the tax code is extremely long and complex). They should find all your deductions based on your inputs. The software programs do not help you with planning (preinput) and behavior modifications (for instance, changing from an LLC to an S corporation), which is where tax professionals can make a large difference and save you a lot of money.

Taxes are usually paid at the time of earning and are calculated on a yearly basis. If you are employed, this means the company calculates your total yearly taxes due and deducts the average from each paycheck. At the end of the year, the Internal Revenue Service (IRS—the federal tax authority) asks you to submit details about all of your income and expenditures to determine if you paid the proper amount throughout the year. The deadline to submit your IRS balance paperwork is April 15 (unless that is a weekend or holiday, in which case it is the next business day). Many states have their own filing requirements {search: when do you have to file taxes in _____}.

The IRS has a large problem with people impersonating them. The IRS will almost always contact you by physical mail first. The IRS website includes more information on tax scams, including the following:

REMEMBER: The IRS doesn't initiate contact with taxpayers by e-mail, text messages or social media channels to request personal or financial information. In addition, IRS does not threaten taxpayers with lawsuits, imprisonment or other enforcement action. Recognizing these telltale signs of a phishing or tax scam could save you from becoming a victim.[1]

End of TL; DR.

> April 15th. In a functioning democratic society, that would be a day of celebration, the day you hand in your taxes. You would be saying: "All right, we got together, we worked out some plans and programs that we think ought to be implemented and we're now participating in providing the funding to get these things done."
>
> —NOAM CHOMSKY, AMERICAN LINGUIST,
> COGNITIVE SCIENTIST, HISTORIAN,
> AND POLITICAL ACTIVIST

Each government, from local to national, levies what it considers "necessary" taxes. The national government spends approximately 15 percent (as of 2016) of its funding on the military, ensuring our safety.[2] Local governments spend a lot of their money (about one-third) on education.[3] The court systems are publicly funded, designed (ideally) so that no matter who you are, your actions have consequences. There are many forms of taxation. Some taxes are imposed locally, like property and sales tax, while some are imposed federally, like income, Medicare, and social security taxes.

The government has evolved taxation in an attempt to incentivize various behaviors:

1. For better health: tax cigarettes and alcohol

2. For better health: tax those who do not purchase health insurance

3. For a better-educated society: grant deductions for education

4. For a fairer society: tax high wages more than low wages

5. For more jobs: grant deductions for research and business start-up costs

6. For more jobs: reduce taxes on investments

7. For more jobs: tax other countries for selling in the United States

8. To ease pressure and create a larger population: grant deductions for having children

9. To encourage helping others: grant deductions for charitable contributions

10. To encourage home ownership: grant deductions for mortgages and property taxes

11. To encourage retirement saving: grant deductions for saving in retirement accounts

And then there's the tax-free status of religious institutions. In a country with such profound expressed respect for the separation of church and state, should this be the case? A small but pronounced example is the "parsonage" deduction, whereby members of the clergy can deduct from their taxes the amount they pay each year in living expenses—whether or not they actually lead any sort of religious congregation.

I have several friends who are clergy working at, e.g., academic or nonprofit institutions, who still gain the parsonage deduction. To a person, they admit it is a ludicrous loophole; but, because they are not idiots, they take advantage of it.

–STEPHEN J. DUBNER, JOURNALIST/COAUTHOR OF *FREAKONOMICS*

We could make arguments for and against each of these as being "right" or "wrong," but that is why we vote and elect representatives. (The House of Representatives is where all federal taxation originates.)

There are many more examples—thousands actually—of how the tax code incentivizes various behaviors.

The basic rundown that the average person without a ton of investments needs to know.

When you make money, a portion of your paycheck gets taken out and paid to the government. This math isn't always perfect, and it depends on assumptions that may have changed (e.g. promotion or job change or something). So at the end of the year, you submit the full story, everything you earned/paid that year. Sometimes you overpaid and are basically saying "hey IRS, I paid too much, give me my change back." Sometimes you underpaid and need to pay a little bit more to make up the difference.

Deductions/credits/tax brackets add a little bit of complexity to this math, but any free/cheap tax program…will do it all for you, you just need to make sure the information is correct. And typically your job sends you a document called a W2 form that contains all of your income info, so it's super easy to just copy it over.

One thing to note about this is that when you sign up for employment, you probably are able to sign up for "withholdings" [form w-4]. This is telling your job some deductions you KNOW you're going to take (spouse, kids, home, military, disability, etc.). This way your job can take less out of your paychecks because they know you're not paying as much tax.

Things get more complicated if you own a business, work as an independent contractor, or have a large investment portfolio. But what I mentioned above is pretty much all you need to know to file.

—VIDYOGAMASTA ON REDDIT.COM

KEY TAX TIPS

Stay on the alert for the latest scams and fraud, including tax ID theft, phishing emails, and dishonest tax professionals!

Things to consider when filing your tax return include credits and deductions, filing options, sources of income, and more.

Getting married, buying a house, or other life events can affect your taxes. Learn the keys to doing your taxes.

Gather your tax forms and paperwork:
• W-2s and 1099 income, 1095-A for health insurance
• Interest statements, receipts, mileage

Check for deductions and credits:
• Charitable contributions, education & child care expenses
• Earned Income Tax Credit (EITC)

Add up your sources of income:
• Salary, interest, investments, & retirement accounts

If you owe money, you may be able to divide the payments over time with an IRS installment agreement.

Get help from the Volunteer Income Tax Assistance (VITA) and Tax Counseling for the Elderly (TCE) programs.

Choose how to file your taxes:
• Online (IRS Free File, paid software, or e-file provider)
• Mailed paper return
• Tax professional

Do you owe money or get a refund?

Get more tax information at https://www.usa.gov/features/five-tips-for-a-smooth-tax-season

Brought to you by usa gov

For many, tax software is great and provides a cheap and effective way to do taxes. Those programs take whatever you tell them and generate the best possible outcome. However, what the software lacks is an intimate understanding of your other options and how to minimize your taxes due for next year. The software is backward facing, while a tax professional is forward facing. Each of us is unique, and finding a tax professional who understands your situation is paramount in reducing your taxes. If you are starting a business, are a homeowner, have children, and so on, it is probably best to at least have a consultation with an accountant to see how you may be able to plan better. Even if you are not in one of these groups, it may still be a good idea to speak with a professional to learn more about your personal situation. Companies pay accountants a lot of money because when they make a small change, it can produce a big (monetary) result. Many say to treat yourself like a business. Maybe, at least, treat your taxes like a business.

Chapter 7

Economics

TL; DR:

> It's how people get what they want, or need, especially when other people want or need the same thing.
>
> —STEPHEN J. DUBNER, JOURNALIST/COAUTHOR OF *FREAKONOMICS*

ECONOMIC FALLACIES USUALLY STEM FROM looking at short-term gains and forgetting long-term consequences.

End of TL; DR.

Basically, economics is the study of behaviors of commerce and how people react to incentives. Economists generally believe that people seek to recognize all opportunities and pick the best choices, given their knowledge and understanding. When people make choices, they are also making a choice to forego other opportunities. Most resources have an element of scarcity to them, whether it is time, knowledge, or physical limitations.

Opportunity costs generally refer to "the next best option"—what people would have chosen if they hadn't already spent their resources—but often include all options that were foregone. This concept recognizes that once you spend your (scarce) resources on something, you cannot spend them again. When you invest your money in X, your opportunity cost is what you would have done with your money had you not invested it in X (like an investment in

Y or Z or a vacation). Every day we engage in these decisions, which can range from whether we go to work to whom we choose to interact with to where we live to how we choose to spend our money, and more. Everything we choose comes with an opportunity cost.

Supply and demand are possibly the most basic concepts in economics and can be seen all around us. However, supply-and-demand curves are often muddled in the simple narrative of "an increase in demand equals a higher price. A decrease in supply equals a higher price. Conversely, the reverse of those are also true." However, it only tells the consumer side of the supply-and-demand curve.

What happens to the producers of goods when there is a decrease in demand? We know from the curve that a decrease in demand leads to a decrease in price and profit. The producers, in response, produce less. A decrease in production leads to a decrease in supply, and we know that a decrease in supply leads to a higher price. What about an increase in demand? An increase in price. But with an increase in price there is more profit, so more producers are willing to create a specific good. With more producers (more supply), price decreases. It is an interesting concept: an increase in price creates an increase in supply due to more entrepreneurs who are willing to make the goods.

Many say opportunity cost is the most basic idea of economics because it seeks to measure everything against another. Let's say you earn twenty dollars per hour, and it takes you two hours to do your laundry. Then, in theory, if it costs less than forty dollars to have someone else do your laundry, you would do better (economically/monetarily) to work an extra two hours and pay someone else to do your laundry. However, life doesn't always work out this way. Maybe there are other benefits that the forty dollars doesn't take into account, or perhaps you are not able to work an extra two hours for forty dollars.

Many people choose to grow tomatoes, blueberries, carrots, and other fruits and vegetables in small home gardens, devoting a lot of their time and resources to these crops, even though it is far easier and more cost-effective to purchase them from a store. Maybe there are other benefits that they gain from having their own small farms. Economics deals in and adapts theories from reality over time, but everyone is different, and humans are often unpredictable.

It is impossible to know the future. The best we can do is make educated guesses. The guesses inherently contain risk, but we must take risks. Not doing anything is a choice in itself and is also fraught with risk.

Various Economic Schools of Thought

Austrian: Reduce or eliminate the government.
Rationale: The free market will eventually solve the problems and will do so in a better/more lasting way. If we teach people to not rely on the government to "fix" our problems, they will stop relying on the government, and everyone will be better off.

Behavioral: Government should intervene where studies show it is best due to human irrationality.
Rationale: People are poor with money, their health, and more. The government may need to intervene in order to help everyone be better off.

Classical: Eliminate the government.
Rationale: The free market and the "invisible hand" will move the economy without a need for government. (This is the first original form of economics by Adam Smith, Wealth of Nations.)

New Classical: Reduce government, but be ready to act/help when technology or other factors throw the system temporarily out of balance (and then exit again).
Rationale: Utilize research and the past to determine the best course for the future.

Chartalism: Allow the government to help in all aspects, ensuring all demands are met.
Rationale: Money only has value due to governments (fiat currency), and capitalism is flawed—cut taxes and guarantee jobs to anyone who wants to work.

Market Monetarism: Limit government except in nominal gross domestic product targets by increasing or decreasing the money supply.

Rationale: Less government except to keep steady growth.

Marxian:

> To each according to his need, from each according to his ability.
> —KARL MARX, *THE COMMUNIST MANIFESTO*

All people should work how they are able to and be given what they need.

Rationale: Full employment and distributions based on need rather than a "wage" economy based on capitalism.

New Keynesian: Government regulation to stabilize the economy and produce desired outcomes on large scales.
Rationale: Economics can influence any area, and we should utilize the government in order to create the outcome desired.

Post-Keynesian/Keynesian: Government intervention in downturns.
Rationale: Stimulate the economy when necessary, but leaving the economy alone most of the time is ideal.

The *Laffer curve* is a theoretical relationship that shows that the more an activity is taxed, the less of that activity occurs. At a 0 percent tax rate, the government earns $0 (but production is high), and at a 100 percent tax rate, the government also earns $0 (because there is no production).

> Most, if not all, people would stop working at a 100% tax rate.
> The black market would become the only market.
> —RAUL IZQUIERDO, CREDIT RISK AND ANALYSIS PROFESSIONAL

Somewhere in the middle there is an optimum tax rate for government revenue, and an optimum tax rate for economic activity, and those two rates are probably not the same. (But that optimum tax rate for revenue does not necessarily mean optimum tax rate for economic activity).

▲ ▲ ▲

Alvin Chester, when he was invited to an economics class at the University of Illinois in 1993, prepared the following lecture:

I think it is only fair to tell you something about myself. You have probably come close to recognizing my age, which is sixty-six.

I have been retired for a little more than eight years.

I owned a small company, which made about eight million dollars in sales. I was fortunate enough to make it a very profitable venture.

Was it because I was a great businessman? Well, I think I was pretty good…but that wasn't the whole picture.

I started work in 1949…with a worthless BS degree (but a good education) and after serving a hitch in the army. It was shortly before my twenty-second birthday. (By the way, I started work for the same company that I ended up owning.)

The US economy was growing at a tremendous speed. Everything was booming. The American dollar had a high international value, and I reaped huge profits from imports. Taxes were fairly high, but capital gains were only 15 percent. Therefore, I could take a lesser salary and plow profits back into the corporation, helping it grow…building a large capital gain for my retirement.

I was a good businessman, but I didn't have to be. We ALL made money in those days, but that same situation that was good for me is not here today. Our economy has not been expanding. In real terms, it has been constricting. Our dollar buys less. It can only buy half of what it bought in Germany in 1983…and even less in Japan.

It's harder now. I know it. YOU should know it too. That is not to say that there are no opportunities now. There are always opportunities, but they are fewer and harder to come by.

What is our country like today…besides having an economy that is in trouble?

We have more poor people.

We have fewer educated people.

We have what may be as much as 50 percent illiteracy.

We have more crime.

We are becoming more and more balkanized.

I could go on and on…and I am sure you can also.

We also have a greater dependence on our government. Over the last sixty years, we have been more and more willing to have our government regulate our society. There certainly have been BENEFITS. However, there have been problems as well.

Now that we are finding more and more problems with our society, we are reaching more and more to the government to find answers for them.

How effective have our governmental resolutions been? How effective will they be? You, each of you, can answer for yourselves. But the fact is that government is going to play a greater and greater role in our lives.

It will affect almost everything about your futures. It will affect whether you make a lot of money…and what limits might be placed on that income.

Will it give you LESS or MORE opportunities than I had?

I think you will have it much tougher than I did.

I no longer look at our economy with the thought of potential SALARY INCOME. I have to look at the possibilities for invested income. What industries does it seem to make sense for me to invest in for future income?

I don't really know. A few years ago, I, and others like myself, could avoid making the decision by utilizing the high interest rates and investing in CDs. That is no longer an option…and hence the proliferation of FUNDS…which make us think our investments are in the hands of real professionals…and are SAFE.

I don't know.

I, right or wrong, in my own mind, feel too many industries are at risk for the future.

You must also think about which YOU WANT TO HAVE CAREERS IN.

YOU can afford SOME mistakes…but the fewer the better.

Many of my considerations respond to how we are resolving our country's problems. This will also affect you…but you for a longer period of time.

I will raise only a few questions we are trying to answer. You (and I) can produce many, many more. My list includes, mostly, those currently in the news.

An important thing for us to note is that we must find (or apparently must, anyhow) most of the solutions through GOVERNMENT ACTION.

By the way—I do not necessarily accept or oppose any of the items on this list.

♦♦♦

POLITICS

Should omnibus laws be disallowed and only items directly relational to each other be allowed into a single law?

Should we have (federally) a single-item veto?

What should be done to make elections fairer so that incumbents do not have so much of an advantage?

Should we have term limits?

What about PACs [political action committees] and lobbyists who give a lot of money to (and spend a lot of money on) legislators? Should this be allowed?

If a law is passed that certain amounts of money must go to a trust fund with a specific purpose, should legislators be allowed in the future to use those funds for a different purpose? Would this indicate some legal malfeasance in office?

If (as in the previous) the restrictions are not mandated but can be altered by the whims of a new legislature, what security do these laws offer us?

CRIME

Should convicted criminals be forced to serve their full sentences?

If prisons do not rehabilitate, should we keep violent criminals locked in jails and out of society to protect society?

What do we do with criminals who are still juveniles?

BUSINESS

What rights should employees have against being fired or laid off if the termination was for reasons other than serious offenses?

Should businesses be allowed to arbitrarily decide to replace an employee with one they feel will be better at the job? Should employees feel free to leave for what they think will be a better job? How can business organize itself so that employees will be secure in their jobs because they are allowed to and are assisted in performing better?

Should business profits be restricted or limited?

Medical/Health

If individuals refuse to lead medically responsible lives, are they still entitled to unlimited medical care?

Are people entitled to VERY COSTLY medical care...?

Even when close to the ends of their lives?

Even when there is very little chance for medical success?

Even if it will leave them, at best, with very poor-quality lives?

Should pharmaceutical companies be forced to restrict their profits?

Should research and development of medical techniques be taken from their current sources and put solely into the hands of government...in order to control their costs?

In an effort to control health-care costs, should our government restrict what doctors can earn? If so, should they be allowed to earn as much as lawyers, accountants, and bricklayers?

If doctors' incomes are restricted, who should be responsible for their errors, accidents, and judgments that go wrong?

If drug and alcohol addictions are determined to be health problems and are eligible for medical care, then what about overeating, smoking, habitual child abuse, criminal tendencies, and so on. Are these HEALTH-CARE problems?

Foods

Should government make and enforce standards on meat quality, fats in foods, salts in foods, or overall food quality?

Should all foods sold have to conform to rigorous health standards regardless of the cost of maintaining that conformity?

Should all insecticides in or on foods be banned even if it means food production will be smaller, prices will be increased, and exports will be diminished?

Schools

Should ALL teaching staff be required to spend paid-for time in the act of teaching? Should their efforts at research and publishing be considered extracurricular activities and not part of their paid-for jobs?

Should universities have separate research departments, not staffed by teachers?

Who, if anyone, should determine correct (politically or personal) speech and/or actions on campuses?

Should they also determine correct speech and/or actions OFF campus?

Should they be moral laws or legal ones?

What punishments for violators should be allowed?

Should these laws be any different than those that affect ALL persons in society?

Should student judicial boards be allowed to mete out punishments to students? How severe? Should they be allowed even to prevent opportunity for future education? To what standards must they be held? What rights must they offer accused offenders? What liabilities and legal responsibilities should they have?

Law (Misc)

Handicapped: Is poor vision (not only loss of all or most) a handicap? Poor hearing? Being very short...or tall? What about reduced INTELLIGENCE (but not retarded) or an inability to take any kind of stress (i.e., while working)?

What limits are there to the definition of "handicapped" and to the responsibility of society to make the lives of those so defined as full as possible?

If newspapers are protected by the First Amendment, then why not radio and television? We get most of our news from them.

If cable television charges can be regulated...why not newspaper prices?

If a personal injury lawyer sues for a client on a contingency basis and loses...

should the defendant be allowed to sue the client AND the lawyer for the cost of the defense? What about anguish and grief? What about punitive damages?

♦♦♦

These are only a fraction of the problems that our society faces today…and they should be solved.

The solutions are all interrelated.

The real question is this: What should our society be like for the twenty-first century?

We cannot begin to resolve these things with Band-Aids. That has been the problem we have faced all through these years of trying to LEGISLATE OUR SOCIETY. We have provided Band-Aid restrictions on some things and have freed other, similar things from restrictions. We have afforded some freedoms and entitlements without noting the complete effects of those actions…restrictions on others.

Maybe we do have to legislate society. But we cannot correct one item without the knowledge of how that resolution will affect ALL THE OTHER ASPECTS OF SOCIETY.

We must determine what our IDEAL AMERICAN DEMOCRACY is. We must have a predetermined goal. Once that is found, there is the possibility that we can change…not all at once, but in some order of importance those aspects that need changing with full knowledge that these changes will lead…without contradiction…to that goal.

Who is going to do this for us? Can we trust our legislatures as they now exist? I doubt it. Their track record is not very good.

We have just gone through an election wherein one of the most notable factors was a public outcry for change. One problem is that people are looking only for changes that benefit themselves.

But the knowledge that change is needed is there.

You are the new elite. What is your position? Will you be at the forefront of the desire for comprehensive change, or will you seek only that which you think will profit yourselves without recognizing that your greatest potential can best be served within the most ideal society?

I regret to say that we who have preceded you have failed. YOU ARE THE FUTURE, AND YOUR FUTURE WILL BE DETERMINED BY THE DECISIONS YOU MAKE NOW. TOMORROW'S AMERICA IS YOURS TO FASHION. WHAT WILL YOU MAKE IT?

What does all that have to do with YOUR making a LOT of MONEY? PLENTY. The SOCIETY we live in has a tremendous effect on the viability of our economic structure. KNOWLEDGE and TRAINING have supplanted LABOR in the world's economies, including ours. But our society has not found the way of preparing enough of our population to play a part in the NEW ECONOMICS.

YOU—who are well educated, will be assets. However, your achievement potential will be limited due to our social problems. Hence, the importance I give to them.

As for any ADVICE to YOU, I doubt it is necessary. I feel certain that by now you have set GOALS: long-range goals and the shorter ones that are the stepping stones along the way.

And I am sure you are determining that the economic NICHES you plan to fill that will fulfill your monetary goals...those niches...ARE THERE... AND WILL CONTINUE TO BE THERE.

I'm sure you are reading people like Stan Davis, Lester Thurow, Peter Drucker, and others. All economists do not concur with each other on everything...but they share, basically, similar anticipations for the next twenty years or more.

Do YOUR PLANS FOR YOURSELF allow you to achieve what you want BASED ON THEIR PREDICTIONS...or at least on YOUR OWN CAREFULLY ASSESSED FORECASTS?

I rather feel you know all of this, and it might be presumptuous for me to try to add.

However, I will try to answer any questions you may have...or challenges you offer to what I have said

The Way to Wealth

Benjamin Franklin

(An essay included in his 1758 almanack)

Courteous Reader,

I HAVE HEARD THAT NOTHING gives an author so great pleasure, as to find his works respectfully quoted by other learned authors. This pleasure I have seldom enjoyed; for tho' I have been, if I may say it without vanity, an eminent author of almanacks annually now a full quarter of a century, my brother authors in the same way, for what reason I know not, have ever been very sparing in their applauses; and no other author has taken the least notice of me, so that did not my writing produce me some solid pudding, the great deficiency of praise would have quite discouraged me.

I concluded at length, that the people were the best judges of my merit; for they buy my works; and besides, in my rambles, where I am not personally known, I have frequently heard one or other of my adages repeated, with, as Poor Richard says, at the end on't; this gave me some satisfaction, as it showed not only that my instructions were regarded, but discovered likewise some respect for my authority; and I own, that to encourage the practice of remembering and repeating those wise sentences, I have sometimes quoted myself with great gravity.

Judge then how much I must have been gratified by an incident I am going to relate to you. I stopped my horse, lately, where a great number of people were collected at a vendue of merchant goods. The hour of sale not being come, they were conversing on the badness of the times, and one of the company called to a plain clean old man, with white locks, "Pray, Father Abraham, what think you of the times? Won't these heavy taxes quite ruin the country? How shall we be ever able to pay them? What would you advise us to?"

Father Abraham stood up, and replied, "If you'd have my advice, I'll give it you in short, for *a word to the wise is enough, and many words won't fill a bushel*, as Poor Richard says." They joined in desiring him to speak his mind, and gathering round him, he proceeded as follows:

Friends and neighbors, the taxes are indeed very heavy, and if those laid on by the government were the only ones we had to pay, we might more easily discharge them; but we have many others, and much more grievous to some of us. We are taxed twice as much by our idleness, three times as much by our pride, and four times as much by our folly, and from these taxes the commissioners cannot ease or deliver us by allowing an abatement. However let us hearken to good advice, and something may be done for us; *God helps them that help themselves*, as Poor Richard says.

It would be thought a hard government that should tax its people one tenth part of their time, to be employed in its service. But idleness taxes many of us much more, if we reckon all that is spent in absolute sloth, or doing of nothing, with that which is spent in idle employments or amusements, that amount to nothing. Sloth, by bringing on diseases, absolutely shortens life. *Sloth, like rust, consumes faster than labor wears, while the used key is always bright*, as Poor Richard says. *But dost thou love life, then do not squander time, for that's the stuff life is made of,* as Poor Richard says.

How much more than is necessary do we spend in sleep, forgetting that *the sleeping fox catches no poultry,* and that *there will be sleeping enough in the grave,* as Poor Richard says. If time be of all things the most precious, *wasting time must be,* as Poor Richard says, *the greatest prodigality,* since, as he elsewhere tells us, *lost time is never found again,* and what we call *time-enough, always proves little enough:* let us then up and be doing, and doing to the purpose; so by diligence shall we do more with less perplexity. *Sloth makes all things difficult, but industry all easy,* as Poor Richard says; and *he that riseth late, must trot all day, and shall scarce overtake his business at night. While laziness travels so slowly, that poverty soon overtakes him,* as we read in Poor Richard, who adds, *drive thy business, let not that drive thee;* and *early to bed, and early to rise, makes a man healthy, wealthy and wise.*

So what signifies wishing and hoping for better times? We may make these times better if we bestir ourselves. *Industry need not wish,* as Poor Richard says, and *he that lives upon hope will die fasting. There are no gains, without pains,* then *help hands, for I have no lands,* or if I have, they are smartly taxed. And, as Poor Richard likewise observes, *he that hath a trade hath an estate,* and *he that hath a calling hath an office of profit and honor;* but then the trade must be worked at, and the calling well followed, or neither the estate, nor the office, will enable us to pay our taxes.

If we are industrious we shall never starve; for, as Poor Richard says, *at the working man's house hunger looks in, but dares not enter.* Nor will the bailiff nor the constable enter, for *industry pays debts, while despair encreaseth them,* says Poor Richard.

What though you have found no treasure, nor has any rich relation left you a legacy, *diligence is the mother of good luck,* as Poor Richard says, and *God gives all things to industry.* Then *plough deep, while sluggards sleep, and you shall have corn to sell and to keep,* says Poor Dick. Work while it is called today, for you know not how much you may be hindered tomorrow, which makes Poor Richard say, *one today is worth two tomorrows;* and farther, *have you somewhat to do tomorrow, do it today.* If you were a servant, would you not be ashamed that a good master should catch you idle? Are you then your own master, *be ashamed to catch yourself idle,* as Poor Dick says. When there is so much to be done for yourself, your family, your country, and your gracious king, be up by peep of day; *let not the sun look down and say, inglorious here he lies.* Handle your tools without mittens; remember that *the cat in gloves catches no mice,* as Poor Richard says. 'Tis true there is much to be done, and perhaps you are weak handed, but stick to it steadily, and you will see great effects, for *constant dropping wears away stones,* and by *diligence and patience the mouse ate in two the cable;* and *little strokes fell great oaks,* as Poor Richard says in his almanack, the year I cannot just now remember.

Methinks I hear some of you say, must a man afford himself no leisure? I will tell thee, my friend, what Poor Richard says, employ thy time well if thou meanest to gain leisure; and, since thou art not sure of a minute, throw not away an hour. Leisure is time for doing something useful; this leisure the diligent man will obtain, but the lazy man never; so that, as Poor Richard says, a life of leisure and a life of laziness are two things. Do you imagine that sloth will afford you more comfort than labor? No, for as Poor Richard says, trouble springs from idleness, and grievous toil from needless ease. Many without labor would live by their wits only, but they break for want of stock. Whereas industry gives comfort, and plenty, and respect: fly pleasures, and they'll follow you. The diligent spinner has a large shift, and now I have a sheep and a cow, everybody bids me good morrow; all which is well said by Poor Richard.

But with our industry, we must likewise be steady, settled and careful, and oversee our own affairs with our own eyes, and not trust too much to others; for, as Poor Richard says, I never saw an oft removed tree, nor yet an oft removed family, that throve so well as those that settled be.

And again, three removes is as bad as a fire, and again, keep thy shop, and thy shop will keep thee; and again, if you would have your business done, go; if not, send. And again, he that by the plough would thrive, himself must either hold or drive.

And again, the eye of a master will do more work than both his hands; and again, want of care does us more damage than want of knowledge; and again, not to oversee workmen is to leave them your purse open. Trusting too much to others care is the ruin of many; for, as the almanack says, in the affairs of this world men are saved not by faith, but by the want of it; but a man's own care is profitable; for, saith Poor Dick, learning is to the studious, and riches to the careful, as well as power to the bold, and heaven to the virtuous. And farther, if you would have a faithful servant, and one that you like, serve yourself. And again, he adviseth to circumspection and care, even in the smallest matters, because sometimes a little neglect may breed great mischief; adding, for want of a nail the shoe was lost; for want of a shoe the horse was lost, and for want of a horse the rider was lost, being overtaken and slain by the enemy, all for want of care about a horse-shoe nail.

So much for industry, my friends, and attention to one's own business; but to these we must add frugality, if we would make our industry more certainly successful. A man may, if he knows not how to save as he gets, keep his nose all his life to the grindstone, and die not worth a groat at last. A fat kitchen makes a lean will, as Poor Richard says; and, many estates are spent in the getting, since women for tea forsook spinning and knitting, and men for punch forsook hewing and splitting.

If you would be wealthy, says he, in another almanack, think of saving as well as of getting: the Indies have not made Spain rich, because her outgoes are greater than her incomes. Away then with your expensive follies, and you will not have so much cause to complain of hard times, heavy taxes, and chargeable families; for, as Poor Dick says, women and wine, game and deceit, make the wealth small, and the wants great.

And farther, what maintains one vice, would bring up two children. You may think perhaps that a little tea, or a little punch now and then, diet a little more costly, clothes a little finer, and a little entertainment now and then, can be no great matter; but remember what Poor Richard says, many a little makes a mickle, and farther, beware of little expenses; a small leak will sink a great ship, and again, who dainties love, shall beggars prove, and moreover, fools make feasts, and wise men eat them.

Here you are all got together at this vendue of fineries and knicknacks. You call them goods, but if you do not take care, they will prove evils to some of you. You expect they will be sold cheap, and perhaps they may for less than they cost; but if you have no occasion for them, they must be dear to you. Remember what Poor Richard says, *buy what thou hast no need of, and ere long thou shalt sell thy necessaries.* And again, *at a great pennyworth pause a while*: he means, that perhaps the cheapness is apparent only, and not real; or the bargain, by straitning thee in thy business, may do thee more harm than good. For in another place he says, *many have been ruined by buying good pennyworths*. Again, Poor Richard says, *'tis foolish to lay our money in a purchase of repentance*; and yet this folly is practiced every day at vendues, for want of minding the almanack. *Wise men*, as Poor Dick says, *learn by others' harms, fools scarcely by their own*, but, *Felix quem faciunt aliena pericula cautum*. Many a one, for the sake of finery on the back, have gone with a hungry belly, and half-starved their families; *silks and satins, scarlet and velvets*, as Poor Richard says, *put out the kitchen fire*. These are not the necessaries of life; they can scarcely be called the conveniences, and yet only because they look pretty, how many want to have them. The artificial wants of mankind thus become more numerous than the natural; and, as Poor Dick says, *for one poor person, there are an hundred indigent*. By these, and other extravagancies, the genteel are reduced to poverty, and forced to borrow of those whom they formerly despised, but who through industry and frugality have maintained their standing; in which case it appears plainly, that a *ploughman on his legs is higher than a gentleman on his knees*, as Poor Richard says. Perhaps they have had a small estate left them, which they knew not the getting off; they think *'tis day, and will never be night*; that a little to be spent out of so much, is not worth minding; *(a child and a fool*, as Poor Richard says, *imagine twenty shillings and twenty years can never be spent)* but, *always taking out of the meal-tub, and never putting in, soon comes to the bottom*; then, as Poor Dick says, *when the well's dry, they know the worth of water*. But this they might have known before, if they had taken his advice; *if you would know the value of money, go and try to borrow some*, for, *he that goes a borrowing goes a sorrowing*, and indeed so does he that lends to such people, when he goes to get it in again.

Poor Dick farther advises, and says, fond pride of dress, is sure a very curse; e'er fancy you consult, consult your purse. And again, pride is as loud a beggar as want, and a great deal more saucy. When you have bought one fine thing you must buy ten more, that your appearance may be all of a piece; but Poor Dick says, 'tis easier to suppress the first desire than to satisfy all that follow it. And 'tis as truly folly for the poor to ape the rich, as for the frog to swell, in order to equal the ox.

Great estates may venture more, but little boats should keep near shore.

'Tis however a folly soon punished; for pride that dines on vanity sups on contempt, as Poor Richard says. And in another place, pride breakfasted with plenty, dined with poverty, and supped with infamy. And after all, of what use is this pride of appearance, for which so much is risked, so much is suffered? It cannot promote health, or ease pain; it makes no increase of merit in the person, it creates envy, it hastens misfortune.

What is a butterfly? At best He's but a caterpillar dressed. The gaudy fop's his picture just, as Poor Richard says.

But what madness must it be to run in debt for these superfluities! We are offered, by the terms of this vendue, six months credit; and that perhaps has induced some of us to attend it, because we cannot spare the ready money, and hope now to be fine without it. But, ah, think what you do when you run in debt; you give to another power over your liberty. If you cannot pay at the time, you will be ashamed to see your creditor; you will be in fear when you speak to him, you will make poor pitiful sneaking excuses, and by degrees come to lose you veracity, and sink into base downright lying; for, as Poor Richard says, the second vice is lying, the first is running in debt. And again to the same purpose, lying rides upon debt's back. Whereas a freeborn Englishman ought not to be ashamed or afraid to see or speak to any man living. But poverty often deprives a man of all spirit and virtue: 'tis hard for an empty bag to stand upright, as Poor Richard truly says. What would you think of that prince, or that government, who should issue an edict forbidding you to dress like a gentleman or a gentlewoman, on pain of imprisonment or servitude? Would you not say, that you are free, have a right to dress as you please, and that such an edict would be a breach of your privileges, and such a government tyrannical? And yet you are about to put yourself under that tyranny when you run in debt for such dress! Your creditor has authority at his pleasure to deprive you of your liberty, by confining you in goal [jail] for life, or to sell you for a servant, if you should not be able to pay him! When you have got your bargain, you may, perhaps, think little of payment; but creditors, Poor Richard tells us, have better memories than debtors, and in another place says, creditors are a superstitious sect, great observers of set days and times. The day comes round before you are aware, and the demand is made before you are prepared to satisfy it. Or if you bear your debt in mind, the term which at first seemed so long, will, as it lessens, appear extremely short. Time will seem to have added wings to his heels as well as shoulders. Those have a short lent, saith Poor Richard, who owe money to be paid at Easter. Then since, as he says, the borrower is a slave to the lender, and the debtor to the creditor, disdain the chain, preserve your freedom; and maintain your independency: be industrious and free; be frugal and free. At present, perhaps, you may think yourself in thriving circumstances, and that you can bear a little extravagance without injury; but, for age and want, save while you may; no morning sun lasts a whole day, as Poor Richard says.

Gain may be temporary and uncertain, but ever while you live, expense is constant and certain; and *'tis easier to build two chimneys than to keep one in fuel*, as Poor Richard says. So *rather go to bed supper less than rise in debt.*

Get what you can, and what you get hold; 'Tis the stone that will turn all your lead into gold, as Poor Richard says. And when you have got the philosopher's stone, sure you will no longer complain of bad times, or the difficulty of paying taxes.

This doctrine, my friends, is reason and wisdom; but after all, do not depend too much upon your own industry, and frugality, and prudence, though excellent things, for they may all be blasted without the blessing of heaven; and therefore ask that blessing humbly, and be not uncharitable to those that at present seem to want it, but comfort and help them. Remember Job suffered, and was afterwards prosperous.

And now to conclude, *experience keeps a dear school, but fools will learn in no other, and scarce in that,* for it is true, *we may give advice, but we cannot give conduct*, as Poor Richard says: however, remember this, *they that won't be counseled, can't be helped*, as Poor Richard says: and farther, that *if you will not hear reason, she'll surely rap your knuckles.*

Thus the old gentleman ended his harangue. The people heard it, and approved the doctrine, and immediately practiced the contrary, just as if it had been a common sermon; for the vendue opened, and they began to buy extravagantly, notwithstanding all his cautions, and their own fear of taxes.

I found the good man had thoroughly studied my almanacks, and digested all I had dropped on those topics during the course of five-and-twenty years. The frequent mention he made of me must have tired anyone else, but my vanity was wonderfully delighted with it, though I was conscious that not a tenth part of the wisdom was my own which he ascribed to me, but rather the gleanings I had made of the sense of all ages and nations. However, I resolved to be the better for the echo of it; and though I had at first determined to buy stuff for a new coat, I went away resolved to wear my old one a little longer. Reader, if thou wilt do the same, thy profit will be as great as mine.

I am, as ever,

Thine to serve thee,

July 7, 1757. RICHARD SAUNDERS

Part Three: Sex

Nothing new here

Chapter 8

Sex

TL; DR:

MAKE YOUR OWN DECISIONS REGARDING sex, and make them active decisions. Sex is an act that you should feel comfortable engaging in—from the very beginning through to the very end. Many from your group of friends, family, religious affiliation, and more will likely influence your decisions regarding sex. Make your own determination for when it is right and when it is wrong.

Sex is fantastic and almost always benefits your health, so long as you practice it safely and intelligently[1] {search: health and sex}. Sexually transmitted infections (STIs) and children are potential risks that result from unsafe or unintelligent sex, and some STIs can stick with you for the remainder of your life. It is probably advisable to wait until marriage before engaging in sexual intercourse. Before marriage, both parties should be tested for infections, diseases, and other health anomalies.

Since you probably won't wait until marriage, know that you are much more likely to catch an STI. The Centers for Disease Control and Prevention (CDC) estimates that one in four persons in the United States currently has HPV,[2] and the American Sexual Health Association estimates that 80 percent of sexually active persons will be infected with HPV at some point in their lives.[3] In most HPV cases, the virus disappears on its own within a few years. The CDC also estimates that 54 percent of the US population age fourteen to forty-nine has oral herpes.[4] The National Institute of Health estimates that one in every seven people living with HIV (the virus that leads to AIDS) is unaware of it.[5]

Ensure that one partner wears a condom when engaging in sexual intercourse in order to prevent STIs and pregnancy. It is further recommended that at least one of the partners uses a backup method of birth control and for everyone involved in the sexual activities to get tested for STIs every six months while they are sexually active. Discussing birth control and STIs prior to engaging in sexual relations is recommended and may put both partners at ease. These practices help reduce unwanted pregnancies and will also help to prevent the spread of infectious diseases.

After sex, all parties should pee in order to reduce the risk of a bacterial infection.[6] Lastly, know that cuddling with your partner after sex increases your connection with one another through the production of the hormone oxytocin and is extremely healthy for you—just as sex is usually incredibly healthy for you {search: cuddle hormone}.

End of TL; DR.

ON PICKING UP YOUR MATE

How should you speak with those you are interested in? There is an abundance of information and various guides available to both genders. Different acts work for different people. You'll need to figure out your own version of how to pick someone up. The best advice I can give is that no matter what other people think you should do—how to talk, where to go, and so on—remain true to yourself and make it your own, rather than copying someone. (Note that this mentality holds true for most everything in life. While others may give advice on what to do, act, say, and so on, you must adapt their advice to your own personality and style, whether it be selling, interviewing, writing, managing, or similar.)

My go-to line for trying to get to know women better stems from being honest with them: "I want to get to know you better. Are you available to grab ice cream with me tomorrow at seven thirty at the greatest ice cream shop in all the land?" Use other people's ideas, but be yourself. Maybe you don't like ice cream. "You seem really interesting. Are you free tomorrow evening for a late coffee date? Four p.m. at the student union? I know, I think four p.m. is late—I'm so old."

When asking someone out, it's usually better to be direct rather than vague. "How about we get coffee tomorrow at three at the coffee shop next to the student union?" is better than "How about we hang out sometime in the near future?" By asking for a specific action, time, and date, you come across as more confident, and it is easier for the person to respond. If you get an "I'm busy" response (but you believe there is genuine interest), ask the person to recommend a time and place. If you leave anything vague, you have another hurdle—asking the person out again. If you reject a person's advances, do so nicely, firmly, and in a way he or she will understand. "Thank you, but I'm not interested." In some cultures, maybe basically means yes, and no means maybe.

Not ready to ask the person out? Say anything, even if it's "Um…hi" and nothing else. Some will think it's cute. Some will keep talking. If the person's reply is an equally awkward "Um…hi," you may have found your match. An easy way to keep a conversation going is to be genuinely interested in the person you're talking to. Listen to the things the person says and ask questions based on those things.

Anyone who is going to actually like you will need to respect you. If you're asked if you're a cat or dog person, and you respond cat while the other person says dog, that's OK! That's a great conversation starter, and you can discuss those differences. If you respond with "Oh, I love dogs too!" you may come off as trying to appease the other person without showing your true personality, which may kill a relationship before one even begins. Be your honest self (but not a jerk). Much of communication is how you say something rather than what you're saying.

If you are unsure if someone is interested in going out with you, ask! You could try one of the following two lines recommended by Al Vernacchio:

"I'm trying to figure something out and I could use your help. I'm feeling a bit confused about what you think of me. I'm wondering, can you be honest with me and tell me whether you like me or not?"

Or

"It's hard for me to figure out if someone likes me or not. I'd be a lot less anxious if I knew for sure. So I was just wondering, do you like me?"[7]

On Consent

Before you have sex, you need a willing partner. *Obtain enthusiastic consent.*

If your partner is under the age of consent, intoxicated or under the influence of drugs, is pressured or threatened in any way, or asks you to stop at any point, you may be charged with rape, even if you thought it was completely consensual.[8]

On Sex

1. It may be best to wait until you find your life partner to begin engaging in sex. Nearly every religion advocates for this, and there is probably a lot of truth in it due to the emotional roller coaster (hormones) that sex helps to create. However, depending on your culture and upbringing, waiting too long to have sex has been shown to be detrimental to a person's psyche. This is a decision only you can make. (Note: I have not provided research here because in my opinion, there are inadequate research studies.)

    Here is something very personal to me; I still think about nearly every person I have been with from time to time. I hope to get married and be in a committed relationship, and I wonder how much the experiences of these other women will taint my sexual and personal connection with that person. Sex helps to create attachment. While I don't regret what I've done, there is definitely a part of me that thinks about how different (and possibly for the best) my life would be with that special person once I find her.

2. Sex gets better as you learn what your partner enjoys and as both partners become more comfortable with one another. Your body was designed to enjoy sex, and, most of the time, it will {search: how to become better at sex}.

3. Any time a woman has sex, there is a chance that she can become pregnant.

The United Kingdom's NHS choices' website writes,

"When a woman has vaginal sex for the first time, it can be a little painful. There may also be a small amount of blood, but this isn't always the case and usually occurs because the hymen has been broken during sexual intercourse.

The hymen is a small piece of thin skin (membrane) that can either partially or totally cover the entrance to the vagina. A woman might already have broken her hymen without knowing about it; this can happen when playing sports or using a tampon.

When a man has sex for the first time, it shouldn't hurt, but he can make it easier for his partner by using foreplay, making sure there is plenty of lubrication and by being gentle and going slowly."[9]

On Pregnancy

If you want to have a child, for healthiest/best sperm, it's best if the male is in top physical condition and hasn't been using any drugs for three months prior to the female becoming pregnant.[10] The female should also be in top physical condition, be free from drugs for two weeks prior to becoming pregnant, and refrain from all drug use throughout the pregnancy and breastfeeding {search: healthy pregnancy}. If you are planning a pregnancy, speak with a medically licensed doctor for the best, most up-to-date information.

If you are pregnant, avoid rough lovemaking…but still make plenty of love.[11]

If you are menstruating, you are still able to get pregnant and are still able to engage in sex safely.[12]

If you have working female parts, the only time you are not at risk of becoming pregnant when engaging in sexual relations is when you already are pregnant.

If you don't want a child, use birth control. Any time the penis (or sperm) is on or near the vagina, pregnancy is possible. The best forms of birth control are those where there is no room for human error. "Effectiveness" in the birth control table below shows the percentage of times that the method will prevent pregnancy in a couple having regular sex over the course of a year (i.e., the effectiveness of that birth control method over a one-year period).

The difference between "observed effectiveness" and "ideal effectiveness" in the chart is the human element. Examples of the human element include initially placing a condom on incorrectly and continuing to use it (which poses both a pregnancy and an STI risk) *or* taking a daily birth control pill at different times of day (or skipping a day or two).

Birth Control Method	Observed Effectiveness	Ideal Effectiveness
Male condom	85%	98%
Female condom	79%	95%
Birth control pill	91%	99%
Birth control implant	99%	99%
Birth control shot	94%	99%
Intrauterine device	99%	99%
Vasectomy	99%	99%
Pull-out method	78%	96%
Fertility awareness	76%	88%
Abstinence	100%	100%

(Table information acquired from Planned Parenthood)[13]

Most birth control methods may be used in conjunction with others. The most common exception to this is using multiple condoms. Only one condom (either a male condom or a female condom) should be used at a time. Condoms work well because they are specifically designed for one purpose:

sex. They are designed to give the maximum amount of pleasure with the maximum amount of protection. Other forms of latex (like a glove) are not designed with this in mind and are never recommended as a protection against pregnancy or STIs. If a condom gets dry in the middle of sex, you are at risk of that condom falling off or breaking, so it is advisable to pull out entirely and replace the condom with a new one.

On Sexually Transmitted Infections (STIs)

Many types of birth control do not protect against STIs, which have the potential to make you (both men and women) infertile.[14] Undiagnosed STIs cause more than twenty thousand US women to become infertile annually.[15] You could also contract an incurable disease or require prompt medical attention to ensure that no lasting effects occur.[16]

> If someone tells you to wear a condom, wear a condom.
> If someone tells you that there is no need to wear a condom,
> you *really* need to wear a condom!
>
> —Jeremy Hofstein, my older brother

This is much easier said than done (so always keep a condom nearby). STIs have been around for a long time, and every generation has thought that their medicine was the best. They were right, but diseases are ever changing and evolving. We were unaware of AIDS and HIV until many people around the globe had already contracted it.

The older someone is, the more likely he or she is to have an incurable STI.

The best way to avoid STIs while engaging in sexual activity is to be in a monogamous relationship. First ensure that both partners get tested and have refrained from sexual activity with anyone for a period of ninety days. Discuss the results of the tests with each other. Until the ninety-day period has passed and testing has occurred, *at least wear a condom*, and make sure you do not transfer any fluid from either party's genital region to the others. (Keep in mind that oral STIs are also possible and an area of concern.)

On Pleasure

If you ride a horse, sit close and tight; if you ride a man, sit easy and light.

—Benjamin Franklin, founding father and businessman

Being relaxed and comfortable is one of the most important aspects of enjoying sex, whether it's your first time or you're thousandth. If you are concerned about your partner's condom use or if the person you are with is concerned, that alone may make the sex worse. (Conversely, if a person is upset about wearing a condom, that may make sex worse. Psychology deeply affects sex and pleasure.)

Be honest. If you fake something, then the person you are engaging with is likely to continue not "doing it" well. If you express that something feels good, your partner is likely to continue doing that, and if you say something doesn't feel good, your partner will stop! Faking orgasms does no one any favors. Communication in sexual relationships is just as important as it is in any other relationship. Talk through what you want. If you are dissatisfied and fake being satisfied, then it will never get better. If you feel uncomfortable talking, do something to let your partner know what feels good—moan or, when you are finished, say you'd like next time to be similar {search: how to have better sex}.

Intimacy is worth mastering if we want to nourish, expand, and protect what is the most important relationship that we choose in this lifetime.

—Jonah Zachary Lavitt, dating and intimacy coach

Chapter 9

Parenting

TL; DR:

> Parents just don't matter as much as we think they do.
> —STEPHEN J. DUBNER, JOURNALIST/COAUTHOR OF *FREAKONOMICS*

ARE YOU RAISING YOUR CHILD "right"? My mother scolded us if we did something wrong, while my father ignored us. Which one was right? Some say that my mother was. In order to teach good discipline and to reward good behavior, some method of punishment and reward is required. Others say that my father was right because any attention given to a child is likely perceived as good by the child. My philosophy is to never reward bad behavior with anyone—but what does a child perceive as a reward?

There are many ways in which you can choose to parent, and children will grow up either way. People will give suggestions, but even if they have raised a dozen children, that advice may not be feasible for others. Every person is different, every child is different, and every relationship is different. If you have a specific problem with a child (or anyone for that matter), you can research the specifics and find expert advice for your situation. You will have to adapt strategies to your own unique characteristics and relationship to achieve your desired outcome. Realize, however, that children are their own people, and that even the worst of parents can create the best of adults, and vice versa.

A father with his son

The manner in which you interact with and treat others is highly contagious. It seems that children are fairly "monkey see, monkey do."[1] How you converse with people—the babysitter, the server, the teacher—your child will likely copy. Kids who grow up around parents who smoke and drink are much more likely to smoke and drink as well. Kids who grow up with parents who are not fiscally responsible are less likely to be fiscally responsible.

End of TL; DR.

There are an endless number of ways to parent, and most parents want the absolute best for their children. Sometimes this involves unknowingly harming both themselves and their children, such as when they spend too much money on the children to give them everything they can and then basically live in poverty.

A debate often comes down to nature versus nurture with children. Which is correct? Likely, they both are.

How much influence do parents have on their children? In chapter 5 of *Freakonomics*, "What Makes a Perfect Parent?" Stephen Dubner and Steven Levitt wrote the following:

"The (U.S.) Department of Education study isolated sixteen distinct factors that, one might think, play a major role in a child's development. Eight of these sixteen factors have been shown to play a major role in the child's development: 1) The child has highly educated parents; 2) The child's parents have high socioeconomic status; 3) The child's mother is thirty or older at the time of her first child's birth; 4) The child had low birth weight; 5) The child's parents speak English in the home; 6) The child is adopted; 7) The child's parents are involved in the PTA (Parent Teacher Association); and 8) The child has many books in his house.

The study also identified eight factors that are, somewhat surprisingly, not correlated with the child's development: 1) The child's family is intact; 2) The child's parents recently moved into a better neighborhood; 3) The child's mother didn't work between birth and kindergarten; 4) The child attended Head Start; 5) The child's parents regularly take him to museums; 6) The child is regularly spanked; 7) The child frequently watches television; and 8) The child's parents read to him nearly every day."

These authors go on to show that, of the eight factors that had an influence on test scores, six were positive and two were negative. The negative two were (1) the child had low birth weight and (2) the child was adopted. (Note: the study looked at test scores. The study did not look at mental health, success later in life, or most anything else.)

Rest assured that these are statistics, and individuals may buck the trend for better or worse, no matter what upbringing they had.

One of the things that I think is true is that obsessive parenting has few rewards.

—STEVEN LEVITT, ECONOMIST/COAUTHOR OF *FREAKONOMICS*

▲ ▲ ▲

Alvin Chester:

1.   Child's tomorrow versus Parent's today

2.   Parents' Part in Education

◆◆◆

CHILD'S TOMORROW VERSUS PARENT'S TODAY

Children need nurturing. They need it from childhood until adulthood, albeit in different forms at different times.

We have been told that repeatedly about children, and we are told that the best environment for children is one within a loving, caring, rational family.

(Actually, I only remember "family." I have added "loving, caring, rational" because I am convinced that just the idea of "family" is not enough. For a child to be developed into a reasonable entity, the family should be loving, caring and rational. However, for the time being we shall consider the family as having all these attributes.)

What the FAMILY NEEDS is the opportunity to sustain itself as an entity in the economic environment it lives in. The economic world does not consider loving or caring to be rational. In the economic world, one performs a task so desired by others that others are willing to pay for the task to be done. If one could perform a task more in demand, or harder to be done, one is paid more.

The old "traditional" family had the father as the wage earner, the one who went out into the economic world and performed tasks. The mother stayed at home, stretched the father's income as much as possible, and was the one who nurtured the children.

As time went on, the father's role changed. Performing his tasks took less of his time, and he was paid more for those tasks and so brought home more to the wife and children.

Advantages to the father grew quickly. The workplace provided him with another environment wherein he could role-play and gain and give admiration. Less time on the job freed the father for more leisure activities or "nights out with the boys." They also had the opportunity to spend more nights home with the family too, and at least some of them did.

For a long time, the mother didn't get much out of the "better society." Her work continued just as it had before, with little opportunity to be anything but a mother.

However, things didn't stop there. The "better society" got much better. Things started to improve for the mother also. In the beginning, these opportunities were primarily work-savers. The vacuum cleaner and carpet sweeper were joined by the washing machine. Time also brought the dryer to complete the clothes-cleaning operation and then the dishwasher and a multitude of electrical appliances. These were joined by the innovation of products that required little to no care at all in furniture, flooring, and especially clothing, which went from little to no care right to the complete throw-a-ways such as diapers.

It isn't necessary to list everything. The changes in food style and packaging availability would be a long list by itself. THINGS GOT BETTER FOR MOTHER ALSO.

What did mothers do with their newfound leisure?

Some emulated the men. Instead of "nights out with the boys," there were "afternoons out with the girls."

There were also mothers who had established such a hectic pace of life that they needed more opportunities for expression. These women often did volunteer work in their communities. Some of them went to work. They weren't trained for the economic world and often had to take lesser positions, but they wanted both the extra expression a job gave them and also the extra income the family was thus afforded.

World War II, with the great manpower shortage, brought many women to the workplace where they found they could perform these tasks required to be wage-earners. Even though great numbers did not remain in the workforce, what did remain in the women was a newfound confidence in themselves as being viable in the economic world.

The period following World War II was one of prosperity. Things were progressively better for almost everyone. Great societies were developed to make sure that everyone would have a place in the sun, a seat at the community table, and the recognition that each individual was the greatest achievement of man.

We could do pretty much what we wanted to do and be pretty much what we wanted to be, and that was our right.

There was a complete new world available for women. No longer must they be relegated to motherhood. All the achievements hitherto available only for men were now also within women's domain.

There is no honorable challenge to equal rights and equal opportunity. Nor should there be.

As this idea got into full swing, another bit of economic history developed.

The growth of the American economy hesitated, faltered. To sustain the living standards previously achieved, a second income became necessary in the family. Women's economic achievements became economic necessities. It's a good thing that new opportunities for women had been in the works for a while. We now have a really viable, productive women's work force.

Well, all's well that ends well, doesn't it?

Not NECESSARILY. WHAT HAPPENED TO THE CHILDREN? Remember that we were told that children need nurturing? Remember that we were told that the best place for children to get this was within a loving, caring, rational family?

What is this family like now?

Both Mother and Father work very hard every day. Among their needs are the opportunity for some expression, some relaxation outside of their jobs. They are entitled to a number of "nights out." We have been brought up with the idea that the individual's right for need-satisfaction is ultimate in society. Go and get it. You deserve it. There are lots of pretty good babysitters around.

And the children? Well, after birth, as soon as Mommy and Daddy can do it, they must go back to work. So the little ones are going to be in day care until they are school age. (You know, we are going to have to make the government do something about regulating day care. Children should get the same nurturing there as if their parents were home taking care of them.) Day care takes very young children from a tight-knit, loving mother/family environment and puts them into a larger (day-care) society along with other children [who are] equally unprepared.

When they are old enough to start school, they shall go to good schools. We shall have to make sure the government guarantees that children get morality within their curriculum, mustn't we? And also there must be courses on how to live within society. We had better teach sex in the schools [to] help them become well-adjusted individuals. And, by all means, educate them. Yes, education is very important. They must be prepared to meet the challenges of the future. It would really be nice if school could teach them to love and respect their parents. It's just amazing what we parents have to think about in the rearing of our children.

After school they can let themselves into their homes. We will have all the latest electronic games and television for them to amuse themselves with. (You know, many of the television shows and electronic games are really education, aren't they?)

I must apologize for being sardonic, I know that parents do mean well. I understand the necessity, in many cases, for both of them working. I know that life can be stifling for people unless there is some regular relief from daily cares.

But I also know that we are taking real potential away from our children. CHILDREN DO NEED PARENTS. PARENTS CANNOT RELY ON THE SCHOOLS. THE SCHOOLS HAVE FAILED, AND THEY WILL CONTINUE TO FAIL. And it is not because the schools are not good. Schools are not meant to supplant parents; they must supplement them. Parents must send children to school who are psychologically prepared to learn. This preparation can only come from the parents and the continuing parental stimulus must remain all through the learning years.

It seems we are at an impasse. Parents are certainly entitled to be as complete and fulfilled individuals as they can be. There is no question about that.

The children we parents have brought into the world are also "entitled."

Well, it seems obvious that the children cannot make the decision; the parents will have to.

It also seems obvious that the parents have already made the decision.

LET THE GOVERNMENT DO IT. IF THE KIDS DON'T DEVELOP WELL, IT WILL BE THE GOVERNMENT'S FAULT THE SCHOOL'S FAULT…SOCIETY'S FAULT…ANY FAULT BUT OUR FAULT.

Well, thank God we have figured that out.

♦♦♦

Parents' Part In Education

Do you send your child to school and then complain that your child does not learn enough? Is it obvious to you that the schools are at fault? Well, someone or something had to be at fault.

Consider…what did YOU do for your child's education? What did YOU do to make him/her understand the importance of learning? What did YOU do to help that child learn?

Rate yourself as a parent. Are you GIVING TO THE CHILD…or only offering sustenance?

Children who come to the school wanting to learn WILL LEARN, whether they are in the best or worst of schools. It is much more the CHILDREN who make the difference, and not the schools nor the teachers.

YOU ARE THE MOST IMPORTANT FACTOR IN YOUR CHILD'S LEARNING.

Now, the question is…HOW ARE YOU GOING TO CORRECT YOUR ERRORS? HOW WILL YOU HELP YOUR CHILDREN?

Chapter 10

Generational Differences
and Similarities

TL; DR:

> The more things change, the more they stay the same.

> —Jean-Baptiste Alphonse Karr,
> nineteenth-century French writer

PEOPLE HAVE TERRIBLE MEMORIES, ESPECIALLY when it comes to past generations. We tend to have similar feelings at similar stages in our lives from one generation to the next, but the specifics of our actions change based on the times. We used to paint pictures of food and hang those paintings, but now we take pictures of food and post them on social media (likely many in each generation thought this was stupid).

Recently, the specifics have been changing at an accelerated rate, but this has been true for many generations. One hundred years ago, they saw rapid change with the increasing usage of electricity. Today we continue to see rapid change with the increasing dependency on the Internet. Yes, change is happening faster now than ever before, but that was true for the people who lived one hundred years ago too.

End of TL; DR:

We can assert with some confidence that our own period is one of decline; that the standards of culture are lower than they were fifty years ago; and that the evidences of this decline are visible in every department of human activity.

—T. S. Eliot, twentieth-century poet, quoted in 1948

Every generation imagines itself to be more intelligent than the one that went before it, and then the one that comes after it.

—George Orwell, author

The "golden-age fallacy" is the belief that the past was better than the present. The past can sometimes seem better in retrospect, especially when a country is dragged into a war, famine, or some other hardship(s). However, more often than not, the golden-age fallacy is just that—a fallacy.

The golden age never was the present age.

—Benjamin Franklin, founding father and businessman

"Children used to respect their elders." Fake news. "Music used to be better." Fake news. "Games are ruining the new generation." Fake news. The truth is, children have always been children. Music may have seemed to be better in the past because only the best music of any generation is still played today, and people have always enjoyed playing the most recent games (which the older generation does not understand). Finally, nearly every generation has been called the "me" generation at one point or another.

A fearful multitude of untutored savages...[boys] with dogs at their heels and other evidence of dissolute habits...[girls who] drive coal-carts, ride astride upon horses, drink, swear, fight, smoke, whistle, and care for nobody...the morals of children are tenfold worse than formerly.

—Anthony Ashley Cooper, seventh Earl of Shaftesbury, quoted in 1843

A pernicious excitement to learn and play chess has spread all over the country, and numerous clubs for practicing this game have been formed in cities and villages...chess is a mere amusement of a very inferior character, which robs the mind of valuable time that might be devoted to nobler acquirements, while it affords no benefit whatever to the body. Chess has acquired a high reputation as being a means to discipline the mind, but persons engaged in sedentary occupations should never practice this cheerless game; they require out-door exercises—not this sort of mental gladiator ship.

—JULY 1859 ISSUE OF *SCIENTIFIC AMERICAN*

The indecent foreign dance called the Waltz was introduced... at the English Court on Friday last...It is quite sufficient to cast one's eyes on the voluptuous intertwining of the limbs, and close compressure of the bodies...to see that it is far indeed removed from the modest reserve which has hitherto been considered distinctive of English females...[Now that it is] forced on the respectable classes of society by the evil example of their superiors, we feel it a duty to warn every parent against exposing his daughter to so fatal a contagion.

—*THE LONDON TIMES*, CIRCA 1816

Once upon a time, there was a generation of parents who were certain that Elvis Presley's unashamed hip-swiveling was most certainly the end of society.

—CHARLIE CARUSO, *UNDERSTANDING Y*

The following is some of the advice given by Quintus Tullius Cicero, a Roman politician in 64 BCE, to his brother, who was seeking to be elected:

1. "Be aware, politics is full of deceit, treachery, and betrayal.

2. Learn the art of flattery. It is disgraceful in normal life, but essential when you are running for office.

3. The most important part of your campaign is to bring hope to people and a feeling of goodwill toward you...stick to vague generalities.

4. Remind the voters what scoundrels your opponents are and smear these men at every opportunity with the crimes, sex scandals, and corruption they have brought on themselves.

5. There are three things that will guarantee votes in an election: favors, hope, and personal attachment. Work to give these incentives to the right people.

6. It will help your campaign tremendously to have the enthusiasm and energy of young people on your side to canvass voters, gain supporters, spread news, and make you look good.

7. If you break a promise, the outcome is uncertain and the number of people affected is small. But if you refuse to make a promise, the result is certain and produces immediate anger in a larger number of voters.

8. So long as the request was not directly contrary to moral duty, tell the people what they want to hear, for the future is uncertain, is prospective, and only affects a few; but if you refuse, the offence given is certain, immediate, and more widely diffused."

Generations *can* be different from one another, and they often are. When times in the past were bad—food disruptions, political instability, war—and the current generation of parents lived through those bad times, the present is seen as wonderful. Often, when our lives are similar to the generations of the past, we look at the present with scorn and the past with rose colored glasses. This is easily seen throughout history and in current days. In the days of King Solomon (approximately 900 BCE), when times had been prosperous and relatively peaceful in his region for a couple of generations, he continued to improve their lands (with the construction of the first Hebrew temple) and wrote in Ecclesiastes 7:10: "Do not say, 'Why were the old days better than these?' For it is not wise to ask such questions."

History doesn't repeat itself, but it does rhyme.

—MARK TWAIN, NINETEENTH-CENTURY WRITER

Society has changed, but human emotions evolve at a much slower rate than society. We feel the same way about similar ideals at similar stages in our lives—both about older and younger generations, as well as about ourselves.

Part Four: Laws

*Ignorance of the law does not
excuse you from it*

Chapter 11

Laws

Disclosure: I am not a lawyer. Nothing contained herein should be construed as legal advice. If you are arrested, it is advisable to get a lawyer who specializes in your local government and in the specific area of law in which you were arrested. If you are signing a contract of importance, opening a business, or filing a lawsuit, and in many more situations, it is prudent to hire a lawyer who can advise you properly.

TL; DR:

> Ours is a government of liberty, by, through and under the law. No man is above it, and no man is below it.
>
> —Theodore Roosevelt,
> twenty-sixth US president (1901–1909)

When you turn eighteen, you are immediately responsible for your actions on a level that you may not have been prior to this age. With any activity you choose to engage in, educate yourself on the surrounding laws.

The idea of law is simple: actions have consequences. No matter who produced the action (social status, political standing, title, etc.), the punishment will be the same. (Note: there are exceptions to this. When you become licensed in a regulated profession, you give up some rights and gain others.)

Laws were created to maintain order, but they can be complex. The government is not responsible for your knowledge of the rules. Even if you do something that wasn't meant to harm, you could end up enduring dire consequences.

Similar actions can produce different consequences, depending on the actual outcomes of those actions. Imagine that you are at a pool and play a prank by pushing the lifeguard into the water. In one scenario, the lifeguard falls into the water, and everyone laughs. The worst thing that happens is that you're kicked out of the pool.

In a second scenario, the lifeguard's neck is broken, resulting in death. You are found guilty of manslaughter and sentenced to seven to twenty years in prison for the same action.

The rule is sometimes no harm, no foul, as in the first scenario in this example, but many actions, like drunk driving, are illegal even if no one gets hurt.

There are many "speed limit" types of laws. These are laws that many people break, but for which police officers usually do not hold a person accountable. These speed-limit types of laws are good reasons to stay quiet when interacting with the police. With a brief interrogation, the police will usually be able to find a speed-limit type law that you've broken, which may give them "probable cause," the legal requirement to search a person, car, and so on, without a warrant, or worse—arrest and charge you with a crime.

You may have heard, "Never say anything to the police." That is impractical advice. The time to take that advice literally is after you've been arrested. Prior to that, you should choose your actions and words carefully. After arrest, only speak with the police with your lawyer present.

Officers may lie to you, but if you lie to them, you may land in serious trouble. The police are trained interrogators and can interrogate you with or without you being aware that an interrogation is happening.

It's important to maintain a high level of respect for our officers. (Note: this does not mean adhering to their every request.)

End of TL; DR.

This chapter is not a debate about laws or what they should be. It's about making you more aware of your rights as a citizen and how to best go about exercising those rights.

TYPES OF LAWS

CRIMINAL LAW

Felonies are criminal laws that carry sentences of more than one year in jail or prison, while misdemeanors are criminal laws that carry sentences of less than one year in jail or prison. Police officers are concerned with criminal law. Police are often incentivized to find out "dirt" on you if they can. What does that mean? Basically, as long as the officers are adhering to the law, they may do anything to get "the truth" out of you, from asking how fast you were going to something more devious like trying to rile you up so that they can have "probable cause" to search your car without a warrant.

Once you are arrested, you will likely be read your Miranda rights. Whether they are read to you or not, they still apply.

Your Miranda rights are the following:

- **You have the right to remain silent.** This applies once you are arrested. You won't say anything after arrest to change the officer's mind about arresting you—that point in time is long gone. You are able to remain silent beforehand too, but this may come off as suspicious and give an officer more reason to investigate.

- **Anything you say can and will be used against you in a court of law.** Wait for your lawyer. We often think of the "bad cop" scenario, where one officer threatens the suspect, but it is often the "good cop" who gains a person's trust and uses it against him or her. If you do want to speak with police and do want to help them catch the bad guys, then do so with your lawyer's help to be certain that what you say will help get you out of charges rather than into more trouble. If you are arrested with a friend, the police may lie to you and say, "Your friend confessed and places the blame on you. If you talk now, we'll go easy on you." They will gain your trust and/or intimidate you. If you cannot afford an attorney, they are required to provide one for you.

- **You have the right to talk to a lawyer and to have one present with you while you are being questioned.** The only words you should utter once you are arrested are "I will only speak with my lawyer present."

- **If you cannot afford to hire a lawyer, one will be assigned to represent you before you are questioned, if you wish.** My advice here is the same as above.

- **You can decide at any time to exercise these rights and not answer any questions or make any statements.** Listen to your lawyer's advice.

On being an accomplice: The dictionary defines an accomplice as someone who knowingly helps another person commit a crime. However, there are plenty of cases where the person was just along for the ride, the friend commits a crime, and the "innocent" person still gets in trouble.

On sexual acts: It's a good idea to research the law in your area and maybe check IDs because you can be charged with statutory rape even if you truly believed that sex was consensual.

On public indecency: You may put having sex in a plane on your bucket list, but remember that it's still in a public place and therefore illegal. The same is true of having sex in a car in a parking lot. Peeing on the side of a building may get you charged with indecent exposure and have you branded as a sex offender. Keep your privates private.

On privacy: If the police don't have a warrant and ask to search your car, home, person, or otherwise, respond with "I do not consent to any searches." If they choose to search you (or your car) anyway, let them (while continuing to verbally tell them, "I do not consent"). Resisting police can be another crime and is unlikely to help your case. At the worst, resisting police may give them the excuse they were looking for to legally search your car.

For the police to search you during a traffic stop without a warrant (prior to arrest), they need "probable cause," which is generally known as facts or evidence that provide justification for the search. This is one of the many areas of law that is vague. (Note: if you are responding to questions and suddenly stop, they may take that as evidence. If an officer asks to search you, and you respond, "No, because there may or may not be something illegal inside," that will likely be used as probable cause.)

> In real life, the most-used reason for searching a car is not probable cause but "Search Incident to Arrest."
>
> —DERRON WOODFORK, CRIMINAL DEFENSE ATTORNEY

On attorney/client privilege: Your lawyer may not repeat anything you say to him or her in private. Your lawyer will use that information to better defend you but may not lie or knowingly allow you to lie. If you inform your attorney that you shot a person and are asking for help, the attorney can help. However, the attorney may not help you lie in court by putting you on the stand and asking questions when he or she knows you will lie. If your attorney asks you questions and you begin to lie (on the stand), your attorney may stop the questioning and ask to be dismissed from the case. Check with your lawyer on all of the details. Most exceptions to the rules of attorney/client privilege deal with future crimes. You may ask how to avoid doing something illegal.

> If a lawyer knows his client is going to lie in court, he must allow him to testify in "narrative form."
>
> —DERRON WOODFORK, CRIMINAL DEFENSE ATTORNEY

CIVIL LAW

Another type of law is civil law, which includes private disputes like contracts, property, and family law. For instance, a civil law would be a dispute when you are getting divorced, at which time, a court may make a decision. If you fail to follow through with a civil court decision, the failure to comply with a court decision may be deemed a criminal offense.

On contracts: When you sign something, you are agreeing to every provision, whether you read it or not. Pay particular attention to the larger contracts like housing/rental agreements and service contracts that bind you for long periods of time. The only aspects of contracts that matter are what is written down. If people tell you, "I will do XYZ," but it is not written in the signed contract, they may forget (I have seen this happen to the smartest and most honest of people). If they sent you an e-mail agreeing to do something that is not written in the contract, they are likely not legally bound to it.

On employment: W-2 employees (salaried and hourly employees) are the most common type of employee in the United States and are afforded many rights by all employers. Employers will generally automatically withdraw taxes from their paychecks. 1099 employees (work-for-hire, freelancer, project-based employment, and other forms of self-employment) are treated as their own business, and there are varying laws that mostly rely upon the individual earner to follow. Internship laws are interesting, especially *unpaid* internship law {search: unpaid internship law}. There are many different statuses you may take on when making money, and different laws (and tax laws) are associated with each type. Educate yourself on the laws pertaining to your specific type of employment.

ADMINISTRATIVE LAW

Administrative laws are carried out through the authority of an agency. The Federal Department of Agriculture (FDA) is an example of one such agency. If you fail to comply, you will be fined and/or brought to a civil court proceeding or, in extreme cases, a criminal court proceeding.

Lastly, the "Commerce Clause" found in Article 1, Section 8, Clause 3 of the United States Constitution is what generally regulates private companies at a federal level.

If there is no rule on something, it often makes that something legal until it is abused.

In general, criminal laws are those that have been forced upon you. Civil and administrative laws you (kind of) elect into. If you choose to engage in sexual activity that results in a child, you elect into the civil laws surrounding child-rearing. If you choose to open a business, you elect into the administrative (and state and local) laws surrounding that business.

Two Personal Stories

1) My Arrest

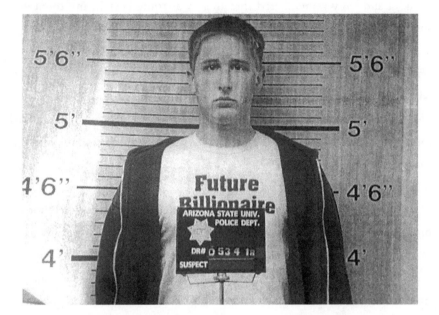

In 2005, I was arrested during my first semester at Arizona State University on felony charges. I was not innocent. Well, I was innocent of some of the charges, like possession of prescription drugs—those prescriptions belonged to my roommate—but I was guilty. All charges were eventually dismissed but not due to any help from me.

It was a school night, and my roommates and I were hosting a small get-together in our dorm room (a small two-bedroom apartment). A half-dozen people were playing beer pong in the living room/kitchen area, and another half-dozen were in my room smoking marijuana. This was not our first time doing any of this.

The resident assistants (RAs) who walked the halls at night to make sure no one was too loud and disrupting other students knocked on our door. A friend of mine, in his drunken stupor, opened the door. The RAs quickly saw the beer pong and asked us to dump all the alcohol down the drain and throw everything away. After complying with their requests, I asked why they were sticking around, to which they replied, "When we opened the door, we smelled marijuana, so we called the police. They should be here soon." I suddenly remembered that there was some beer in my room and suggested that my friends and I clean that up.

There was, of course, also a plethora of marijuana and marijuana paraphernalia in there that we proceeded to mostly take care of. In my infinite wisdom, I decided that it would be wise to leave a little for the police to find; you know, throw them off the hunt for larger stashes. I left one half-smoked joint and a lighter inside my desk drawer. I threw a grinder full of weed out the window. We threw everything else away, and, before the police came, the RAs let someone take all the trash out.

When the police finally arrived, one of the officers immediately took a big whiff and exclaimed, "I smell marijuana. Whose is it?" I raised my hand or stood up—I don't really remember—and took him to the half-smoked joint inside my desk. (Note: I thought I would be hailed as a hero among my friends for taking the fall and not giving up anyone. I was wrong. No one seemed to care and probably just thought of me as the kid who was arrested.) Then the officer sat me down and read me my Miranda rights. "You have the right to remain silent…"

The police searched my room and found more marijuana paraphernalia that I had forgotten about. I had a locked safe in my room that contained fake IDs. The officer said that if I didn't open the safe, he would call a judge and get a warrant to search it because they clearly had "probable cause." He emphasized that a warranted search would be much more detailed and invasive. I told him there was personal stuff in it that I didn't want anyone to see. So we worked out a deal. I would open the safe, he would glance inside, and, if there was no drug paraphernalia, I would promptly close it. I agreed, and he kept his word. I was probably stupid to open it. He was a police officer and didn't have to keep his word on anything.

I was arrested for 1.3 grams of marijuana, marijuana paraphernalia, alcohol, and prescription drugs. I was released on my own recognizance shortly after my arrest, which meant they let me go without any bail, immediately after taking my fingerprints, on the agreement that I would return when summoned by the courts.

Not knowing what to do, I simply did nothing. I didn't tell my parents; I didn't contact a lawyer. I simply waited…until about three weeks later, when I sobbingly confessed to my parents while visiting home for the holidays. I confessed that I had failed every class, was kicked out of the dorms, and had been arrested on felony drug charges. (Note: what most people probably see as the best time of my life, at least from a fun-and-party perspective, was truly anything but. I was failing—and that is not cool. I was not getting laid, probably because failures are not cool. I was spending my money on weed and smoking weed all day, happy because of the weed and not caring about much at all.)

The day after I told my mom what happened, she called a lawyer, who knew a guy who worked in the state where I was arrested. He informed me that had I contacted him within the first few days of being arrested, his friend in the state could have made a call, and my case would never have been inputted into the system: no record, no court, no anything. (Note: I include this to show one way that the system is flawed.)

It was too late for that, so I found a lawyer and told him everything, including how guilty I was. He told me there was a chance I would never be prosecuted because the state was backed up. They had one year to try the case, or it would be dropped. A couple of months before the year mark, I was processed.

I was guilty and ready to proclaim it, but my lawyer told me to plead "not guilty." I had described everything to him, including how guilty I was. "Why?" I asked. I was guilty, and a judge was about to ask me if I was guilty or not. Wouldn't I get into more trouble by lying? I didn't feel right lying to the judge. I was so nervous in the courtroom that I asked my lawyer again, in front of the judge, what to say. "Not guilty." It turned out my lawyer knew what he was doing.

There are many procedures that you have to go through before being convicted, and pleading "not guilty" is basically a formality in many circumstances. The only way I knew how to plead, and to ultimately have a felony charge dismissed, was to follow the advice of my lawyer.

ANDREW P THOMAS
MARICOPA COUNTY ATTORNEY

Sarah L. Corcoran
Deputy County Attorney
Bar Id #: 020131
222 East Javelina, Suite 1750A
Mesa, AZ 85210
Telephone: (602) 506-0855
MCAO Firm #: 00032000
Attorney for Plaintiff

FILED
FEB 2 1 2007   10:00 A.m.
MICHAEL K. JEANES, Clerk
By_____
A. Pagel-Spaulding, Deputy

IN THE SUPERIOR COURT OF THE STATE OF ARIZONA

IN AND FOR THE COUNTY OF MARICOPA

THE STATE OF ARIZONA,	)
Plaintiff,	)
vs.	)
DANIEL GARRETT HOFSTEIN,	) CR2006-031227-001 SE
Defendant.	) **O R D E R**

Having read the foregoing Motion to Dismiss with Prejudice, the court hereby finds that the County Attorney has stated good cause; therefore, the Defendant having successfully completed the requirement of the Maricopa County Attorney\TASC Drug Diversion Program, and

IT IS ORDERED that the case be dismissed with prejudice.

DONE IN OPEN COURT February _16_2007.

_____
JUDGE/COMMISSIONER OF THE SUPERIOR COURT

The state offered to dismiss all charges if I completed the drug-diversion program for first-time offenders. I began random drug testing in a ninety-day drug-and-alcohol-free program.

Each time I was tested, I had to pee in a cup while someone watched. There was a sign in the room that read, "273 282 people have been caught trying to use fake pee this year." Sure enough, every time I went back, the number had been crossed out and increased. If I had failed to show up or failed a test, the state retained the right to prosecute me—or something like that. I don't know.

The ninety-day mark would have brought me into my winter vacation, and I requested that the time allotted be reduced slightly to allow me to go home to my family. The state agreed, and, after about eighty-three days, my duties to the state were completed. My case was dismissed soon after.

2) Drunk Driving

I am often the designated driver—the person who agrees to not drink alcohol (or do any drugs) in order to safely drive everyone else around. The year was 2010, I was twenty-three, and I was driving a sport-utility vehicle (SUV). I had driven to California with a friend from Las Vegas, and we were going barhopping with his older brother. At the first bar, my friends pressured me to try their drinks, but I refused. We had a bottle of whiskey in the *trunk* of the car, and, between the first and second bar, they opened the bottle for a taste. They again pressured me to take a swig; this time, just to shut them up, I took what I consider to be the smallest swig a person can take. We put everything back in the trunk and went on our way. (Note: trunk is technically the wrong word for the back compartment of an SUV. Open compartment is more proper.)

After coming to a stoplight with seemingly no one around and following the directions of the brother in the backseat, I made a left turn from a "straight" lane. After a mile on this road, I was pulled over.

Note: police officers have one of the toughest jobs in the world. They put their lives on the line every day for societal safety. Imagine if one in every thousand traffic stops resulted in a "serious situation" that threatens an officer's life. If an officer makes an average of ten traffic stops a day, then every hundred days, that officer is facing a life-or-death situation.

Every day, they risk their lives and are often on edge before they even meet you. They have to be. Aim to put an officer at ease, but know your rights so that you may properly assert them.

What can/should you say to police? Here are some guidelines:

- Be respectful. Even if you are right, an officer can make your life harder.

- Put the cops at ease by turning on the lights in your car, turning the radio off, and keeping your hands on the top part of the steering wheel where they can be seen (and keep them there). Keep your seat belt on (or they may issue you a ticket for not wearing a seat belt). This allows the officers to see everything in the car easier, hear everything easier, and know where your hands are, altogether letting them know that you are not a threat. Talk through your actions and ask permission before you do them. If an officer asks for your driver's license and your wallet is in your pocket, say, "My wallet is in my pocket. May I grab it now?" In addition to putting the officer at greater ease, those few steps also show respect. To further make the officer's job easier, pull onto a side street or somewhere with lighter traffic so that oncoming traffic will not cause an issue to the officer—but ensure that it doesn't look like you're trying to delay the stop in order to hide something or as though you are about to take off and evade the police.

Naturally, the first question the officer asked after pulling me over was "Do you know why I pulled you over?" In this instance, I actually didn't know why. (Note: at this point in time, the officer is performing the beginning of his or her interrogation, trying to gather information and see if you are cooperative. If I admit, "Yes, I was speeding, and I am sorry," or otherwise, the officer will often go back to the vehicle and write in his or her personal notes, "The first thing I asked the suspect was if they were aware why I pulled them over, and the suspect admitted guilt to speeding.")

When I responded, "No," the officer asked if I had been drinking that evening and how recent it was, to which I replied with the truth: "I have had less than a half drink, but it was recent." He promptly asked me to turn the car off and step out of the vehicle. He gave me a sobriety test.

The officer demonstrated what I was to do, and I mimicked him and asked, "Like this?"

He got a few inches from my face and yelled, *"Did I tell you to begin? Do you have a problem following directions? I did not tell you to begin yet."*

My heart, which was already racing, was now pounding furiously. The officer, in my opinion, was trying to rile me up ("bad cop") and elicit a response that could give him enough reason to arrest me. I passed all of the officer's tests. He responded that since I had recently drunk, the alcohol might not be in my system yet, and he would hold me for twenty to thirty minutes and then administer another test.

In the meantime, his partner cozied up to me, began small talk, and casually asked if he could search my car while we weren't doing anything but waiting. I responded, "No." He then began to question me in a friendly way.

Officer: "Why not?"

Me: "No reason."

Officer: "Are you hiding something from me?"

Me: "No."

Officer: "It'll be OK if you tell me. Is there something you don't want me to find?"

Me: "No."

The officer asked me these questions and others in a curious manner ("good cop"), and if I hadn't responded appropriately, it might have given him probable cause to search my vehicle. What if one of my passengers had drugs and placed them underneath a seat due to fear of a search? Who would be held responsible? Me.

In the end, I calmly responded, "My father taught me that if an officer asks to search my car to say no."

The officer grinned and responded, "I tell the same thing to my children. Have a good day." And he and his partner left (never having given me a second sobriety test).

My father never said those words. He always told me to comply with an officer's every wish, and that if you have nothing to hide, then you are fine. But I did have something to hide. I was not drunk driving. I thought I was being responsible. But there was an open bottle in the back of the SUV that was accessible from the main cabin. That alone could have landed me in jail for drunk driving, and maybe there was something else I was unaware of.

Driving drunk is one of the worst offenses a person can commit. Driving (without being drunk) is one of the most extreme responsibilities any of us will ever have. We are controlling machines that are capable of death and destruction. Driving while intoxicated subjects others to this extreme danger while we are in poor control of our motor skills.

I have driven drunk before, and I deeply regret it. I was not caught, nor did I injure anyone, but I should not have been behind the wheel. It's easy enough to take a cab home or call a friend and return the next day for your car. There truly is no excuse to drive while drunk. In my case, a friend who was supposed to be the designated driver left me (with my car) because I didn't want to leave yet. I can come up with many excuses for my actions, but, ultimately, *I was in the wrong.*

My personal belief is that you should be able to ruin your own life if you so choose (drugs, poor money habits, personal choices, etc.). However, drinking and driving is a quick way to ruin the lives of others. Because of this, it is one of the most serious offenses in our legal system. It stays on your record for a long time, employers can and will discriminate against you for it, and state licensing boards often won't give you a license if you have a drunk-driving conviction on your record. In short, being caught driving while intoxicated will ruin your life.

Chapter 12

The Bill of Rights Applied

TL; DR:

> The constitution is not an instrument for the government to restrain the people; it is an instrument for the people to restrain the government—lest it come to dominate our lives and interests.
>
> —PATRICK HENRY, FOUNDING FATHER AND ATTORNEY

I INTERVIEWED MANY POLICE OFFICERS off the record while writing this book and always asked, "What is the most important thing everyone should know?" A common response was this: "Know your rights. Your federal constitutional rights hold true in every jurisdiction, so if you know those, you know your most basic rights everywhere [in the United States]."

End of TL; DR.

> The basis of our political systems is the right of the people to make and to alter their constitutions of government.
>
> —GEORGE WASHINGTON, FOUNDING FATHER
> AND FIRST US PRESIDENT (1789–1797)

The founding fathers who wrote the US Constitution understood this:

> Times must and always do change.
>
> —PRINCE AKEEM, COMING TO AMERICA

With this in mind, they allowed for the Constitution to change (and thus stay relevant) through the use of amendments. The first ten amendments are known as the Bill of Rights and will be further illuminated here.

In essence, the federal government has written laws as "the supreme law of the land," and anything they do not address, the states are free to address (or not address). If the federal Constitution protects your free speech rights, state and local governments may not infringe on that right. However, our freedoms are only guaranteed protections from the government—a private organization does not have to abide by them.

It is impossible to cover every law because there are probably over a million in the United States. There are an estimated twenty thousand laws governing the use and ownership of guns, even though the Second Amendment is clear: "A well-regulated militia, being necessary to the security of a Free State, the right of the people to keep and bear arms, shall not be infringed."

OK; it is not perfectly clear. Laws are rarely black and white, and that includes those found in the Constitution.

The amendments are the protections and rights of the people from the government (except the Thirteenth Amendment, which was a protection of the people from other people: outlawing slavery).

THE FIRST AMENDMENT—FREEDOM OF THOUGHT AND WORD

"Congress shall make no law respecting an establishment of religion, or prohibiting the free exercise thereof; or abridging the freedom of speech, or of the press; or the right of the people peaceably to assemble, and to petition the Government for a redress of grievances."

Without Freedom of thought, there can be no such thing as wisdom; and no such thing as public liberty, without freedom of speech.

—BENJAMIN FRANKLIN, FOUNDING FATHER AND BUSINESSMAN

As an American, you have the right to say almost anything you want without being penalized by the government. Hate speech is protected pretty strongly here in the United States. In Whitney v. California, the Supreme Court ruled, "To justify suppression of free speech, there must be reasonable ground to fear that serious evil will result if free speech is practiced" and "there must be reasonable ground to believe that the danger apprehended is imminent."

Congratulations. You can call some random person a "Nazi cunt" on social media or in person, and the government will not do anything about it (though your employer, friends, social media, etc., might). The First Amendment does not protect your right to privacy, criticism, shame, mockery, or consequences from others—and others may exercise *their own free speech rights* by calling you out personally, criticizing, shaming, mocking, and so on.

Basically, speech combats speech. If you say or do something, other people are allowed to exercise their free speech rights against you. Everyone gets to say stuff, but with that freedom come the relevant repercussions. Free speech laws mainly protect unpopular views. If the idea were popular, there would be no need to protect it.

> You need a First Amendment to protect speech that people regard as intolerable or outrageous or offensive—because that is when the majority will wield its power to censor or suppress, and we have a First Amendment to prevent the government from doing that.[1]
>
> —STEVEN SHAPIRO, AMERICAN CIVIL LIBERTIES UNION
> LEGAL DIRECTOR

> Where there is a great deal of free speech there is always a certain amount of foolish speech.
>
> —WINSTON CHURCHILL, PRIME MINISTER OF THE UNITED KINGDOM
> (1940–1945 AND 1951–1955)

FREEDOM OF SPEECH INCLUDES THE RIGHT

- Not to speak (specifically, the right not to salute the flag). West Virginia Board of Education v. Barnette, 319 U.S. 624 (1943).

- Of students to wear black armbands to school to protest a war ("Students do not shed their constitutional rights at the schoolhouse gate"). Tinker v. Des Moines, 393 U.S. 503 (1969).

- To use certain offensive words and phrases to convey political messages. Cohen v. California, 403 U.S. 15 (1971).

- To contribute money (under certain circumstances) to political campaigns. Buckley v. Valeo, 424 U.S. 1 (1976).

- To advertise commercial products and professional services (with some restrictions). Virginia Board of Pharmacy v. Virginia Consumer Council, 425 U.S. 748 (1976); Bates v. State Bar of Arizona, 433 U.S. 350 (1977).

- To engage in symbolic speech, (e.g., burning the flag in protest). Texas v. Johnson, 491 U.S. 397 (1989); United States v. Eichman, 496 U.S. 310 (1990).

FREEDOM OF SPEECH DOES NOT INCLUDE THE RIGHT

- To incite actions that would harm others (e.g., "shout[ing] 'fire' in a crowded theater"). Schenck v. United States, 249 U.S. 47 (1919).

- To make or distribute obscene materials. Roth v. United States, 354 U.S. 476 (1957).

- To burn draft cards as an antiwar protest. United States v. O'Brien, 391 U.S. 367 (1968).

- To permit students to print articles in a school newspaper over the objections of the school administration. Hazelwood School District v. Kuhlmeier, 484 U.S. 260 (1988).

- Of students to make an obscene speech at a school-sponsored event. Bethel School District #43 v. Fraser, 478 U.S. 675 (1986).

- Of students to advocate illegal drug use at a school-sponsored event. Morse v. Frederick, __ U.S. __ (2007).[2]

—ADMINISTRATIVE OFFICE OF THE US COURTS
ON BEHALF OF THE FEDERAL JUDICIARY

THE SECOND AMENDMENT—GUNS

"A well-regulated militia, being necessary to the security of a Free State, the right of the people to keep and bear arms, shall not be infringed."

The strongest reason for the people to retain the right to keep and bear arms is, as a last resort, to protect themselves against a tyranny in government.

—THOMAS JEFFERSON, FOUNDING FATHER
AND THIRD US PRESIDENT (1801–1809)

Each state has its own laws on gun ownership. This amendment has largely been interpreted as "the federal government" will not infringe on your gun-ownership rights, and each state may make its own laws regarding how guns are regulated. Sometimes those state laws are found unconstitutional but not always.

THE THIRD AMENDMENT—STATIONING TROOPS IN HOME (YOUR HOME IS YOUR CASTLE)

"No Soldier shall, in time of peace be quartered in any house, without the consent of the Owner, nor in time of war, but in a manner to be prescribed by law."

The Fourth Amendment—Right to Privacy

> "The right of the people to be secure in their persons, houses, papers, and effects, against unreasonable searches and seizures, shall not be violated, and no Warrants shall issue, but upon probable cause, supported by Oath or affirmation, and particularly describing the place to be searched, and the persons or things to be seized."

Some of the wording in this amendment is vague. While we have the right to not be "unreasonably" searched (or possessions seized), who determines what is reasonable? The same holds true with "probable cause." Our judges determine this, and many police officers assess it for themselves.

In general, police may search a person who is being arrested, items within plain view or reach of that person, and things or places in control of that person. Typically, a warrant is not needed if a crime is being committed or about to be committed; there need only be reasonable suspicion. Reasonable suspicion is often the first step to stopping a suspect, while a warrant and/or "probable cause" are often needed for anything more. Warrantless searches can also be made if a person gives consent to search. If you are unsure (and do not want to be searched), inform the officer that you do not consent to a search. Continue to repeat that you do not consent if the officer persists.

The Fifth Amendment—Witness against Self and the Right to Remain Silent

> "No person shall be held to answer for a capital, or otherwise infamous crime, unless on a presentment of a Grand Jury, except in cases arising in the land of naval forces, or in the Militia, when in actual service in time of War of public danger; nor shall any person be subject for the same offence to be twice put in jeopardy of life or limb; nor shall be compelled in any criminal case to be a witness against himself, nor be deprived of life, liberty, or property, without due process of law; nor shall private property be taken for public use, without just compensation."

"The right to remain silent" is derived from this amendment. The Fifth Amendment gives you the right to wait to speak to a lawyer before making a statement. If you do speak to the police and you are innocent, but you tell the officer a lie (even accidentally), it can and will be used against you. It is said that the law protects the innocent as well as the guilty, because truthful responses of an innocent person may still provide ambiguous circumstances of which a reasonable person may be suspicious.

> Time has not shown that protection from the evils against which this safeguard was directed is needless or unwarranted. This constitutional protection must not be interpreted in a hostile [redacted] spirit. Too many, even those who should be better advised, view this privilege as a shelter for wrongdoers. They too readily assume that those who invoke it are either guilty of crime or commit perjury in claiming the privilege. [3]
>
> —FELIX FRANKFURTER, US SUPREME COURT JUSTICE (1939–1962)

This law came about because in England in the 1600s, people would be called to the courts for crimes they were not even aware that they had committed. The courts would not tell them what crimes they were being accused of. They would then place them on the stands and bully them into answering incriminating questions. If they failed to respond truthfully, they were held in contempt of court.

Lawyers are generally excellent at language and speaking, while many persons accused of crimes are not. Be innocent and tell the truth 100 percent, and it can still be used against you. Imagine you say, "Sure, I never liked him, but I wouldn't kill the guy." The prosecuting attorney will likely pick out that you admitted to not liking the victim and will plaster that image in the jury's mind.

If those accused of a crime are innocent but poor when it comes to verbal expression, then lawyers may be able to run circles around them and get them to inadvertently say almost anything. Even if they later deny whatever the lawyers came up with and had them accidentally admit, the jury has heard it, and it will affect them. So even if the accused are innocent, defending lawyers will sometimes ask them not to take the stand out of fear of how the opposing lawyers may approach their clients. They don't want their clients' inability to defend themselves to have a negative effect upon the case.

The Sixth Amendment—Right to a Speedy Trial

> "In all criminal prosecutions, the accused shall enjoy the right to a speedy and public trial, by an impartial jury of the State and district wherein the crime shall have been committed, which district shall have been previously ascertained by law, and to be informed of the nature and cause of the accusation; to be confronted with the witnesses against him; to have compulsory process for obtaining witnesses in his favor, and to have the Assistance of Counsel for his defense."

If you are accused of a crime, you are allowed to ask for a trial by jury. You have a right to a lawyer to aid in your defense. Today this means that if you do not have the money to afford a lawyer, a public defender will be provided for you. It should be noted that an estimated 95 percent of all criminal prosecutions end up in plea bargains. A "plea bargain" means that before defendants go to trial, they make deals with the prosecutors. Usually in plea bargains, the defendant agrees to plead guilty but to a lesser charge. For example, that charge might be third-degree murder rather than first-degree murder.

The Seventh Amendment—Common Law Procedures

> "In Suits at common law, where the value in controversy shall exceed twenty dollars, the right of trial by jury shall be preserved, and no fact tried by a jury shall be otherwise re-examined in any Court of the United States, than according to the rules of the common law."

This amendment largely allows for federal civil disputes to be afforded a trial by jury.

The Eighth Amendment—Excessive Bail

> "Excessive bail shall not be required, nor excessive fines imposed, nor cruel or unusual punishments inflicted."

Bail is an amount of money that the defendant gives to the court upon release from jail to ensure that he or she returns for all court appearances. Bail is returned when the defendant appears in court. If a defendant doesn't appear in court, a warrant will be issued for his or her arrest. Bail will likely not be offered again, and the bail that was already put up will be forfeited.

Bail bonds, companies that put up bail for you, generally require you to pay them a fee of 10 percent of the bail. When you appear in court, the bail bond company gets back the full amount, while you spent 10 percent of the amount of bail and do not receive it back.

Example: Bail is set at $20,000 (refunded upon appearance in court) and a court date in thirty days. You do not have $20,000, but you also do not want to spend thirty days in jail waiting for your day in court. You do have $2,000 (and/or a credit card). You contact a bail bond service and agree to pay them 10 percent of the bail amount, $2,000, and they agree to post your full $20,000 bail. Your $2,000 is nonrefundable, but you also did not spend thirty days in jail waiting for your court date.

The cruel and unusual punishment clause is vague and will likely change through history based on what is considered cruel and unusual in the current society.

The Ninth Amendment—Right to (More) Rights

> "The enumeration in the Constitution of certain rights shall not be construed to deny or disparage others retained by the people."

This amendment ensures that the people and the government understand that people are entitled to many other rights that are not specifically listed. There was a great fear that the people's rights would be infringed upon if they were not explicitly stated. Originally, there was no Bill of Rights, but the "antifederalist" colonies would only agree to the Constitution if the Bill of Rights was included. The federalists argued that the rights were already there and didn't need to be explicitly stated, but the antifederalists were worried about government power creep. This amendment sought to ensure that everyone knew that this list was not exhaustive.

The Tenth Amendment—Rights of States

"The powers not delegated to the United States by the Constitution, nor prohibited by it to the States, are reserved to the States respectively, or to the people."

In conjunction with the Ninth Amendment, this amendment sought to protect the rights of the states. The states (and people) would be allowed to do anything outside the scope of the Constitution.

Chapter 13

Last Will and Testament

No TL; DR.

IF YOU DON'T HAVE A legal last will and testament, then your assets will be distributed based on your state's court procedures. In general, your assets will be distributed in the following order, with the first person on the list receiving everything unless he or she is unavailable to receive it, at which point everything will go to the next person on the list:

1. Spouse

2. Children (minors are particularly susceptible to inheritance fraud by the people taking care of them)

3. Parents

4. Siblings

5. Closest blood relatives

I have created a mock will below that is not a legally binding document and, if used, serves only to inform of your wishes; most courts will not admit this if there is any sort of dispute (and there will likely be a dispute).

Reminder: this will is nonbinding. You are placing an immense amount of trust in those who read this. It is highly recommended that you pay a couple of hundred dollars to create a proper will to ensure that when you do pass away, there are no large fees imposed by the state and others for the dissolution of your assets.

When the will is completed, inform someone (or a few people) close to you that you have something written for them that, upon your untimely death, you would like them to read and carry out those wishes. You can also make copies and distribute them or, if you do not want it read before your death, place your will in an envelope.

I, _____, of healthy and sound body and mind, wish for the following actions to be taken upon my death:

_____

_____

_____

_____

_____

_____

_____

To those who are receiving my assets:
(Example: Take 10 percent of my assets and donate them to the following charity: XYZ. Divide my remaining assets equally among my siblings.)

_____

_____

_____

_____

_____

_____

_____

Social media accounts:

(Example: Please write the following message on Social Wahoo: "I lived a wonderful life. Thank you for being a part of it." After three weeks, write the message, "Back from the dead! Just kidding. I wanted to play one last joke on everyone :) Hope you are all living your lives to the fullest! Remember: it can end unexpectedly!")

_____

_____

_____

_____

_____

_____

_____

_____

Pets:

(Example: Please give my cat, Moon, to my friend Cindy. She loves taking care of stupid animals, and Moon is as dumb as they come. Love you, Moon! Thank you, Cindy!)

_____

_____

_____

_____

_____

_____

_____

_____

Special wishes:

(Example: Cremate my body, and distribute the ashes into a volcano. I have researched a local cremation place, To Ashes Cremation LLC, which should cost approximately $800. Please tell Cathy that I love her more than anything in the world. Please advise people that instead of flowers or whatever, my request is that they look into themselves and resolve to become better persons. That is the primary gift to society that one can make.)

_____

_____

_____

_____

_____

_____

_____

_____

Other important information:

(It may help to let people know your passwords—or at least a way to access your passwords, lawyer's information, accountant's information, and anything else that may assist them upon your death.)

_____

_____

_____

_____

_____

_____

_____

_____

Chapter 14

Politics

TL; DR:

In this country it is not only permissible to question our leaders, it is our responsibility.

−LEWIS ROTHSCHILD, *THE AMERICAN PRESIDENT*

THIS CHAPTER ISN'T ABOUT ANYONE being right or wrong or telling people how to think. This is a brief explanation of how our government works, general advice for involvement, and how to better understand another's point of view.

I have heard many Democrats say, "I vote my conscience. If I voted Republican, I personally would be better off, but I believe that this is better for the whole in the long run."

I have heard many Republicans say, "I vote for what will make everyone better off in the long run, even if it does not benefit me today. I vote my conscience."

Democrats and Republicans are the two most prominent political parties in the United States, but political parties do not have to exist in our nation. Political parties arose due to efficiency and to allow a lot of people to act together through a broad political philosophy.

The American government is made up of the people (most citizens of proper age can be elected), voted on by the people (most citizens age eighteen and older may vote), to represent the people (themselves). The people are given the power to vote for who they feel best represents them.

It may be simple to hear different points of view but mighty difficult to understand them.

> It is the mark of an educated mind to be able to entertain a thought without accepting it.
>
> —ARISTOTLE, ANCIENT GREEK PHILOSOPHER

Most people want the economy to improve, but the way to make that happen is often viewed differently and can be achieved in a multitude of ways. It is probably for the best that we disagree, have active discussions, and test many hypotheses.

Socrates believed that no one does wrong knowingly; he claimed that all wrong is done out of ignorance. If we never discuss our differences, we rarely learn, and we are less likely to understand those differences.

Politics can be difficult to discuss due to the emotions and divisiveness involved in having a belief system or choosing a "side." We may think, "My position is moral, and others are immoral," or "My position is one from thought and thinking, and others are from emotion and stupidity," or "My position is right, and others are wrong."

Politics are often divisive because we associate people's positions with their characters, intelligence, and more. Most people believe that their current thinking is right, and that if they are proven wrong, they will change their opinions (and then be "right" again). No doubt that all of us have had a change of mind at some point in our lives. Our previous state of thinking was wrong. We—each of us—always seem to be "right" in our current state of thinking.

End of TL; DR.

Government consists of a group of people who exert a set of conditions or laws over a given society. Politics is how power is distributed within a given government. People are elected by rallying constituents in their district to vote for them. When we vote for representatives, we decide some of how that power is distributed within our government. When we lobby our representatives, when we discuss issues with our family and friends, and when we protest, we are engaging in the political process.

The United States of America is a democratic republic. Representatives of the people are elected by a majority or plurality vote of its own citizens (the people) in order to govern themselves (the people).

Of the people, by the people, for the people.

—ABRAHAM LINCOLN, SIXTEENTH US PRESIDENT (1861–1865)

This chapter will cover the following concepts:

1. Structure
   a) Federal
   b) State
   c) Local

2. Forming opinions
   a) Statistics
   b) Lobbying
   c) Incentives

3. Getting involved
   a) Voting
   b) Public
   c) Private

4. Debates
   a) Abortion
   b) Health care
   c) Minimum wage

5. Conclusion

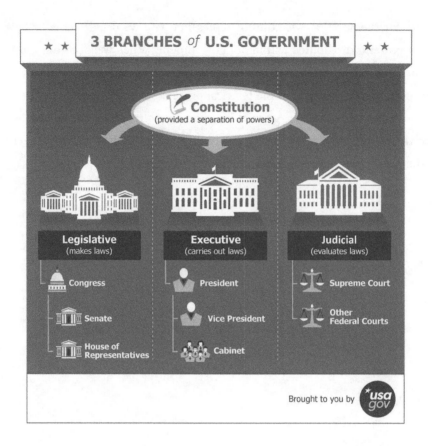

1) STRUCTURE

As the most centralized group, the federal government writes laws to provide universal basic rights for all people. The various institutions then make specific laws pertaining only to the people of that region, state, county, city, neighborhood, community, and so on, and all may make additional laws at the behest of the people.

> The powers not delegated to the United States by the Constitution, nor prohibited by it to the States, are reserved to the States respectively or to the people.
>
> —CONSTITUTION OF THE UNITED STATES OF AMERICA,
> TENTH AMENDMENT

Congress's three major activities include lawmaking, budgets, and oversight.

A) FEDERAL

Each state is usually represented on the national level through the Senate, and the citizens are further represented through their district representatives (House of Representatives).

This gives more power to the states, requiring more uniformity among the states (which requires uniformity within the states as well) for national laws to be passed (rather than a simple majority of the citizens in the country).

This idea of state power is starkly in contrast to many other countries. In many other democratic countries, people vote for parties and party leaders. If in the national election, a party receives 5 percent of the votes, that party is awarded 5 percent of the seats in that congress. This allows for minority parties to be better represented. Because each party is given seats according to total votes, each vote "counts," whereas in our "state" system, if I vote for a candidate who loses, my views may not be represented in the government.

Andy Bookman, a political campaign manager wrote (in review of this chapter):

> "The vote matters and is important in the long-term political calculus of 'political movements' (i.e., the Tea Party, civil-rights movement, progressives, etc.)."

Each state is one of many in the United States of America, and the citizens of each state elect representatives to positions in the federal government. Each state is like a semi sovereign country acting within a union. For the federal Constitution to be amended, besides passing through both the House and Senate with a two-thirds majority, the amendment must also be approved by three-fourths of the states (or vice versa, where it is first passed by the states with two-thirds majority, and then both the House and Senate with three-fourths).

B) STATE

Each state has its own constitution (all of which are longer than the federal Constitution). The state constitution addresses that state's priorities and specific issues while giving power to local authorities. Each state acts somewhat differently but, for the most part, in a similar fashion to the federal government. There is a governor (like the president), and a state senate and state house of representatives (often called an assembly). Districts within the state vote for their representatives. Though people pay less attention to these elections (evidenced through lower voter turnouts),[1] they often have a greater impact on a person's day-to-day life than federal elections.[2]

C) LOCAL

Local authorities may make laws as long as they do not violate state and federal laws. Local authorities may continue to arise as people engage and agree to contracts with one another. At their roots, laws are contracts that we have elected into, either through our representatives or through ourselves. If we personally did not elect into them by virtue of being born in a particular place, then usually our parents did, or our parents' parents, and so on, by virtue of moving to a place.

2) FORMING OPINIONS

> The scientific process can only provide evidence that something is true. The more evidence you have, the more likely it is that it's true, but you can never say that something is scientifically proven. This was hammered into me by my high school science classes, but I don't think it's really being taught anymore.
>
> —JDMAN1699 ON REDDIT.COM

(Note: this is not a rejection of science. It means that science tells us what is probably true but recognizes that it cannot be definitive. We research constantly in order to prove ourselves wrong. If a person discovered that evolution or climate change or any scientifically accepted "truth" were not true, that person would likely win a Nobel Prize.)

How much leeway do we allow the people who represent us to be right or wrong and to change their minds? When new information is presented that goes against my way of thinking, I can change my mind. However, politicians struggle with this. Do we, the voters, allow our elected representatives the ability to change their stances on positions?

Barack Obama was elected in 2008 through our political process and, prior to the election, said he would close Guantanamo Bay. He did not close Guantanamo Bay. Maybe he learned something that he is unable to tell us because it is classified information (like that they were using it as a storage facility for nuclear weapons, secrets, illegal intelligence gathering, etc.), and maybe "politics" got in the way (parts of Congress didn't allow it to be closed).

On the other hand, did we elect someone who was uninformed when making a promise that in part prompted people to elect him? Or did he say this to get elected, not planning to follow through? Is that right? If we allow too much leeway, our representatives may abuse this power and say anything to get elected.

When politicians change their positions, like on trade, foreign policy, labor laws, or Guantanamo Bay closure, they are known as "flip-floppers." Most of us don't want to elect people who change their minds midway through their terms. That's not why we voted for them. Right?

A) STATISTICS

There are three kinds of lies. Lies, damned lies, and statistics.

—BENJAMIN DISRAELI, PRIME MINISTER OF THE UNITED KINGDOM
(1868, 1874–1880)

Researchers are supposed to be like referees, providing an unbiased review. However, they are often given money from institutions to perform research. If a women's advocacy group pays for research on the gender-wage gap, it may be more biased than if an economic-research institution performed the same study.

Benjamin Disraeli posed an interesting point: a "good" statistician can use data and statistics to "say" almost anything. Given the same set of data, two people can come to different conclusions.

In the gender-wage gap example, for example, both of these statements are true:[3]

1. Women earn 77 percent as much as men.

2. Women earn 95 percent as much as men.

Statement one is referring to a broad category: women who are employed full time versus men who are employed full time. Statement two is factoring out time off, chosen professions, education levels, work experience, and more. Neither statement is fully accurate because both leave out important details. The statements are "sensationalist"—they are trying to get a rise out of people.

In short, check your sources, and find multiple sources with differing incentives.

B) LOBBYING

Lobbying usually refers to the act of organized influence on representatives. It began with constituents waiting for their representatives in the *lobbies* of their hotels and meeting spaces. Lobbying can be done by nearly anyone. I went to my state capitol and lobbied my representatives on issues that I felt were important and about which I wanted to share my point of view. (I joined a local nonprofit organization that helped set it up.) The politicians were much easier to reach than I had expected. I literally showed up and waited for some time in the halls near their offices, and every one of them spoke with me for at least a few minutes.

Today, companies employ people to speak with representatives on their behalf. They feel it is more efficient for a large company to have a dedicated member learn the issues and form a relationship with the representatives, rather than the CEO or employees spending their valuable time doing so. Is this good or bad? It may be both. It may just be the way it is, or maybe it's something that should change. If the goal is for representatives to learn as much as possible and govern based on what they have learned, what is the best way for them to learn?

How would you learn about the needs of the people you represent? Would you learn from the media? Would you rely on academic, governmental, and industry statistics? There is nothing inherently wrong with any of these, but isn't it possible that the best sources would be the constituents themselves? Are businesses constituents? No, but if politicians want to improve the lives of their constituents, then taking businesses into consideration may be important. Also, we should be very wary of what a lobbyist or special interest group tells us.

Lobbying Pro/Con Worksheet

Pros	Cons
Representatives learn from direct, knowledgeable sources.	Businesses may have perverse incentives.
Anyone may engage in lobbying efforts; paid lobbyists must disclose that they are being paid.	It is difficult for an average person to lobby as it takes time and energy, and if too many lobby, voices would go unheard.

There are many more pros and cons to lobbying {search: pros and cons of lobbying}.

C) Incentives

Incentive (definition): a reward that motivates or encourages an action.

The government has set up many incentive programs like subsidies, grants, and tax credits in an effort to improve and safeguard our society.

For instance, the government incentivizes

- **Farmers**, through subsidies; this helps ensure that we can sustain ourselves in war time.

- **Alternative energy**, through subsidies; this benefits our shared environment and decreases reliance on foreign energy.

- **Marriage**, by allowing for joint income taxes and other common law; this promotes the success of the next generation.

- **Businesses**, through various measures; this encourages new investments in research and development (innovation/tech-nology) and employment.

- **Health**, by taxing cigarettes and alcohol more than other items; this helps to offset some of the negative impact of people's poor life choices.

The government also incentivizes businesses on large levels. If a company is going to build a headquarters and bring ten thousand new jobs to an area, would it be wise for a city to give that company a discount (for example, tax breaks on property tax)? Some argue yes, and others argue no. What if the city has ten thousand unemployed people, and this will help them immense-ly? How much should the city offer the company? These incentive situations happen on both large and small scales in our society. Many cities have low property taxes to encourage retired people to move there, while others have high property taxes to encourage families to move there as property tax is often tied to education spending. Each city makes its own choices.

3) GETTING INVOLVED

A) VOTING

> The vote is the most powerful instrument ever devised by man for breaking down injustice and destroying the terrible walls which imprison men because they are different from other men.
>
> –LYNDON B. JOHNSON, THIRTY-SIXTH US PRESIDENT (1963–1969)

Discussion can only go so far; eventually action must take place. The most visible way to take action is through voting. You might think, "My vote doesn't matter!" Perhaps, but if people like you don't vote, people like you won't be represented. If you are not being represented, others may take ad-vantage of you. By not voting, you give a louder voice to everyone else, and you leave your fate in their hands.

How to vote {search: register to vote}:

There are multiple ways to vote: early voting, day of, by mail (absentee ballot), and so on. There are few excuses for not voting. Choosing not to vote is an indication that you have chosen not to have a voice in a particular political debate.

When we elect a person, we want that person to have power. Then that person can effect the changes we were hoping for. Over time, power creep (slowly growing power) happens on nearly every scale. The government has become larger, due in part to this power creep. Each person, when elected, seeks to wield more influence. And with everyone trying to do this, the total influence of government has grown.[4]

The two-party system is not mandated, but due to efficiency, the two parties have gained a lot of power. In today's political arena, there are subgroups within each party that advocate for the party as a whole. Each subgroup has a specific issue (or set of issues) and influences friends and acquaintances about why its candidate is the best. Each party seeks to implant their party members in all areas of government, from local elections like mayor and city council to federal elections, like the House of Representatives, Senate, and president.

The "party" system continues to propagate because the parties are now institutions: well organized and a part of every facet of government. If you want to be "lazy" in voting, you can vote for a party whose broad philosophy you already know and generally agree with. The parties in power want to remain in power, and they enact laws that make it easier to perpetuate their power.[5]

A) PUBLIC

There are many ways you can get involved in politics and be in the public eye.

Lobbying can be done by anyone. Visit, call, e-mail, write, send social media messages…any form of contact is better than no contact {search: contact a politician}.

Letter writing is interesting. Emailing is interesting. Phone calls are good. But there is nothing more valuable, nor spontaneous, than showing up at an event that a member of congress is at and asking them, "Why did you vote a certain way? What's your position on a certain issue?"

—STEVE ISRAEL, MEMBER OF THE US HOUSE OF REPRESENTATIVES (2001–2017)

B) PRIVATE

Discuss your positions with your family, friends, associates, and strangers. Try to have an open mind and respect (if not attempt to understand) other people's points of view. Word-of-mouth advertising is possibly the best form of advertising for businesses and politicians alike.

Be aware: your right to free speech ends with the government. Your employer (or supplier, distributor, etc.) may be able to terminate you for exercising free speech.

4) DEBATES

The animals listened first to Napoleon, then to Snowball, and could not make up their minds which was right; indeed, they always found themselves in agreement with the one who was speaking at the moment.

—GEORGE ORWELL, *ANIMAL FARM*

In politics, the Animal Farm conundrum, as George Orwell pointed out, can easily happen. I will attempt to illustrate this with the following debates, illuminating good arguments for both (or many) sides of each situation.

I want to understand the good and the logic in opposing arguments rather than believing a person is acting out of malice, hate, or ignorance. I have friends who are one-issue voters (they vote for a candidate based on a single belief), and abortion is often that one issue.

A) ABORTION

Status quo: Since Roe v. Wade in 1973, all women have the legal right to an abortion.

Questions:

1. Should abortion be a legally protected right?

2. Do unborn children have legal rights, and, if so, what should they be?

Pro-life (abortions should be illegal)	Pro-choice (abortions should be legal)
There is a child in the womb who should have rights from when the sperm enters the egg.	There is no child (and no human rights) until birth (exit from womb).
People chose to engage in an activity; the unborn child has not made a choice and should not be affected by a new choice.	People should always have a choice if it is their bodies and selves.
Unborn children have no voices, so I must act as their voice.	What about in cases of rape, deformities, and life-threatening conditions to the mother?
This should be a local decision (not federally legalized).	This should be a decision between a doctor and his or her patient—no one else.

Debates abound, and there may be no "right" answer, but, hopefully, we can understand the other's point of view. As in the above debate, the ones below will not cover every issue but are meant to illuminate that there is logical reasoning and "good" on each side. The goal of the debate is for a person to be exposed to another's point of view, hopefully learning to listen better. All debates here will focus on a national level.

B) HEALTH CARE

Status quo: The Patient Protection and Affordable Care Act (PPACA) has been law since 2010, requiring all persons to have health insurance.

Here are a few provisions of the current law:

a) Insurers must charge the same rates, regardless of preexisting conditions or sex.

b) Insurers must provide certain "essential health benefits."

c) All citizens must purchase health insurance, with help given to households under 400 percent of the poverty line. (Part of this, the individual mandate, was repealed in the 2017 tax reform bill, effective in 2019.)

Question:

What is the effect of the PPACA?

Pros	Cons
Lower net health-care costs; everyone buying insurance creates a larger purchasing power, allowing everyone to benefit.	Young person's subsidizing old persons means young people (who, on average, make less money and are healthier) are paying for older people (who, on average, make more money and are sicker).
Persons born with diseases and other ailments should have access to affordable health care.	People of all ages who take care of their health will be paying for those who neglect their health.
Access to preventative care will benefit individuals and society through improved public health and long-term increased productivity.	People will be more inclined to use health-care services when it does not directly impact their finances, utilizing unnecessary testing and resources.
Everyone should be entitled to health care and not go bankrupt because of it (in 2007, about 62 percent of all US bankruptcies were related to health care).[6]	Because more people will utilize unnecessary resources, wait times for necessary procedures will increase (limited resources in doctors, nurses, beds, machinery, etc.) and could lower the quality of treatment.

The number of uninsured in the United States since 2010 has fallen by twenty million, from forty-nine million to twenty-nine million.[7]	The PPACA focuses on providing insurance rather than lowering health-care costs. We should focus on lowering costs to make health care more accessible and affordable.

C) MINIMUM WAGE

Status quo: Minimum wage is $7.25 per hour.

Question: Should minimum wage be increased to a "livable" wage? (Many argue for a minimum wage that starts at fifteen dollars per hour as of 2016.)

Pros	Cons
Everyone working forty hours a week should be able to live a comfortable life.	The definition of "comfortable" changes, and people are free to organize and/or quit.
The economy would expand because the poorest would be able to afford more and would likely be spending almost all of it.	Growth would slow. Less capital for research and development and/or layoffs would result, creating worse conditions and more disparity.
Graduated increases to minimum wage have a minimal effect on unemployment.	Minimum wage increases would increase unemployment and encourage more automation.
Welfare programs would be reduced, forcing the companies to take care of their own employees.	Minimum wage increases are a temporary solution to a different problem: welfare. Welfare programs provide an incentive for people to stay working at their current employers at their current levels. If anything, welfare (and "corporate welfare") should be reevaluated, as well as the idea of a minimum wage.

There is research to back up each argument. Some research shows increased economic growth, while other research shows decreased. Some research shows increased unemployment and increased welfare, while other research shows decreased unemployment and decreased welfare. No one knows the impact of such programs until implementation, and even then, there are many factors that contribute to unemployment, poverty, and prosperity. We will likely never be certain that one has caused the other.

5) CONCLUSION

A just society is a society that if you knew everything about it, you'd be willing to enter it in a random place.

–JOHN RAWLS, ADAPTED FROM *A THEORY OF JUSTICE*

Government can never duplicate the variety and diversity of individual action. At any moment in time, by imposing uniform standards in housing, or nutrition, or clothing, government could undoubtedly improve the level of living of many individuals; by imposing uniform standards in schooling, road construction or sanitation, central government could undoubtedly improve the level of performance in many local areas and perhaps even on the average of all communities. But in the process, government would replace progress by stagnation, it would substitute uniform mediocrity for the variety essential for that experimentation which can bring tomorrow's laggards above today's mean.

–MILTON FRIEDMAN, *CAPITALISM AND FREEDOM*

Is he correct? Martin Luther King Jr. advocated for a universal basic income in the 1960s. Thousands of years ago in Rome, politicians debated these same questions. I hope that you continue to ask such questions and question such ideas.

▲ ▲ ▲

Alvin Chester:

With Justice For All

In the early development of the United States, a federation was established… a government divided into parts that would serve the best interest of individuals…of the states…and the country as a whole.

Separate powers were granted to the states and the federal government. Basic powers were the states'…but it was obvious that there would be times when a national government would have to act in those situations wherein states could not act effectively.

Congress was established to be the national law-making body. The fact that Congress would consist of persons chosen by the states (senators) and portions of the states (congressmen) and these combined delegates would protect their constituencies while enacting laws for the entire country. This was a great innovation in politics. It was not considered that the federal government would pass laws other than very broad ones.

However, the United States grew beyond sectionalism, and the powers of the federal government grew and grew and grew. It was only right that ALL of the persons, regardless of the area they lived in, should be entitled to joint participation in the benefits of our society.

Today we are controlled more by the federal government than by our local ones. Even in many areas wherein the local government has control powers, much of the funding comes from Washington…and with that funding is the power to exercise its own controls.

At the same time the various sections of the United States have become more similar than different, thus lending convenience to national laws and regulations.

One would think that this would affect the responsibilities of the elected national legislators. They would not be passing laws that would affect all citizens and would (should) benefit all persons equally.

Is this the case?

I believe it is in many, many instances.

However, there has been another change our founding fathers did not anticipate. They did not anticipate that people would become CAREER POLITICIANS.

Now, there is nothing wrong with a career politician…EXCEPT that the most important responsibility of the career politician is TO GET REELECTED. To accomplish this, the constituents must be made aware that "their" career politician is doing things for the CONSTITUENTS. No laws should be passed that negatively affect these voters…and some should be passed that are especially good for them.

And…as has been a fairly recent trend…electioneering has become very expensive…so constituents (and others, even outside of the constituency) who can contribute dollars to fundraising campaigns are just a little more important than voters.

It being that no one senator nor one congressperson can pass (or keep from passing) laws all alone…there developed a process wherein the legislators learned to work together. "You vote for my idea and I will vote for yours." Of course, with so many legislators around…this is a fairly complicated process.

But, it must be done. The voters and contributors get value for their votes and contributions BECAUSE REELECTION IS THAT MOST IMPORTANT GOAL.

At the same time, this complicated process of working "together" has extra complications. Some legislators are more powerful than others. They may control legislative committees. Therefore, they are in positions to get MORE for their voters and contributors. There have been instances of known-to-be corrupt legislators being reelected regularly because they were so powerful in the federal government. "Better to have a crook who can get things for us than an honorable person who may not."

And the more federal laws that are passed, the more the federal government impacts the lives of people, the more "for show" opportunities the federal legislators have.

Now…within the states themselves, everything works quite the same way. And state legislators can try to work up to becoming national ones.

I am not the first person to bring this matter up. Certainly in 1997 during the election-fundraising scandals and the subsequent conversations about how to regulate political fundraising…this dilemma has been presented over and over again. It has even been suggested that this is one of the reasons for poor voter turnout at elections…and the general public's apathy to government.

I get the feeling that the best interests of all the people and all the states and localities are NOT BEING EQUALLY SERVED.

What can be done about this? I don't know. The same persons that should be more regulated are the ones that must pass the laws to regulate themselves. What do you think the odds on that are?

We know there is dishonor, even immorality, in our officials, but we have no available way of changing it.

We, the citizens, must resist, renounce, and rebel. It is our obligation to correct the system. But…who will lead us?

Part Five: Miscellaneous

*Much is uncertain in
mind, body, and soul*

Chapter 15

Drugs

Upon writing this chapter, there could have been a source for nearly every sentence, and I chose not to do that. I attempted to use my best judgment. Additionally, there are many definitions and differing uses for drugs. For instance, drug use and abuse are different, and drug addiction and dependence are different, but we do not go (much) into those here. Do your own research and check with a medical professional before using any prescription, legal, or illegal drug. Nothing contained herein should be construed as medical advice.

TL; DR:

> The drug and alcohol thing it seems to me comes down to this: drugs and these things are wonderful. They're wonderful when you try them first: they're not around for all these millennia for no reason. First time: mostly pleasure, very little pain (maybe a hangover). And as you increase and keep using whatever it is, the pleasure part decreases, and the pain part (the price you pay), increases, until the balance is completely the other way, and it's almost all pain and there's hardly any pleasure.
>
> —GEORGE CARLIN, COMEDIAN

WHEN PEOPLE INGEST NICOTINE, THEY immediately relax (de-stress). However, over time, people who consistently ingest nicotine become more stressed (less relaxed), becoming addicted to the nicotine's relaxation effect.[1]

The more they ingest nicotine (both quantity and length of time), the more stress they perceive in everyday life. This is the basic way many drugs work: at first they provide relief, but then your body begins to need that relief (things that would have not stressed you out before are stressing you out now).

> Many a Man thinks he is buying Pleasure, when he is really selling himself a Slave to it.
>
> —BENJAMIN FRANKLIN, FOUNDING FATHER AND BUSINESSMAN

I want you to choose whether to use drugs rather than being pressured into using them by doctors, parents, peers, colleagues, or whomever, with much knowledge of what you are getting yourself into. I want you to want to take drugs when you want to take them—not when others want you to—and only if it will contribute to your happiness, both short and long term.

End of TL; DR.

> Many educators are loathe to admit that the pursuit of pleasure might be a valid reason for drug use, or to recognize young people's curiosity, their need to experiment, to take risks and define their own boundaries.
>
> —TOM FEILING, COCAINE NATION: HOW THE WHITE TRADE TOOK OVER THE WORLD

Don't do drugs. Or do them. Whatever. It's your choice. But if you choose to do them, know what you're getting yourself into and realize that we are all different and the same drugs may have different effects on each of us.

> It's all about the relationship between the person and that object or substance. The interaction between a person and alcohol may be more robust than their interaction between heroin - it all depends on neurochemistry.
>
> —PAIGE SHAFFER, EPIDEMIOLOGIST FOR THE BUREAU OF SUBSTANCE ABUSE SERVICES

For the purposes of this chapter, a drug is something put into your bloodstream that then affects your brain. Love and sex are not drugs. Gambling is not a drug. Sugar is not a drug because it is mostly the taste of sugar and not the substance hitting your bloodstream that produces those immediate "brain" effects.[2] (For more on how sugar affects the brain, see the TED-Ed lesson "How Sugar Affects the Brain," by Nicole Avena.) The aforementioned activities may be addictive, with withdrawal, too, but they are not drugs. I apologize to any psychologist, neuroscientist, and other professional, as this is not a perfect definition. I had a lot of trouble finding a good definition.

In general, drugs can be harmful to your body (damaging your heart, tissues, brain, etc.) and distort reality (your brain adapts and changes with the drug).[3] Nearly every drug—even those that seek to repair or strengthen—has an alternate effect. The more you use a drug, the more harmful it becomes.

Joshua Schorr, an emergency medicine medical doctor wrote (in review of this chapter):

"Antidepressants often times only work after taking them for 2+ weeks and the side effects can also diminish with time, so using them more may actually be less harmful."

The first time you use a drug, while it probably won't kill you (as long as you are safe and doing it properly), it often makes it easier and more appealing to do it a second time. In fact, you can never do anything a second time, or a third, if you never do it in the first place. Any drug can be viewed as a gateway to other drugs and to more drug use, because finding or using or any drug teaches a person where to obtain more drugs.

Don't kid yourself by saying that one time can't make you addicted. It can. I believed it couldn't too when I first tried meth. I was so, so wrong. The worst part about it is that you won't realize what has happened immediately afterward. Addiction is a gradual process and it doesn't happen overnight. But trust me when I tell you that one time is all that it takes to set this into motion. It can and it will.

—ASHLY LORENZANA, *SEX, DRUGS, AND BEING AN ESCORT*

Drugs can make you feel almost anything. However, there's a huge risk: you may not feel the emotion you first experienced on the drug as easily the next time due to brain adaptation.[4]

Drugs produce the illusion of alternate realities. Want to not feel like yourself for a while? Use some drugs. When we take painkillers, we are hoping that our body will cure whatever is causing our pain by the time the painkiller wears off.[5] The painkiller itself (the drug) is not curing our bodies. It is simply masking the pain (temporarily). Our brains alter reality by shutting down various parts of our interpretations of "reality" (in the case of painkillers, the pain receptors in our brain).

Drugs work by changing our brains. Some shut down parts, while others increase receptibility. Unfortunately (and sometimes fortunately) for us, our bodies are great at adapting to these changes. If we have pain and take a painkiller, but the cause isn't cured by the time it wears off, we may need more painkillers than what we initially took in order to produce the same painkilling effect. Our body's natural painkilling ability has been diminished due to the use of drugs, and the pain will likely be greater.

If our bodies get used to external resources, they will usually come to rely on those external resources (known as dependence). This is what creates that "increased" pain from painkillers above. With recreational "fun" drugs, reality may seem worse afterward because our bodies are either not producing as many mood-elevating hormones as they were prior to our taking the drug, or they are producing the same amount as before but became accustomed to the higher production levels throughout the use of the drug.

> Even when I took the drugs I realized that this just wasn't fun anymore. The drugs had become a part of my routine. Something to wake me up. Something to help me sleep. Something to calm my nerves. There was a time when I was able to wake up, go to sleep, and have fun without a pill or a line to help me function. These days it felt like I might have a nervous breakdown if I didn't have them.
>
> —CHERIE CURRIE, MUSICIAN

I wish we knew exactly how drugs affect the human brain. If it were true that "by elevating today, I am depressed tomorrow," and the reverse were also true, I might try becoming depressed today for elevation (long-term happiness) tomorrow…but I fear it doesn't work this way. We don't know exactly how drugs affect the human brain and body, but, like every generation in the past, we (think we) know a great deal.

> Medicine is not a science; it is empiricism founded on a network of blunders.
>
> —EMMET DENSMORE, HOW NATURE CURES

> Before you treat a man with a condition, know that not all cures can heal all people. For the chemistry that works on one patient may not work for the next, because even medicine has its own conditions.
>
> —SUZY KASSEM, RISE UP AND SALUTE THE SUN

The following are a few generalized notes on drugs:

1. The first time you take a drug, it usually has the most profound effect in terms of how long it lasts as well as the rush/feeling you get.

2. Drugs affect different people differently. Even if most people experience euphoria on a drug, there is a chance that very same drug could have the opposite effect on you or a different effect or no effect at all.

3. The short-term withdrawal (the next day) for most drugs will have the opposite effect that the drug had on you. For instance, if a drug, like ecstasy, made you extremely happy, the next day (or sometimes even for consecutive days), you will feel very depressed and be easily agitated. (Note: for many drugs, there is a hangover, where your body is in need of other nourishments, like water and vitamins, and not the drug you had used before.)

During a withdrawal period, your body is adapting to go back to equilibrium - which in effect actually tricks you into thinking you need something else to "cure" those unpleasant feelings

—Paige Shaffer, epidemiologist for
The Bureau of Substance Abuse Services

4. The longer you use a drug, the less profound the short-term effects are, and the less noticeable the short-term withdrawal effects will be. If you quit, those withdrawal effects will become more noticeable.

5. When you use a drug regularly, the less profound the short-term effects are (due to your body adjusting to it), and the less noticeable the short-term withdrawal effects will be (because you still have some of the drug resonating in your system).

6. If you choose to quit after regularly using the drug (dependency), the short-term withdrawal effects may take longer to notice due to your body having an excess buildup of the drug in your system. When withdrawal symptoms do appear, they will likely be more intense and last longer.

7. Drugs are great at convincing you that it's not the drug that controls your behavior and that you are in complete control of your addiction.

8. The longer you use a drug, the more your brain adapts to it, and the longer it will take for your brain to go back to "normal" once you stop using. The sooner you stop doing a drug, usually, the better.[6]

9. Physical dependence is only one factor in the addictiveness of a drug. The mental aspect of addiction often lasts for life {search: physical versus psychological addiction}.

10. Consult a medical professional before using or stopping the use of any drug.

11. Be honest with your medical professionals. If you use any drug, legal or illegal, tell them. Your medical records are confidential (unless you are in immediate danger). Medical professionals can help you be saf-

er about your usage and inform you of what steps to take to preserve your health as best as possible. (Note: if you have illegal drugs on you, you can be arrested for possession, but the act simply notifying your medical professional and having drugs in your system should fall under Health Insurance Portability and Accountability Act of 1996 [HIPAA] or 42 CFR Part 2 and remain confidential. Additionally, nearly 100 percent of medical professionals just want to help.)

12. If you are ever thinking about taking your own life due to depression or any other reason, call 1-800-273-TALK (8255), the National Suicide Prevention Lifeline. It is completely anonymous, and they do not call 911 (unless you request they do so) and are always available to help you or a friend. Or you can text HOME to 741741 for the Crisis Text Line. There are many people who are willing to help if you let them {search: where can I find help with _____}.

13. Visit https://www.drugabuse.gov/ to further research drug abuse.

14. Nearly every resource shows that the younger you are when you start to use drugs, the more damage they do to your brain in the long term, lowering IQ and decreasing happiness, among many more potentially negative consequences.[7]

15. If you are determined to use drugs, do so safely (have a non-user with you), and do your own research beforehand. I do not recommend any drug usage (except that which you've consulted a medical professional for). However, the following are a few resources for more information on drugs (Warning: not everything in these are scientifically validated and may contain false or harmful information):

    a) http://www.erowid.org/

    b) http://www.thegooddrugsguide.com

    c) http://www.drugsand.me/

Please verify details for yourself, be cautious, and research from external sources before using any drug; it may save your life and/or happiness {search: what should I know before I do _____}.

The list below is far from all-inclusive. There are many more dangers and effects from each drug mentioned, and many of the drugs, like the birth control pill, is only one form of the drug. This list is in alphabetical order, and the legal, illegal, or prescription-only status applies generally to federal regulations (for instance, cannabis is listed as ILLEGAL although many states have begun legalizing it for recreational and/or medicinal use).

Alcohol—LEGAL (after the age of twenty-one). It is estimated that approximately 70.1 percent of adults in the United States have consumed alcohol in the past year, and 56.9 percent of adults have consumed it within the past month.[8] Short-term effects, which last about two hours, may include euphoria, increased self-confidence, and/or a depressive state. If you cease using alcohol after prolonged, heavy usage, you may be at risk of seizures (and death) due to withdrawal effects.[9] Most withdrawal symptoms will be gone within seven days, but they can persist for several weeks. Heavy drinking is defined by the Centers for Disease Control and Prevention (CDC) as fifteen or more drinks per week for men and eight or more drinks per week for women. Alcohol has a low to moderate level of addictiveness, but the numbers are difficult to determine due to the extreme societal acceptance of this drug.

The CDC recommends that if you are thinking about getting pregnant, refrain from the use of all drugs except those that have been medically recommended. They advise that pregnant women (and those trying to conceive) stop consuming alcohol entirely.

There has been quite a lot of research about alcohol, and most researchers and doctors regard alcohol as a fairly dangerous drug. There are plenty of studies that show the benefits of alcohol. We can find nearly anything if we look hard enough. However, rather than drinking for stress reduction, it is healthier (and longer lasting) to do yoga or meditate. Rather than drinking wine for antioxidants, eat a piece of fruit. The benefits rarely outweigh the negative effects. A benefit of being punched in the face is an increased resistance to pain, but I would not recommend getting punched in the face in order to increase your pain tolerance. This holds true for most drugs, except when medically recommended. Just because a lot of people are jumping off a bridge does not mean you should do so too.

The most common way to consume alcohol is by drinking it. Overdose is possible and is much more likely when ingesting hard alcohols, in competition, or in combination with other drugs (specifically benzodiazepines, opioids, or any other central nervous system depressant).

> Drink does not drown Care, but waters it, and makes it grow faster.
>
> —BENJAMIN FRANKLIN, FOUNDING FATHER AND BUSINESSMAN

Anabolic steroids—PRESCRIPTION ONLY. It is estimated that about 25 percent of college and professional athletes use (or have used) anabolic steroids regularly.

> Anecdotal evidence suggests the widespread usage of anabolic steroids among athletes (20-90%), particularly at the professional and elite amateur levels. In contrast, scientific studies indicate that usage is rare and no higher than 6%.
>
> —THE JOURNAL OF STRENGTH AND CONDITIONING RESEARCH[10]

Steroids produce short-term increases in muscle mass, strength, and athleticism, which, when the athletes train properly, can produce more long-term increases in each. Other, less desirable short-term effects include acne, mood swings, decreased sperm count (in men) or shrinking of breasts (in women), and trouble sleeping. They are highly addictive, with a moderate chance of overdose.

Withdrawal symptoms can last up to two weeks and include depression, decreased sex drive, joint pain, muscle pain, and fatigue. Long-term side effects may include shrinking of testicles (in men) or breasts (in women), deepening voice, growth of breast tissue in men, menstrual irregularities in women, fertility issues, heart problems, other stress on organs due to irregular size, and more.

Arecoline (betel nut)—LEGAL. While not popular in the United States, approximately 10–20 percent of the world's population chew areca nut in some form.[11] This drug is not regulated by the Food and Drug Administration, which means it is legal (for now). It acts similarly to nicotine and chewing tobacco and is often described as a moderate hybrid of caffeine and nicotine.

Benzodiazepine (over fifteen prescriptions contain this)—PRESCRIP-TION ONLY. It is estimated that about 5.6 percent of people in the United States are prescribed a type of benzodiazepine yearly, and about 8.5 percent of people in the United States have used these for nonmedical uses in their life-time.[12] Short-term effects include muscle relaxation, anxiety relief, sleepiness, memory loss, and more. Withdrawal can last up to two weeks and includes problems sleeping, headaches, nausea, weight loss, muscle pain, seizures, and more. When prescribed, they are usually meant to be taken as short-term solutions for less than one month. Because this is one of the most commonly prescribed drugs, it is often overlooked as being dangerous or addictive. Ben-zodiazepines are both very addictive and deadly. These are some of the most popular central nervous system depressants, and any central nervous system depressant used with other drugs has the potential for serious harm. Other central nervous system depressants include alcohol, heroin, and opioids.

Caffeine—LEGAL. It is estimated that 90 percent of the world consumes some form of caffeine daily (which includes chocolate, tea, coffee, and en-ergy drinks).[13] Short-term effects include a positive and energized mood, which lasts for approximately three hours. If you cease using caffeine after prolonged and heavy usage, it may take up to seventy-two hours before you notice any withdrawal effects, which can include sleepiness and headaches. Most withdrawal symptoms will cease after two weeks without use; for heavy users, they may persist for up to two months. There has been quite a lot of research done on caffeine, and most regard it as generally safe. However, it has a high level of addictiveness. The most common way to take caffeine is through a coffee beverage. Overdose on caffeine is possible and is much more likely when it is ingested in pill form.

Cannabis (marijuana, weed, pot)—ILLEGAL. It is estimated that in the United States, 19.8 percent of the eighteen-to-twenty-five-year-old popula-tion has used marijuana in the past thirty days and that 6.5 percent of those twenty-six and older have used marijuana in the past thirty days.[14] Short-term effects, which last approximately three hours, include euphoria, relaxation, and hunger. If you cease to use marijuana after prolonged and heavy usage, you will likely experience decreased appetite, increased irritability, depression, and sleep difficulty. These withdrawal effects will mostly be gone within ten days but may last up to four weeks. If you were a heavy smoker, you may cough up tar from your lungs for up to two years. Marijuana has a low level of physical addictiveness.[15]

The most common way to take marijuana is by smoking, although it is also commonly swallowed. There is no known overdose amount, but vomiting and other undesirable side effects may occur.

> But the thing is, I didn't make my friends happy and they didn't make me happy. All we did was get stoned out of our minds. That didn't have anything to do with happiness.
>
> —BENJAMIN ALIRE SÁENZ, *LAST NIGHT I SANG TO THE MONSTER*

> I had tried marijuana several times, but in the words of my friend and longtime assistant Janet Stark, "When I smoke pot, it makes me want to hide under the bed with a box of graham crackers and not share."
>
> —LINDA RONSTADT, *SIMPLE DREAMS: A MUSICAL MEMOIR*

Cocaine (powder/crack)—ILLEGAL. It is estimated that in the United States, 1.7 percent of the eighteen-to-twenty-five-year-old population have used cocaine in the past thirty days, and that 0.6 percent of those twenty-six and older have used cocaine in the past thirty days.[16] It is estimated that approximately 1 percent of people in the United States consume this regularly, and 10 percent have used it during their lives. Short-term effects include euphoria, energy, alertness, and talkativeness. The differences between powder and crack cocaine are how they are consumed. Due to the differences in consumption, the effects hit you faster or slower. When injecting (powder mixed with water) or smoking (crack), the high will be almost immediate, with the peak occurring soon after and lasting three to five minutes and the residual effects lasting an additional twenty to thirty minutes. The effects of snorting (powder) cocaine will come on within one to five minutes, peak after fifteen to twenty minutes, and last for about an hour. Withdrawal can come fairly soon after, within ninety minutes, and can last up to forty-eight hours. If you cease to use cocaine after prolonged use, you will experience more severe withdrawal symptoms lasting for up to two weeks. Cocaine is one of the most addictive drugs due to the quick onset of its effects and the quick appearance of withdrawal symptoms. Due to the shortness of the high and the quick onset of withdrawal, people often engage in binge behavior with the drug, which results in a higher risk of overdose and addiction.

Joshua Schorr, an emergency medicine medical doctor wrote (in review of this chapter):

"Medically, cocaine/amphetamines can lead to heart attack, stroke, congestive heart failure, kidney failure, and more. The higher the dose and duration appears to increase these risks."

That was the first time I did coke. My body, it was electric. For the first time in my life I felt as if I had a real heart and a real body and I knew that there was this fire in me that could have lit up the entire universe. No book had ever made me feel that way. No human being had ever made me feel like that.

–Benjamin Alire Sáenz, *Last Night I Sang to the Monster*

But even Es and cocaine, over the years they blow holes in your brain, rob you of your memories, your past. Which is fair enough, convenient even.

–Irvine Welsh, *Porno*

You're Superman, thinking Kryptonite makes you invincible.

–J. M. Darhower, *Ghosted*

Heroin—ILLEGAL. It is estimated that in the United States, 0.3 percent of the eighteen-to-twenty-five-year-old population have used heroin in the past thirty days and that 0.1 percent of those twenty-six and older have used heroin in the past thirty days.[17] It is further estimated that 2.1 percent of the twenty-six-and-older population have used heroin in their lifetime.[18] Short-term effects include extreme euphoria, extreme relaxation, extreme happiness, and extreme relief of pain. The extreme euphoria may only last for forty-five seconds, but the relaxation lasts for approximately four hours. If you cease to use heroin after prolonged usage, you may be at risk of suicide or death from the extreme pain and withdrawal effects. The heaviest withdrawal effects will last for about seven days, while some effects may linger longer.

The most common way to take heroin is intravenously with needles or by smoking it. It is easy to overdose on, especially when a user has been clean for a while and thinks it is safe to start consuming again at the previous dosage. This is a very dangerous assumption, as tolerance decreases when the user has avoided abuse of the drug for an extended period of time. It is even easier to overdose if it is combined with other drugs.

Additionally, when purchasing drugs "on the street", it is impossible to know what you are receiving. Drugs purchased in this manner are often cut with other drugs (Heroin often being cut with fentanyl, an opioid which is 50-100 times more potent than morphine), providing an even more dangerous and lethal high.

Heroin is one the most dangerous and addictive "street" drugs.

Heroin—a drug that helps you to escape reality, while making it much harder to cope when you are recaptured.

—NIKKI SIXX, THE HEROIN DIARIES:
A YEAR IN THE LIFE OF A SHATTERED ROCK STAR

Imagine trying to live without air. Now imagine something worse.

—AMY REED, CLEAN

I had someone at the Houston police station shoot me with heroin so I could do a story about it. The experience was a special kind of hell. I came out understanding full well how one could be addicted to "smack," and quickly.

—DAN RATHER, JOURNALIST

Human growth hormone—PRESCRIPTION ONLY. Similar to anabolic steroids, but with less proof of effectiveness on athleticism, and generally regarded as safer. Key part of that last word is safer.

Lysergic acid diethylamide (LSD/acid)—ILLEGAL. It is estimated that 0.6 percent of the eighteen-to-twenty-five-year-old population in the United States has used LSD in the past thirty days and that less than 0.1 percent of those twenty-six or older have used LSD in the past thirty days.[19] Lifetime estimates of any hallucinogenic use (not only LSD but including psilocybin mushrooms, peyote, and mescaline) for person's age twenty-one to sixty-four is 17 percent.[20] Short-term effects are often unpredictable, but some of the more common effects include euphoria, a perception of being outside of your body, distortions of time, and visual illusions where objects appear unusually vivid or distorted and colors become very intense. Some people report experiencing a bad "trip," in which case the euphoria is replaced with fear. The best way to have a good "trip" is to be absolutely positive you want to do this (and are not being pressured into it), be in a good emotional state, and have a sober person (or two) with you to help ensure your safety.

The short-term effects of LSD last for approximately seven hours. Short-term withdrawal effects are unknown; however, some research states that flashbacks from an LSD "trip" may occur at any time throughout your life, including many years and even decades postures. Addiction to LSD is possible, but there is a low likelihood of it. Overdoses on LSD are rare but possible. More likely scenarios resulting in death from LSD include believing you can fly, engaging in other life-threatening behaviors while on the drug, mixing the drug with other drugs, or being predisposed to mental illness (therefore causing a bad trip).

The most common way to take LSD is through a small piece of paper that has been doused in LSD and is then placed beneath the tongue. It is highly recommended that a user consult with a guide (like the one on http://www.tripsafe.org) before consuming.

LSD was an incredible experience. Not that I'm recommending it for anybody else; but for me it kind of–it hammered home to me that reality was not a fixed thing. That the reality that we saw about us every day was one reality, and a valid one– but that there were others, different perspectives where different things have meaning that were just as valid. That had a profound effect on me.

—ALAN MOORE, COMIC BOOK WRITER

However, on one occasion, several years ago, I was idiot enough to take a dose of LSD. (I did it to please a woman.) I had what is known as a "bad trip." It was a very bad trip. I shall not attempt to describe what I experienced on that dreadful and rather shameful occasion. (I will only add: it concerned entrails.) In fact it would be extremely hard, even impossible, to put it properly into words. It was something morally, spiritually horrible, as if one's stinking inside had emerged and become the universe: a surging emanation of dark half-formed spiritual evil, something never ever to be escaped from. "Undetachable," I remember, was a word which somehow "came along" with the impression of it. In fact the visual images involved were dreadfully clear and, as it were, authoritative ones and they are rising up in front of me at this moment, and I will not write about them. Of course I never took LSD again.

—IRIS MURDOCH, *THE SEA, THE SEA*

Methamphetamine (crystal meth/speed)—ILLEGAL. It is estimated that 0.4 percent of the eighteen-to-twenty-five-year-old population in the United States have used a methamphetamine in the past thirty days and that 0.4 percent of those twenty-six and older have used a methamphetamine in the past thirty days.[21] Short-term effects include euphoria, increased energy (loss of need for sleep), increased sexual arousal, grinding of teeth, loss of appetite, itching, disorganized thinking, mood swings, dry mouth, and so on. The euphoria lasts for the first thirty minutes of the high, while many of the other effects last for twelve hours. People often binge on methamphetamine because the craving for the drug is so intense that the user will continue to seek the drug out, not sleeping for days (or even weeks). The street names (crystal meth and speed) refer to the way in which the drug is ingested. Crystal meth comes in crystal form and can be smoked, injected intravenously, or snorted, while speed is available in pill form and can be ingested or crushed and then snorted. Methamphetamines are possibly the most psychologically addictive drugs. The most severe withdrawal symptoms can last for up to two weeks, with some symptoms continuing for up to three months, but methamphetamine addiction is usually (psychologically) lifelong.

Joshua Schorr, an emergency medicine medical doctor wrote (in review of this chapter):

"This is becoming a severe and underestimated problem. Abuse/intoxication often leads to hallucinations, paranoia, and dangerous behavior. Many people are picked up and placed on psychiatric holds for several days as the effects mimic the symptoms of schizophrenia, and long term use possibly leads to changes in the brain similar to schizophrenia."

I think it's better to be comfortable in your skin than to be miserable being who you are. Sure, the meth is horrible. It ruins people from the inside out. It's a waiting game—it's not a matter of if it destroys you, but rather a matter of when it will.

—ASHLY LORENZANA, *PORTRAITS OF A YOUNG ADDICT*

The decision-making part of the brain of an individual who has been using crystal meth is very interesting. When Carly and Andy were in their apartment, they ran out of drugs. They sold every single thing they had except two things: a couch and a blow torch. They had to make a decision because something had to be sold to buy more drugs. A normal person would automatically think, sell the blow torch. But Andy and Carly sat on the couch, looking at the couch and looking at the blow torch, and the choice brought intense confusion. The couch? The blow torch? I mean, we may not need the blow torch today, but what about tomorrow? If we sell the couch, we can still sit wherever we want. But the blow torch? A blow torch is a very specific item. If you're doing a project and you need a blow torch, you can't substitute something else for it. You would have to have a blow torch, right? In the end, they sold the couch.

–DINA KUCERA, *EVERYTHING I NEVER WANTED TO BE*

Midomafetamine (MDMA/ecstasy)—ILLEGAL. It is estimated that in the United States, 0.8 percent of the eighteen-to-twenty-five-year-old population have used MDMA in the past thirty days and that 0.1 percent of those twenty-six and older have used MDMA in the past thirty days.[22] Short-term effects include extreme euphoria, relaxation, empathy, reduced fatigue, and heightened sensory perception. For example, touch and other sensations will feel extremely vivid. Short-term risks include overdose on nearly anything—including water—as you lose many of your body's natural regulators (like peeing, which is how a person can overdose on water because their body no longer tells them to pee). Dehydration is also a large risk on MDMA. The high lasts approximately four hours, and when you come down, you will likely experience opposite effects lasting for four days, with normalcy returning in about one month. There is a low level of addiction associated with MDMA, mostly because your body will be unable to replicate the results for a long time. It is highly recommended to not use MDMA more than once every six months (and recommended to never use it). The most common way to take MDMA is by ingesting a pill, which poses a great risk of overdose because the drug is illegal and unregulated, and it is impossible to know precisely how potent the pill is or if it has been mixed in with another drug with its own negative effects. "The DEA says only 13% of the Molly seized in New York state the last four years actually contained any MDMA, and even then it often was mixed with other drugs."[23] (Molly is a street name, often indicating pure MDMA.) Extreme caution is recommended.

> MDMA, it was beginning to be apparent, could be all things to all people.
>
> —ALEXANDER SHULGIN, *PIHKAL: A CHEMICAL LOVE STORY*

Nicotine (tobacco)—LEGAL (over the age of eighteen). It is estimated that 36.6 percent of the eighteen-to-twenty-five-year-old population in the United States have used nicotine in the past thirty days and that 24.3 percent of those twenty-six and older have used nicotine in the past thirty days.[24] (Approximately 50 percent of those are daily users.) Short-term effects include increased alertness, relaxation, mild euphoria, and decreased appetite. If you cease to use nicotine after prolonged usage, you will likely have difficulty concentrating and experience an increase in anxiety, irritability, and hunger, with the effects being most pronounced around seventy-two hours postcessation and generally subsiding within two weeks. The most common way to take nicotine is through tobacco smoke (cigarettes), but other ways include chewing, vaping, gum, and more.

> Smoking [tobacco] is the leading preventable cause of disease and death in the U.S., responsible for about 1 in every 5 deaths.
>
> —U.S. DEPARTMENT OF HEALTH AND HUMAN SERVICES, CDC
> NATIONAL HEALTH REPORT HIGHLIGHTS (HTTPS://WWW.CDC.GOV/
> HEALTHREPORT/PUBLICATIONS/COMPENDIUM.PDF)

Overdose on nicotine is possible, but your body will likely tell you when to stop. There is a higher possibility of overdosing when chewing gum or using a patch, so follow instructions carefully.

Avoid using cigarettes, alcohol, and drugs as alternatives to being an interesting person.

—MARILYN VOS SAVANT, PERSON WITH THE HIGHEST RECORDED IQ

Opioids (prescriptions include codeine, fentanyl, hydrocodone, morphine, oxycodone, and many more)—PRESCRIPTION ONLY. It is estimated that, in the year 2015, 8.5 percent of the eighteen-to-twenty-five-year-old population in the United States have misused a prescription-only painkiller and that 4.1 percent of those twenty-six and older have misused a prescription-only painkiller. In that same year, approximately 34.8 percent of the eighteen-to-twenty-five-year-old population and 38.3 percent of those twenty-six and older in the United States were given a prescription.[25] The effects are similar to those of heroin, except that due to the method of consuming the drug (usually through a pill), the effects are not as abrupt (and are therefore less addictive). The effects last a bit longer, six to eight hours. The withdrawal symptoms, addictiveness, and likelihood of overdose are similar to those of heroin.

Joshua Schorr, an emergency medicine medical doctor wrote (in review of this chapter):

"Many of these are injected just like heroin. This does not need to be a separate category from heroin as they are all essentially the same other than their mode of ingestion and pharmacokinetics."

Paroxetine (antidepressants)—PRESCRIPTION ONLY. It is estimated that 12.7 percent of Americans use some sort of antidepressant (and paroxetine, a selective serotonin reuptake inhibitor [SSRI] is only one type of them).[26] There is a threat of addiction when combined with other drugs, but it is otherwise low. Short-term positive effects include improvement of mood and increased energy. Short-term side effects may include acne, gastrointestinal issues, weight gain, depression, and many others. Antidepressants are studied often and highly regarded as safe when properly administered by a doctor.

Progestin (female birth control pill)—PRESCRIPTION ONLY. It is estimated that approximately 28 percent of fertile women in the United States are on some sort of birth control pill (which includes other pills that are not progestin only).[27] Short-term effects include 99 percent reduced chance of pregnancy and increased menstrual regularity. Side effects vary from person to person but often include weight gain, acne, decreased libido, and depression.

Psilocybin mushrooms (magic mushrooms)—ILLEGAL. It is estimated that less than 1 percent of Americans have used LSD, mescaline and/or mushrooms within the past month and that 13.4 percent of adults in the United States have used these drugs in their lifetime.[28] Short-term effects include euphoria and vivid hallucinations. The same measures taken for LSD should be taken for psilocybin. Psilocybin mushrooms grow naturally on every continent except Antarctica and are most commonly found on cow dung. (Some speculate that this is why the cow is sacred in India—it may have been a valuable export thousands of years ago!) The most common way to take mushrooms is by eating them, but they taste like shit. A recent article in Scientific Reports states that magic mushrooms may help depression in people by figuratively "resetting" the brain.[29] It should be noted that this research is not definitive, that consumption of psilocybin mushrooms may produce the opposite of intended effects, and "they affect different people, at different places, and at different times, with incredible variability."

> Using mushrooms for depression is like lifting your house up on jacks to get at the foundation. If you do it for fun, you gain nothing. If you don't know what you're doing, you're not really going to fix anything. Sometimes you need to get a professional in there who can teach you how to level that shit out. Hell, dealing with mental issues should start with finding a trusted professional anyway. They can teach a person a lot about how to process these things in a healthy way without leaving a person to the minefield of trial and error.

I hope that nobody seeks out mushrooms believing that it'll just fix everything. There is no pill that magically fixes mental illness and it would honestly be a little frightening if drugs had that power. Even prescription drugs at their best can only help people manage their illness. Mushrooms show potential to do the same and I hope people research it well and respect its effects and limitations.

—IMPOVERISHEDYORICK ON REDDIT.COM

This sentiment should be noted for the use of any drug.

With all drugs, it's best to consult medical professionals. If you are considering using a nonprescribed drug, do your research.

Street drugs are usually more toxic because they contain impurities. In the laboratory, however, most impurities are separated out, resulting in less toxic compounds.

—SANNA MALICK, FORMER SYNTHETIC ORGANIC CHEMISTRY RESEARCHER

These pages are not meant to be medical advice. The safest way to elevate your mood is to be in the company of someone you enjoy and/or by exercising, listening to music, stretching your face, meditating, and more {search: elevate your mood naturally}.

If you feel pressured into taking a drug or doing anything you typically wouldn't do, ask the person pressuring you, "Why do you care if I do it?" Usually, that will take care of the peer pressure. If it doesn't, hopefully you have the willpower to do what you truly want to do.

For a faster recovery time with most anything, eat healthily, drink plenty of water, exercise, stretch, and engage in activities with people who do not do the drugs or activities you are trying to avoid.

For a plethora of information, go to https://www.drugabuse.gov/publications/drugs-brains-behavior-science-addiction/drugs-brain and https://www.samhsa.gov/.

Remember, drugs generally work very well—and with most things in life, if we unnaturally produce euphoria today, tomorrow will be the opposite. Drugs exacerbate this effect to the extreme.

"Nearly three decades of scientific research have yielded 13 fundamental principles that characterize effective drug abuse treatment. These principles are detailed in NIDA's *Principles of Drug Addiction Treatment: A Research-Based Guide* [and outlined and quoted here].

PRINCIPLE OF DRUG ADDICTION TREATMENT:

1. **No single treatment is appropriate for all individuals.** Matching treatment settings, interventions, and services to each patient's problems and needs is critical.

2. **Treatment needs to be readily available.** Treatment applicants can be lost if treatment is not immediately available or readily accessible.

3. **Effective treatment attends to multiple needs of the individual, not just his or her drug use.** Treatment must address the individual's drug use and associated medical, psychological, social, vocational, and legal problems.

4. **At different times during treatment, a patient may develop a need for medical services, family therapy, vocational rehabilitation, and social and legal services.**

5. **Remaining in treatment for an adequate period of time is critical for treatment effectiveness.** The time depends on an individual's needs. For most patients, the threshold of significant improvement is reached at about 3 months in treatment. Additional treatment can produce further progress. Programs should include strategies to prevent patients from leaving treatment prematurely.

6. **Individual and/or group counseling and other behavioral therapies are critical components of effective treatment for addiction.** In therapy, patients address motivation, build skills to resist drug use, replace drug-using activities with constructive and rewarding nondrug-using activities, and improve problem-solving abilities. Behavioral therapy also facilitates interpersonal relationships.

7. **Medications are an important element of treatment for many patients, especially when combined with counseling and other behavioral therapies.** Buprenorphine, methadone, and levo-alpha-acetyl-methodol (LAAM) help persons addicted to opiates stabilize their lives and reduce their drug use. Naltrexone is effective for some opiate addicts and some patients with co-occurring alcohol dependence. Nicotine patches or gum, or an oral medication, such as buproprion, can help persons addicted to nicotine.

8. **Addicted or drug-abusing individuals with coexisting mental disorders should have both disorders treated in an integrated way.**

9. **Medical detoxification is only the first stage of addiction treatment and by itself does little to change long-term drug use.** Medical detoxification manages the acute physical symptoms of withdrawal. For some individuals it is a precursor to effective drug addiction treatment.

10. **Treatment does not need to be voluntary to be effective.** Sanctions or enticements in the family, employment setting, or criminal justice system can significantly increase treatment entry, retention, and success.

11. **Possible drug use during treatment must be monitored continuously.** Monitoring a patient's drug and alcohol use during treatment, such as through urinalysis, can help the patient withstand urges to use drugs. Such monitoring also can provide early evidence of drug use so that treatment can be adjusted.

12. **Treatment programs should provide assessment for HIV/AIDS, hepatitis B and C, tuberculosis and other infectious diseases, and counseling to help patients modify or change behaviors that place them or others at risk of infection.** Counseling can help patients avoid high-risk behavior and help people who are already infected manage their illness.

13. **Recovery from drug addiction can be a long-term process and frequently requires multiple episodes of treatment.** As with other

chronic illnesses, relapses to drug use can occur during or after successful treatment episodes. Participation in self-help support programs during and following treatment often helps maintain abstinence."

Tis easier to suppress the first Desire, than to satisfy all that follow it.

—BENJAMIN FRANKLIN, FOUNDING FATHER AND BUSINESSMAN

Chapter 16

Health

TL; DR:

> The human body seems indestructible when we are young.
> However, it is incredibly fragile and must be cared for if it is
> to serve us for a lifetime. Too often, the abuse it takes during
> early years (from drugs, improper nutrition, sporting injuries,
> etc.) becomes painful handicaps during later years.
>
> —JAMES C. DOBSON, *LIFE ON THE EDGE: THE NEXT GENERATION'S*
> *GUIDE TO A MEANINGFUL FUTURE*

EAT LESS, AND MOVE MORE. Following these two principles will be of benefit to most people. Beyond that, eat real food (food without additives or processing, food that microorganisms would also want to eat), engage in weight-bearing exercises and cardiovascular exercises, and stretch.

If you gain (unhealthy fat) weight, aim to lose it before one year's time, or else it may be with you permanently.

Consistency is the key to health. Aim to improve a little bit each day. One less potato chip, a little more exercise, and so on. Over time, your mindful improvements will add up.

> Clear any new lifestyle plan with your primary health-care
> provider to rule out any preexisting conditions that may be
> causing health problems and hinder progress.
>
> —ROBYN WARD, OCCUPATIONAL THERAPIST

End of TL; DR.

My favorite TED Talk, "Why Dieting Doesn't Usually Work," given by Sandra Aamodt (https://www.ted.com/talks/sandra_aamodt-_why_dieting_doesn_t_usually_work), discusses not only dieting but also reveals that if you gain weight and keep that weight on for too long (about one year), your body may adjust to this "new" weight forever. The TED Talk also explained that having a few healthy habits, even for an obese person, can drastically improve a person's health. I highly recommend you watch it.

Health, medicine, and what we understand about the human body are ever-evolving fields of research.

> Many of us take better care of our automobiles than we do of our own bodies...yet the auto has replaceable parts.
>
> —B. J. PALMER, MIXED MARTIAL ARTS FIGHTER

If you neglect your health long enough, advancement in medicine will not make up for living an unhealthy lifestyle.[1]

> If we could give every individual the right amount of nourishment and exercise, not too little and not too much, we would have found the safest way to health.
>
> —HIPPOCRATES, FATHER OF MEDICINE

For nearly everyone, a few basic principles apply:

1. Eat a variety of foods. The fresher, the better. The way you cook food matters, but not nearly as much as the type of foods you are eating.

> Let food be thy medicine and [otherwise] medicine be thy food.
>
> —HIPPOCRATES, FATHER OF MEDICINE

In army mess halls, foods are often classified as high, moderate, or low performance. High-performance foods are generally considered to be vegetables, small portions of nuts and beans, whole grains, fish, lean meats, and fruits. Moderate-performance foods are generally considered to be stir-fried vegetables, eggs, baked chicken, lean ground beef, and dried fruits. Low-performance foods range from cheeseburgers to pizza, ribs, macaroni and cheese, tempura-battered vegetables, buffalo wings, syrup, pancakes, butter, soda, and nearly all high-processed, long-lasting foods.

> Healthy food choices provide a diet that is nutrient dense with recommended intakes of vitamins and minerals, high fiber, moderate protein, and much lower levels of saturated fat, sodium, sugar, cholesterol, and preservatives than is typical of the most current eating patterns. (2) Healthy foods typically have minimal food processing technologies applied to them. (3) A healthy, balanced diet combined with other lifestyle choices leads to increased resistance to disease, better daily performance, and a better sense of well-being.
>
> —US Army nutrition guidelines, Go for Green Program

2. Avoid food additives. If you do not understand what an ingredient is, it is probably not great for you. There is a good chance that if other bacteria do not want to eat something (highly processed), your gut bacteria won't, either.

> If man makes it, don't eat it.
>
> —Jack LaLanne, godfather of fitness

3. Exercise, and ensure that you perform the exercises you engage in with proper technique.[2] Stretch midway or after exercising (stretch when your body is warm, not cold).[3] The main functions of exercise are twofold: weight-bearing exercises will help you retain bone and muscle mass, and cardiovascular exercises will help to keep your lungs, heart, and overall blood flow (and other internal organs) functioning properly. It often helps to be part of a group for exercise, but some people want to work out alone. What is important is exercising in a manner that you mostly enjoy so that you don't strain yourself or burn yourself out, and you maintain the activity throughout your life.

4. Sleep. If you have trouble sleeping, try following these steps:

- Refrain from caffeine/stimulant use.[4] It may take up to two weeks after cessation of caffeine consumption before the stimulants are no longer affecting your body.

- Exercise during the day.[5]

- Keep electronics out of your bedroom and refrain from use within an hour of going to sleep.[6] If you cannot sleep, read a book by candlelight.

- Meditate. This helps promote the production of melatonin, a hormone that helps you sleep.[7]

- Obtain a weighted comforter.[8]

See a medical doctor if you have continuous issues sleeping. Some sleep issues are due to either a physical or mental health problem. There are many other remedies for insomnia. Sleep is one of the most important aspects of maintaining good health, especially long term[9] {search: how to fall asleep}.

5. The older you get, the harder everything becomes.

> Neglect mending a small fault, and 'twill soon be a great One.
>
> —BENJAMIN FRANKLIN, FOUNDING FATHER AND BUSINESSMAN

No matter how old you are, if you don't use it—you do lose it.[10] (Remember this when you are fifty because it is truer for a fifty-year-old than a thirty-year-old.) To be healthy in the long term, you must combine all facets of health at all stages of your life. If you neglect one area, it will catch up to you.

6. Most Americans should weigh less.[11]

> Eat few suppers, and you'll need few medicines.
>
> —BENJAMIN FRANKLIN, FOUNDING FATHER AND BUSINESSMAN

How to lose weight: burn more calories than you ingest. That is the only way to lose weight. You can eat only candy bars and lose weight, but that doesn't mean you're a healthy person, nor does being thin or buff mean you are necessarily healthy either. (Note: one pound is equal to about thirty-five hundred calories.)[12]

7. Brain health. Your brain grows new cells every day through a process called neurogenesis.[13] How many of these new cells (and current cells) live rather than die depends on what activities you engage in,[14] from drugs to exercise, sleep, and meditation.[15]

8. Anxiety and stress are generally bad.[16] It has been theorized that when you are stressed, your body prepares for physical trauma, and your blood literally thickens to help with blood clotting in the event of an injury. Anxiety has been linked to blood clots.[17]

Western versus Eastern medicine:

Western medicine focuses on society, while Eastern medicine focuses on the individual. Western medicine often masks the pain, while Eastern addresses the root cause of the pain.

- Western medicine finds remedies that work for most of society and that also allow individuals to maintain their lifestyles. While this is not always the case, Western practitioners often prescribe drugs that mask problems rather than address the underlying causes. Western medicine focuses on a person's immediate happiness, often at the expense of long-term happiness. This is usually the patients' fault and not that of the doctors prescribing the medicine. Doctors usually give the information for patients to self-correct without the use of, or at least with limited use of, drugs. Patients, however, often rely on the drugs rather than what they can do (often these are lifestyle changes) to help improve their problems, which eventually diminishes their quality of life.

- Eastern medicine focuses on the individual, customizing a routine or remedy for that person. While Western remedies tend to focus on external factors that are often outside of a person's control, Eastern remedies focus on internal factors that are within an individual's control. For example, if you have knee pain, a Western doctor may prescribe a painkiller, while an Eastern doctor would be more likely to prescribe stretching exercises (and/or yoga). Some Eastern medicine does utilize external treatments; with these, find what works best for you. If the one-size-fits-all method were true with Eastern external treatments, they would be more widely used within Western medicine. Eastern medicine is not always perfectly measurable because it often deals with human effort.

Sometimes the more measurable drives out the most important.

—RENÉ DUBOS (1901–1982), FRENCH AMERICAN ECOLOGIST

Insurance:

Reddit.com user JohnLennonsPenis asked:

"I'm 26. I've only ever had insurance through a past job and didn't use it much if at all. I don't currently have insurance and don't make much money at the moment but I'm trying to take better care of my body. What are my options? Where do I even start? Thanks in advance!"

Reddit.com user Leoparda answered with the following:

"So, that's a big question, and I'll try to cover basics of health/prescription insurance terminology, since that's what I know.

Deductibles: A set amount of money that you must pay on your own before the insurance kicks in. If you have a deductible of $2,000 and a bill for $400, you pay that entire $400. However, after a $400, $300, and $1,300 bill, then your insurance company starts paying for anything else that happens the rest of the year.

Copayments: A set fee you pay every time you use the insurance, whether it be at a doctor's office or for a prescription medication.

In-network/Out-of-network: The insurance company negotiates contracts with hospitals, pharmacies, etc. In-network means the insurance company has a good deal with that entity, and wants to encourage you to use them, since it will be better for them financially if you do. Out-of-network is a less favorable contract, so you can still go there, but you'll be paying more.

Formulary (prescriptions): A list of drugs that your insurance company covers. There are different "tiers"—groups of drugs with set copays. The cheaper copays will be associated with the drugs that are cheaper for the insurance company.

Prior authorizations (prescriptions): When the insurance company doesn't want to pay for a specific drug (too expensive, probably), this is an "appeals" of sorts. The prescriber can fill out a form stating why it is medically necessary for you to have THIS expensive drug instead of THAT cheaper one. The form will then be sent to the insurance company, and a decision will be made."

Reddit.com user cupcakemichiyo added the following:

"u/leoparda covered definitions pretty well, so I won't cover those, but

Dental: Covers anything to do with your teeth, may or may not cover orthodontia (mine doesn't). Usually covers an annual or semi-annual cleaning, and maybe (if you're lucky) some basic services (like filling cavities)

Vision: Most cover an annual eye exam, and some portion of frames or contacts. If you have good eyes, this is all you need. I have bad eyes, and my (expensive) insurance covers more expensive frames, and better lenses (a larger portion of transitions, polycarbonate lenses, and a couple of other things, either for necessity, protecting my eyes from damage, or because it makes life way easier) in addition to my yearly eye exam.

Health insurance: Anything else. If you're lucky, it'll cover misc things like mental health services, but you should absolutely check on the plan before you buy it. It took me hours to comb through the benefits of my employer's health insurance options to find the one I wanted/fit my needs.

As for where you start, that really depends on where you are. If you're in the US, you should start by researching Obamacare options for your state and income.

Health insurance plans can be reviewed and purchased at https://www.healthcare.com/. That site also provides a 24/7 customer service line for answering questions, but many plans exist off-market."

This chapter is not all-inclusive. Much that deals with health will be specific to you individually. Some people enjoy participating in multiple activities, while others find that a similar or entirely different routine works best for them. The key is consistency. Whether you are consistent with one routine or with multiple routines, consistently eating healthily, exercising, stretching, and more, the key is consistency.

Minimize stressful environmental factors, and create a healthy and consistent routine, eating plan, and exercise plan that fits your life now and for years to come.

—ROBYN WARD, OCCUPATIONAL THERAPIST

Chapter 17

Religion

(Note: This chapter was reduced to include only the TL; DR section.)

TL; DR:

RELIGION HAS DIFFERENT MEANINGS FOR different people. It is often associated with a belief in a god, a supernatural Supreme Being (or beings) that transcends the physical laws of this world.

To many, religions have always been the answer to the universal workings of the world and everything around us, often in the form of communication and life practices dictated through spirits or gods, supreme beings, and omnipotent creators. Some sort of god or gods are often seen as accurate because no matter how much evidence we are provided in this world, it is likely that we will never know the definitive origin of ourselves. We have a fixation on beginning and ending; the universe does not seem to be guided by this same principle.

Others (mainly atheists) believe religions were started as a primeval means of organizing large groups of people (an early form of government). Since many people were illiterate, stories were used to convey various laws and workings of society. Holidays were representative of different work modes, such as spring planting, fall harvesting, record keeping (New Year), and others. These demarcations helped to keep the members of these societies in good spirits. Simply because we do not understand something, nor ever will, does not mean gods exist.

To many, religion is a set of core beliefs that helps guide them through their daily lives. Various books often accompany a religion and aim to provide a framework for how to live and go about a person's communities, daily life, and so on.

In much of China, Buddhism is the major religion and one that most of its followers argue has no god. Without having any gods, is it a religion? Some argue yes, and others, no.

Most religions have many commonalities, like a belief in gods (that which we cannot explain), forbidden practices like killing without justification (criminal laws), practices against interest on loans (civil laws), as well as holidays and prayer times (cultural traditions).

As said in the beginning, religion has different meanings for different people.

End of TL; DR.

Chapter 18

Self-Help

TL; DR:

> What you truly want to do, you will do.
>
> —ALEXANDRA PEACOCK SCHARPNICK,
> A FRIEND GIVING ADVICE

To ME, AT LEAST, ALMOST all self-help books are extremely similar.

Step 1: Get motivated. Use that motivation to get started and to...

Step 2: Make a plan. Develop a routine, and use your plan as a guide. If you cheat, you are only cheating yourself. After all, you are the one who designed the plan. And finally...

Step 3: Stay consistent. Discipline is the real key to success. Motivation only lasts for so long. You must adhere to your routine and to your plan. Being dedicated is probably the best way to ensure lasting results.

What you truly want to do in this life, you will do (as long as it's within reason). If you truly want something, chances are you will do what you must to achieve it—and if not, you will not.

> Amateurs sit and wait for inspiration; the rest of us just get up and go to work.
>
> —STEPHEN KING, AUTHOR (OVER 350 MILLION COPIES SOLD)

End of TL; DR.

> Do what makes you great, do what's uncomfortable and scary
> and hard, but pays off in the long run. Be willing to fail…Fail
> in the way and the place where you would want to fail…You
> have to trust your own voice, your own ideas, your honesty,
> vulnerability…You do not have to be fearless, just don't let fear
> stop you. Live like this as best you can and I guarantee you will
> look back on a life well lived. You are capable of greatness.
>
> —CHARLIE DAY, ACTOR, WRITER, AND COMEDIAN

That brief self-help guide in the TL; DR section may be applied to almost any facet of life. Often, people tout *motivation* when they really mean *dedication*. There will be difficult days. On those difficult days, it is not motivation that will help you—because the motivation is not present. It is your self-discipline that will get you there.

> Do you want to know who you are? Don't ask. Act! Action will
> delineate and define you.
>
> —THOMAS JEFFERSON, FOUNDING FATHER
> AND THIRD US PRESIDENT (1801–1809)

There is always an excuse. The truth is, we can always find an excuse.

As stated in the introduction,

> So convenient a thing it is to be a reasonable creature, since it
> enables one to find or make a reason for everything one has
> a mind to.
>
> —BENJAMIN FRANKLIN, FOUNDING FATHER AND BUSINESSMAN

It is never too late to start (a project, a passion, a new skill, etc.). You're eighty years old and can barely move? There are plenty of stories of people taking up yoga and being more active in their eighties than in their sixties or even in their forties. Are you forty years old and want to get an education? Go do it. You will likely crush the other students in your class, and, when you are forty-four, you'll crush life. People are living longer than ever. It is never "too late." As for me, I did not pass a single class in my freshman year of college, was arrested on felony drug charges, and was kicked out of my dorm.

At the end of the year, the summons came for my court date, my transcripts read, "E, E, E, E, E," I had spent nearly all of my savings, and my romantic relationships were poor. I thought my life was ruined. I realize now that one year does not determine my entire life. I eventually had the mindset to get things right. I got motivated, made a plan, and stuck to the plan. I transferred schools a year later and graduated at the top of my class. You can overcome anything if you truly want to.

One of the easiest ways to be happier in life seems to pertain to having specific goals. If you have a goal, whether it is short term (a year or less), medium term (one to five years), or long term (five or more years), you are better able to focus. If you are unsure of what to do, simply pick something that is at least of some interest to you. This will buy you time, and you will still advance yourself in the process. Without any sort of accomplishment, you will simply be older and in the same (or often an even worse) place.

A dream written down with a date becomes a goal. A goal broken down into steps becomes a plan. A plan backed by action becomes reality.

—GREG S. REID, AUTHOR AND SPEAKER

You do not need motivation—you need discipline.

—ANONYMOUS, (OVERHEARD AT THE GYM)

The wisest men follow their own direction.

—EURIPIDES, ANCIENT GREEK PLAYWRIGHT

To achieve great things, two things are needed: a plan, and not quite enough time.

—LEONARD BERNSTEIN, CONDUCTOR, COMPOSER, AUTHOR

Do not wait to strike 'til the iron is hot; but make it hot by striking.

—WILLIAM BUTLER YEATS, POET

He that resolves to mend hereafter, resolves not to mend now.

—BENJAMIN FRANKLIN, FOUNDING FATHER AND BUSINESSMAN

People don't run out of dreams—people just run out of time.

—GLENN FREY, SINGER, SONGWRITER, ACTOR

There is a huge difference between WANTING to change and BEING WILLING to change. Almost everyone wants to change for the better. Very few are willing to take the steps necessary to create that change.

—JOHN T. CHILD, AUTHOR, SPEAKER, DESIGNER

For what it's worth…it's never too late, or in my case too early, to be whoever you want to be. There's no time limit. Start whenever you want. You can change or stay the same. There are no rules to this thing. We can make the best or the worst of it. I hope you make the best of it. I hope you see things that startle you. I hope you feel things you've never felt before. I hope you meet people who have a different point of view. I hope you live a life you're proud of, and if you're not, I hope you have the courage to start over again.

—F. SCOTT FITZGERALD, WRITER

▲ ▲ ▲

Alvin Chester:

IN GOD'S IMAGE (ALSO CALLED CONFESSION)

Why must we go on this way?
Living from moment to moment,

Watching the days pass
In endless succession,

Winding along life's byways,
Pausing nowhere, resting nowhere,

The past lost
In the lie of memory,

The future, without approach or warning,
Arriving with each turn of the eye,

Each step, each breath
Beclouding our dreams,

Making false our desires and ambitions?
Why must I?

What is the cost?
Of discovering one's own true image?

Comfort. And that comfort,
Which we all so augustly disdain the need of,

Is the one barrier
Preventing us from being ourselves.

How great must one be to make the break?
How brave must one become?

And yet, it has been done.
And these few have made weaklings of us all.

A handful of persons
In God's own image

Among millions of
Cowardly nonentities;

Only a smattering
Of the living

In the great
World valley of the dead.

Only a few pure should,
But, nevertheless, a few.

And the cowards,
What do we do?

Nothing.
For that is what makes us so.

And the pity of it is
We go on.

Part Six: Conclusion

Your actions will define you

Chapter 19

Conclusion

No TL; DR.

AT ANY POINT IN YOUR life, you can change, learn, and grow. I hope I continue to realize that I grow every day and that my views from yesterday, while I heartily agreed with them, have changed today. I wonder what I will believe when I am eighty—if I make it to be that old. Given enough time, even the smallest of changes produce large results. Most goals and dreams in life are easier said than done.

Lastly, your experiences help to solidify knowledge. Experience, combined with knowledge, is what really seems to count.

> Reading a book about driving isn't the same as actually driving. Put that in your book!
>
> —LEWIS HOFSTEIN, MY FATHER (WHO EVERY DAY TOLD ME TO GET A JOB BUT NEVER STOPPED TRYING TO HELP WITH THIS BOOK)

⌃ ⌃ ⌃

Alvin Chester:

They Told Me To Choose Happiness:
A Tale Of Youth's End

They told me to choose happiness
When the time for decision came.

And so I chose the carefree way,
Had my fun, played all the games.

Hey there, they cried, and called me back.
We didn't quite mean that.

The joy and bliss we spoke about
Will come tomorrow, so settle back

And work real hard, accept responsibility,
And then, perhaps, will come the day

When you can relax and look back on your life
And pat your back, and then, maybe, play.

And I told myself, they're old; they've had
Years of experience. I guess they must be right.

So I changed my course and turned around,
And worked all day, and then, at night,

When I should have been sleeping, I lay awake
And thought to myself that the life I was leading

Was not for me. That I was crawling down
The road of the Dead, when I could have been speeding

Along the highways of life and romance. And I lay back
And cried dry tears that came from my heart,

For I knew I was lost. I had set a course
From which there was no chance of parting.

The years flew by, and there I was still,
Longing for that tomorrow, a day never to come.

I, a high-spirited fiery stallion, held in harness
By a plodding world, and never allowed to run.

But some say I'll make amends
For the wonderful things I missed.

I'll tell every hot-blooded young soul
I meet what real happiness is.

Turn back, I'll cry, before it's too late,
Before you're caught and made to walk their pace.

Go away from the pack, and lead your own life,
And then, if you want, race

Them all to Hell. And you'll beat them
For sure, but never you care.

You will have had more happiness in any one
Of your days than all of them in their barren

Existence they call life. Run, leave now;
And look not back nor ahead.

Whatever lies before you will come,
And that which is back is dead.

This is your life; here is your day;
The world is yours; your soul is free.

Tomorrow is never. Only now can you determine
Your life and make today your eternity.

Deny yourself not that little which is yours,
Your spark of the divine which God blessed.

Heed well their words…and choose what they say
When they tell you to choose happiness.

And so, if it's true happiness you want,
Choose no one's beaten path

Walk on two feet all your own
And be glad you've vexed their wrath.

Move on in your own heart's fashion.
Hail heaven in your own way.

Now, today, in your own manner work.
Now, today, in your own manner play.

And forever more
      In your own manner
            Be yourself.

you, You, YOU
YOU
are the
Philosopher

Alvin Chester

A guide to developing your
own personal philosophy

you, You, YOU are the Philosopher
Authored by Alvin Chester
Edited by Daniel Hofstein
Originally published by Dano Ventures, LLC

Dedication

*To you (the reader). To society. To all who have
come before me. Without you (everyone), I would
have never been able to do much of what I have done.*
(by Daniel G. Hofstein, editor and grandson of Alvin Chester)

CONTENTS

1

What is Personal Philosophy?

WHAT YOU ARE ABOUT TO read is a personal philosophy for ME. It is NOT meant to be one for YOU. My purpose is to help to stimulate you to start one of your own, to help you to start to form your own personal philosophy. My aim is to encourage your own thinking, not to influence it.

You will notice that this book is printed with many blank spaces. The intention is to leave room for you to write notes of your own—of agreement, disagreement, or added thoughts. It is quite important to make these notes so that you will have them available for future use. I cannot put enough emphasis into this aspect of your reading this...making your own notes as you go along.

Why should you (someone, anyone, and everyone) formulate your own personal philosophy? What does it mean to have one? Why do you need your own personal philosophy?

_____

_____

_____

_____

_____

_____

I believe the extensions of thought from any human being are so profuse they are countless. Normally these thoughts go forth in helter-skelter ways, exhibiting innumerable separate and unrelated facets. There is no cohesiveness of thought. We find we think dissimilarly about similar things. We are neither consistent in our thinking nor in our behavior. There is no central core. We are not wholly integrated persons and cannot, therefore, firmly and positively, achieve inner growth.

Having your own personal philosophy will give you personal unity. It will allow you to maximize your potential. A person with a philosophy is a MOVER; without it one floats and is MOVED.

It is very easy to establish your own personal philosophy, your own YOU. After you finish reading my personal philosophy, you will find a chapter on how to develop your own. The reading of my philosophy AND THE MAKING OF YOUR NOTATIONS is the BEGINNING.

Philosophy, in the way I use it here, is PERSONAL PHILOSOPHY. It is not meant to cover all branches of knowledge and life, only those that concern me (or you). A person with a personal philosophy is not a philosopher. Your personal philosophy will not purport to be valid for anyone else. Therefore, you are not bound by all the obligations of the philosopher.

Your personal philosophy does not have to be perfect. It must only be YOU, albeit a more organized and integrated you than you would be without it.

Religion may or may not be a part of your philosophy; it depends on what religion is to you. Your philosophy does not obligate you to believe anything. It is the ORGANIZATION of what you do believe into a positive, harmonious YOU.

Your personal philosophy will expand your outlook; it will also restrict it.

No PROOF is required for your personal philosophy. That it is YOU is proof.

There is no reference made here to great scholars, philosophers, or teachers. I have certainly learned from them, but my philosophy is reflecting what is ME, now, without reference to what influenced these thoughts, just as your philosophy will reflect what it is to be YOU.

You will note, as you read my philosophy, that not all the questions are answered. That is because I do not have all the answers. (I expect that you will find that same is true for yourself.) It is not vital to know all the answers. With many things, there are no perfect answers (even for oneself); it is sufficient to understand the question. This is NOT to say that one should not SEEK the solutions.

Great knowledge is not a necessary factor in developing a personal philosophy; opinion will suffice. Of course you should be able to distinguish between knowledge and opinion so as not to confuse yourself about their relative values. (See chapter on TRUTH.)

To the true PHILOSOPHER, I offer my most humble apologies for using (and, in the context of true universal philosophy, misusing) that word. I hold the greatest respect for your endeavors and achievements. I only ask that you do not deny us simpler souls the privilege of playing "at the game" in our own way.

2

You

YOU ARE UNIQUE. YOU ARE individual. You are you, and you are no one else, and no one else is you. You are the most important being ever created. It is not even necessary that you feel this or understand it. You are all of those things, whether or not you are cognizant of that status of you.

You are, for you, the beginning, the end, and the in-between. You are, for you, all that exists or ever did. And you can't do anything about it.

There is nothing in your universe that does not, in some way, exist in you. Nothing exists, for you, that you cannot (or did not) see, touch, hear, taste, smell, experience in some way, sense in some way. For you, there is nothing beyond you; for me there is nothing beyond me.

Everything that exists for you exists for you only. You cannot perfectly share anything with anyone else. Any number of people will look at the same object you look at, and you will see it somehow differently than anyone else. You and others will commonly acknowledge that it is a tree, but your tree, the one that you see, will be a little bit different. You are you.

Why is this so absolutely so? Why are you not the same as anyone else? Why are you so very unique? I have this pseudoscientific story that explains it.

———————————————————————————————

———————————————————————————————

———————————————————————————————

———————————————————————————————

_____

_____

_____

_____

_____

_____

_____

Let's begin with the beginning, your beginning. Let's begin with you at the earliest possible stage, a simple organism, and the first moment of your existence. There is a stimulus, an external stimulus. What happens? You respond. You respond with the first and only simple response of your existence, now and forever. (It is not important to know the specifics of that stimulus and response, only to understand their happening.)

Now receive the second stimulus. How do you respond? There is the natural response CONDITIONED by the experience and memory of the first stimulus and response. The third stimulus receives a more complex response; the fourth; the fifth; etc. (And, with all that complication, we must also understand that each response itself brings forth and conditions still another stimulus.)

One could take time to speculate on how many stimuli and responses you experience in each nanosecond and go from there to some arithmetic gyrations and develop to tally astronomical numbers. What difference would it make? We know the meaning and effect for this discussion.

Taking the above into account, can you possibly ever call the smallest and newest child a "simple person"? No. For practical purposes we start out complicated and become more and more different and individual and unique every second.

Do you still doubt your own individuality? Is it necessary to embellish the tale by establishing that this organism (person) started out vastly different than any other person? Shall we add data about genes, chromosomes, DNA?

_____

_____

_____

_____

_____

_____

_____

_____

_____

_____

Let's face it. You are unique. You are the center of your universe.

I hope you have been making the notes I told you were important. You may have observed a couple of obvious continuations of the stimulus/response speculation. Let's look at them.

Firstly, if the theory is correct, one could, having accumulated all the data regarding an organism, including a complete study of all stimuli and responses, thus determine how that organism (person) would respond to any given stimulus and (second objection) that this organism (person) therefore has no control over its responses.

Both comments are certainly valid.

You are you. You are unique. But you are also the universal human. By this I mean that there is in every person all that there is in every other person. Obviously the real NEEDS of existence are common to us all. In addition, however, all the wants, desires, lust, love, hate, all the emotions and passions are also within each of us to some degree or other.

That degree is determined by the combination of the experiences we have had (external forces) and the controls we have developed for ourselves (internal forces). We can be stimulated FROM WITHIN as well as from without.

The emotions and passions that are within us all are controllable only by ourselves. Your inner strength and potential growth are determined by your ability to overcome and control these things which are the subjective you. Only the truly objective you can obtain knowledge and make valid decisions.

You are you, and you are the universe.

Continuing with the first objection, there is a whole field of science today devoted to human responses and how to anticipate them. Much of this effort was made to determine how to stimulate mass (not individual) human motivation. This understanding of the active subjective you (plural) helps predict how you can be moved to act.

Advertising, political campaigning, propaganda of all sorts involve the use of the knowledge about the subjective human to provide data on what stimuli to send forth to elicit a desired response.

Is this what you want yourself to be, a puppet? Do you want ever to be manipulated by people who can use their objective thinking to control the subjective you?

No. And neither, if you are good and humanitarian, do you want to be the puppeteer. The more people who can and do control themselves, the more OBJECTIVE YOU (plural) there are in the world, the better the world will be.

There is in society a corps of misguided though well-meaning persons who wish to amend our laws of responsibility and criminality to make the antisocial acts of persons acting subjectively less abominable. They claim that these acts are the result of environment and, because they are not objective, are not evil. I disagree.

Just as there are in us the subjective forces of emotion, so has there also been implanted in us other natural forces, such as the will to live, the desire to procreate, conscience, and free will. I call these GOD-FORCES.

Antisocial behavior can be controlled and curtailed by the objectiveness in us and also by the GOD-FORCES of conscience and free-will.

We have now established that you are unique, that you are universal, that you are both objective and subjective, and that GOD-FORCES are within you.

You are, indeed, quite a person.

3

GOD and God

I BELIEVE IN GOD. I can't help myself. There is so much outside the possible scope of human experience, of human conception, that I feel some identification must be given. All that is beyond the possible conception, I call GOD.

GOD is before the beginning. GOD is the creator of the beginning. GOD is after the end. GOD is omniscient and omnipresent. GOD exists beyond space and time. GOD IS.

I am not "making a case" for GOD. Nor am I stating that GOD is a "must" in your (or anyone else's) philosophy. These are things that I feel… and I, as you, am unique.

GOD is the creator. All things exist because of GOD but not necessarily by GOD's design.

I do NOT believe that GOD is an omnipotent activist. (However, if it is part of your belief that GOD is that then GOD is that to you.) I do NOT believe that there is GOD to do for me that which I will not do for myself. All that can possibly be done by me is MY responsibility.

GOD is EVERYTHING. GOD is TOTALITY, that which is in my comprehension and that which is beyond it. GOD IS ALL THINGS, KNOWS ALL THINGS. GOD IS TRUTH. GOD IS PERFECTION. GOD IS ALL THINGS AT ALL TIMES.

You have probably heard the expression "Man is created in GOD's image." I don't know what it means to you, if anything, but it does have a vital meaning to me. To me it means that I can become God (not GOD, God) and that I can achieve an oneness with GOD. (Mind you, I said ONE-ness, not SAME-ness.)

It means that Truth, total knowledge, can be in my domain, AND I MUST SEEK IT. (Note that in my expression, Truth is perfect knowledge for humans and not TRUTH, which is GOD. Truth is in the human domain; TRUTH is GOD's.) We will have a separate complete section on TRUTH/Truth/truth later on.

One-ness with GOD is the ultimate Goal of man. We can have, and should have, many goals; all goals must properly exist within the striving toward the Goal—human perfection.

To become God (one-ness with GOD, my own perfect self) is my Goal. GOD is GOD. I cannot comprehend GOD: therefore, I do not try. A quest to be GOD is an impossible goal. I do not let GOD deter me from the Goal of God. I accept GOD. I work to become God. There is nothing to be gained by seeking what you cannot find. No amount of worship or prayer (or anything else) will bring me to GOD. A great deal of effort will help me become closer to God. There is no path, direct or indirect, to lead me to GOD. God, not GOD, is the Goal.

Will I become God? I shall not even begin to come close. I am not only vastly imperfect, but I am also imperfect in my quest for the Goal.

And yet, acknowledgement of the Goal and the efforts I do make will bring me some degree closer than not having any cognizance nor making any effort.

I also feel that if I (and you) move a little bit in the direction of the Goal that we will leave for the ensuing generation(s) a way of life that will make it a little easier for them to take another step. And what if we ALL took a little step…just a little step…wouldn't that be better yet?

you, You, YOU are the Philosopher

_____

_____

_____

_____

_____

_____

_____

_____

_____

_____

_____

4

TRUTH – Truth - truth

THERE ARE THREE WORDS IN this title, not one. Let's look at each of them briefly. TRUTH is GOD's domain. It is PERFECTION. TRUTH is that which is TOTAL TRUTH, all things at all times. TRUTH is GOD. We cannot aspire to TRUTH, as we cannot aspire to GOD. The only way to describe it is to know that it is beyond us. We will not dwell on it.

Truth (T) is the maximum Goal we can ever look to. Truth (T) is all knowledge that humans might attain. It is not the most knowledge that anyone has achieved; it is all knowledge that one can achieve. Truth (T) is the unaberrated, total human being. It is our Goal of perfection.

Truth (t) has two meanings. A truth is an unqualified Fact. It is a Fact now, and there is nothing that we can foresee that might change it. Truth (t) is a part of our conscience (morality; GOD-FORCE) that leads us to manifest truth and not that which is untrue.

Again, as previously stated, we shall expend no additional agonizing nor dreaming regarding TRUTH. Let us continue with Truth and truth.

A fact is a fact is a fact. But a fact may not be a Fact or a FACT. An example: You ask a person what time it is. The reply is that it is four minutes and eleven seconds past six o'clock. (We are going to assume that we all know it is evening.)

We know that time (the o'clock) is a constantly changing thing, and a statement about time can only possibly be true for an instant. We are normally willing to accept as an answer to "What time is it?" a reply which specifies that time for a nearby instant. (Actually, we might be satisfied merely to know it is a "little after six," but, in the case of our example, we have asked a person who is quite "factual" and wants to give us the best possible answer.)

Is the answer a "fact"? Not necessarily. The watch may not be accurate and even if the respondent read it correctly and spoke the truth as he saw it, it is NOT a "fact."

If the watch IS accurate, is it a "fact"? Yes. Is it a "Fact"? No. Timekeeping by a watch or clock still does not fully reflect our ability to measure time. Human scientific knowledge has allowed us to be, if we choose, much more specific. If the response did include those additional factors that are known, then it would have been a "Fact" as the reply would have been made in the most accurate manner that humans are capable of and we are satisfied that no new potential knowledge will alter our understanding of time.

If the reply included ALL OUR CURRENT KNOWLEDGE, THE BEST AND MOST IN THE WORLD, would it be a "FACT"? I think not. I do not know. FACTS are in the world of TRUTH and GOD. I don't know. I can never know. I accept the "idea" of FACT the same way I accept TRUTH and GOD. I "believe" it's there.

I shall not continue to complicate things with words, Words, WORDS. But I do want to aver that when and if we ever achieve Goal, there will be no difference between Truth and truth, Fact and fact, Word and word, et cetera, et cetera.

If Truth is the proper Goal, does that mean it is incumbent upon me to make sure that my watch is always perfectly accurate so that I will always know the Truth about what time it is? I guess the answer is yes. The answer would also have to say that I should know all there is to know about "time." That is the ideal.

We now recognize a "Fact." The author is not perfect, has not achieved Goal, and is a long way from it.

You may think that I have used this example as a deliberate means to further explain "Fact." I did not. I actually wrote myself into the corner.

Finding myself here, I realized, of course, that I had the option of leaving it. To rewrite might make me look better, but leaving it is my obligation to truth. I am, at least, in the "direction" of truth if I leave it.

I will say, in some small defense, that I do have a timepiece that I usually maintain (except for rare instances) within a handful of seconds of the accepted correct time. In a "reasonable" way, if not perfect, I do exert some discipline in that direction.

I am also one of those "sinners" who is apt to reply to your query of the time that it is "four minutes and eleven seconds past six o'clock." However, I am fairly "certain" of the time. If I were not, if I were wearing a watch that I was unsure of, I would probably say, "I think it is…" or "It is about…"

I really would have liked to have said in the above paragraph that "I would say" rather than (as stated) "I would probably say." I almost believe I have the right to, that I have disciplined myself enough (at least about time) to make that statement. But I cannot be absolutely sure. Therefore, "probably" is necessary to firmly establish the truth.

One should learn the discipline of the separation of truth and opinion by using more often the statements of "I think," "I believe," "I read somewhere," "I heard," or any of the others available that will allow the listener to know that you are not certain of the truth of your remark. There is a twofold gain in that constraint. One is, of course, that we have acted more heedfully as to our obligations to truth; the other is that we will remain credible to those with whom we are speaking.

I also think that we have obligations to truth as LISTENERS. We should not automatically accept everything we hear or read as a fact. It is the listener's responsibility to mentally CHALLENGE each new experience and test its validity. As we have the responsibility of seeking the truth, so we must also become the identifiers of truth. We must not allow that which is false but disguised as truth to fool us. The greater the relationship to truth you achieve, the sterner identifier you will become.

The search for Truth/truth is most difficult. It is much easier to accept truth as a simple responsibility to not tell lies. The proper search forces you to challenge everything and everyone, to make almost unlimited demands on yourself and those around you.

Awareness of your attitude about truth will make those in your company cognizant of your demands ON THEM and can make them quite uncomfortable, especially if they do not have that same relationship. There is a stress that comes with this that oftentimes causes emotional distress. How fragile is the relationship of two people, one who has a deep concern for time and the other who has little regard for it.

This search for truth/Truth is demanding. It is more than one can hope to achieve. It is too much to attempt to undertake. It is so all encompassing there is little or nothing left for anything else. Can I really believe that this is the only life?

I have asked this of myself over and over and over. I ask it when I see so many of my own deficiencies (which is almost all the time). I ask it when I violate my own rules. I ask it when I cry for relief from the "hell on earth" that I live with.

Yet, somehow, the difficulties, the cost, the anguish, the pain does not change my belief. The Goal is the Goal.

On the other side, I am sometimes comforted by the glimpses of "heaven on earth" that I am occasionally allowed. I am sometimes succored by the feeling that I have risen a smattering over what I would have been with the Goal.

The Goal is the Goal. I cannot disregard it. I cannot change it.

There is limitation to Truth. Truth is what was and what is, not what WILL BE. The future cannot be Truth. Awareness of Truths can help us to anticipate the future but only that. Truth is absolute; the future is not.

We must understand, therefore, that any thought or statement about the future can never be more than opinion. At the same time, the more Truths we achieve the more positively potential will become our view of that future.

Concepts are another part of truth. Whereas facts are related to what is (was), concepts relate to things as they should be. Concepts are behavioral truths. Concepts are truth with conscience.

5

Conscience

CONSCIENCE IS ONE OF THE GOD-FORCES within us. Because of our conscience, we feel good when we do right, and we have pain when we do wrong. There is no one without conscience.

Truth, added to conscience, is concepts (next chapter) and makes us aware of proper behavior. We know it is wrong to inflict pain onto someone. But we must know what pain is and what actions will inflict pain before we know what our behavior should be. Without the addition of truth, conscience will not properly impact on our lives.

Conscience inspires the behavioral utilization of truth. Conscience is truth in action. Truth (T) may not ever be achieved. The Goal is forever. Conscience is NOW. Truth (T) is the Goal of life. Conscience, with truth, is the way of life. Conscience becomes the identifier of our responsibility.

Conscientious behavior is the performance that justifies our existence, the outward responsibility. (The Goal of Truth is the inward.) The odds on our existence were extremely small. That we have life is sufficient to demand the justification of that life.

Look at these odds. Considering the frequency of coitus, the millions of sperm cells, the potential readiness of the egg, and considering that singular combination that joined to start what would become me, the odds against my particular birth must be astronomically astronomical. And I am here, recipient of the greatest gift of all...life.

What I do with that life is my responsibility. That my existence came to be requires justification on my part. That justification will be to make the world a better place for my having lived. To do this, I must seek the Goal and live conscientiously. It is not necessary that I accomplish great feats; it is necessary that I do my best; Life is the ultimate entitlement. A better life for all is the responsibility, the justification.

We can, each of us, easily work toward a better life for all. There is, at least, the opportunity to be an influence for good.

If we have children, we will exert a great influence on them. We must stimulate our children to seek truth and do good.

We influence ALL we come in contact with. Maybe our sphere of influence seems small to us. So what. We don't have to sway the multitudes. We don't have to accomplish great things. We do what we can.

In a sense it is like saving money. There are those who say it is valueless to save only a little bit at a time; unless one can put away large sums, life will not be changed. They, therefore, never save, because they never have "a lot" to save. Yet there are many who understand that each penny grows on top of every other one, and pennies do add up to dollars and more. In the course of time, the total of the small savings will be enough to make some difference (however small). Something is better than nothing. A "little" good is still *good*.

Just think what would happen if everyone in the world did a little good. The world would certainly become better for all of us. Your little bit is important. Everyone's is.

Let's examine an act of simple courtesy and see what a little positive influence might do.

Sometimes I feel that the least courteous aspect of a person exhibits itself when that person is behind the wheel of an automobile. Oftentimes, the freeways show people at their worst.

What might we do to change this? What small effort can be the constructive influence? Look at this possible example:

A driver is trying to enter, from off the road, into the stream of traffic. No one allows it. Isn't that typical of our roads and drivers? No one adjusts his own vehicle to allow that courtesy.

You do it. You slow your car and wave the other driver on. What happens to the PEOPLE involved? YOU FEEL GOOD. The OTHER DRIVER FEELS GOOD.

What else? From that moment on, that other driver is more apt to extend this courtesy to someone else. And the more times a driver receives the courtesy, the more apt he is to give it, thereby stimulating other drivers the same way.

That wasn't any great feat of accomplishment, but you, in your own small singular way, with no cost to yourself and with the gain of the pleasure in knowing you did good, did one small bit to make the world a better place, to fulfill your responsibility, to live with your conscience.

The thought does come that if everyone has a conscience and if courtesy is conscientious behavior, then why are not all people courteous? Because truth is also necessary. Conscience is the desire to do good. Truth explains the values and tells us how to.

_____

_____

_____

_____

_____

_____

_____

_____

_____

_____

_____

6

Concepts

CONCEPTS IS TAKING WHAT YOU know to be true, infusing the GOD-FORCE of conscience, and extruding rules of behavior. To seek Truth is the Goal; to tell the truth is a concept. That is about as simple an example as I can offer.

The unfortunate aspect of concept is that concepts are normally not so simply developed. One apparently simple concept may not be valid in all circumstances.

"Thou shalt not kill" (or any other preferred expression of the same statement) is a concept. Is it, in an unamended state, a completely valid rule of behavior? I don't think so.

_____

_____

_____

_____

_____

_____

_____

_____

_____

There are those who accept that rule just as it is, and they offer the singular explanation that all animal life is included. They will not eat meat or fish; they will even try to avoid stepping on an ant.

I believe that most people would further restrict the meaning and suggest that the reference is to the taking of a "human" life. All the GOD-FORCES do not exist in lower animals; therefore, this rule can justly apply to human life only.

Of this group, there are those who say one must hold with this rule, as is, with no other amendment, no privilege of altering it in any other way. DO NOT TAKE A HUMAN LIFE (period).

To comply, one must then decide what a human life is. Does human life begin at the moment of conception? Does human life cease with the cessation of the functioning of the brain? What human values must exist in order to determine human life?

There are people who demand further amendments. What, for example, does one do when he sees a person who seems to be about to murder two people? (Note that I said "seems to be," not "is." Remember, there is no truth in future.) Is it then permissible to take one human life in order to save two? Also, what if there were only ONE other life at stake, possibly your own?

What are the rules regarding the taking of life in wartime? In a "just" war? In an "unjust" war?

Should the rule be amended to have a reference to the cost to society for sustaining that life? Is any human life worth every cost? Is every human life worth any cost?

I am sure it would not be difficult to bring more and more questions into this discussion. What I have done here is to illustrate one of the problems in concepts.

How do YOU feel about "Thou shalt not kill"? Mark that feeling as a note on "your" side of this page. Let's look at another conceptual problem. What should we do with people who commit antisocial acts, who violate the laws of society?

_____

_____

_____

_____

_____

_____

_____

_____

_____

_____

Mark it on your side of the page. (You will want to make reference to these notes when reading the chapter on forming your own philosophy.) Concepts is our determination of morality. Add all our concepts together and you will find the sum of our moral values.

Let's go back to truth as a part of concepts. Why is truth there? Isn't this all opinion? Aren't morals always in a state of flux? Our knowledge and scientific and technical understanding has grown by leaps and bounds, but our morals have not. We have less morality today than before. How can we have, accordingly, more valid truth and fewer valid concepts (morality)?

_____

_____

_____

_____

_____

_____

I believe we do have more morality today, perhaps not as easily reflected in our individual activities as in the social order we have established. Certainly the rules for social living that we have instilled into our governments (generally, not totally) are more moral than governments of the past. That is a big step. I do not say I am satisfied with all of our rules (laws), but for the most part, they are better now than before.

I cannot say I am pleased with our individual morality as I see it now. I think we have lost some of the individual humanity we had in our fairly recent past, though I do believe we have more morality now than other times in our past. I would like, also, to see a greater effort toward our development as individuals. (And I think having personal philosophies can help.)

Truth is a big factor in concepts. Truth helps us see the world as it is, to see ourselves as we are, to give us the basis of thought which, together with conscience, leads us to concepts.

Truth is also the unifying factor that adds a cohesiveness to our concepts. The truth-seeking person is a more organized person and has concepts which are more in concert with each other.

7

G(g)oals

ONE OF THE MOST DIFFICULT aspects of adhering to an ideology is what to do when you cannot (or do not) maintain yourself or your actions in perfect harmony with your original design. How do you overcome the disheartenment and frustration? Isn't there the tendency to give up, to quit?

Yes, it is difficult. But we should remember that the Goal (and even a goal) is the quest. Perfect achievement is not necessary; one need only get closer.

It is like someone on a diet. After some successful adherence to orderly eating, a moment of weakness takes place. The dieter takes candy or pizza or cake (or whatever) into the mouth and ingests it before being able to act on the knowledge of the folly.

That eating (overeating) was a small error. The big blunder would be to use that error as a "reason" to give up the quest for a slimmer and healthier body. "Oh, well, I ruined it. I ate wrong. It proves I may do it again. The diet is off." More potentially successful diets are ended this way than any other.

Obviously, the wiser thing to do would be to accept that an error was made (and cannot be undone), understand that the goal has had a slight set-back, and continue forth with the diet regimen as planned. The goal is still the goal and still attainable.

Can you imagine someone who "sins" once, then accepts the fact that he is a "sinner," and begins to lead a "life of sin" in accord with his new opinion of himself?

It is better to acknowledge that, though imperfect, you are striving toward a proper goal. The imperfection is a little of your "hell on earth" but will be well offset by the "heaven on earth" achieved time after time as progress toward the goal continues. There is no happiness in self-defeat.

At the same time, there is danger in setting goals that are too high. I have felt that way from time to time about the Goal. However, I find comfort in realizing that the Goal is more than a goal. The Goal is forever. A goal is now.

Goals (g) should be achievable. Use truth to help in determining goals that can be reached.

I wish I could report that I have achieved all my goals. I am still striving toward most of them.

There is a difference between goals that can be reached and "dreams" that are unobtainable. Too often people set unrealistic goals for themselves. Truth was not used to establish them. Success is not potential. These people are only "dreaming."

I call these people "armchair achievers." They sit in their armchairs and daydream about becoming something they are not. A salesman will "dream" about making a huge sale. He will not set that sale as a goal and make a sincere effort to attain it. He will just "dream" about the possibility. In truth, he had no goal at all, just a dream. Since dreams are more easily attained than goals, he is content merely to dream.

We are all armchair achievers about some things from time to time, but for some people, it is their way of life. They don't want goals, real goals. They don't want to make that commitment.

These people who have no real goals, who spend all of their lives as "armchair achievers," are ever dismayed that they have accomplished no growth in their lives. They are oftentimes disgruntled at a world that has "held them back" from the attainments (dreams) that they feel should be theirs.

Can you conceive of this type of person having a personal philosophy? What truth is there in their lives? What value to society?

Proper goals allow infinite ways for each person to make gains, to have achievements. Truth helps us to determine what these attainments can be and what goals to set. Without goals, all roads lead to nowhere.

The setting of proper goals and their achievement will stimulate you to set new goals and more new goals. Though effort is required, the gains and successes are rewarding. You will delight in your growth, in your stature.

Let's look again at ordinary living and goal setting and problem solving. There are just a few things to keep in mind.

Seek truth. Be as sure as you can be that you are looking at the problem and clearly seeing as many facts as can be seen.

Determine goals. Remember that the Goal of achieving a oneness with GOD is a way of life, and, as such, it is the general Goal.

Other goals may be set without direct reference to the Goal. If the Goal is a part of you, you will set no goals to deter you from it. Set attainable goals.

The brain is a perfect computer. It is as true of the brain as it is of a modern computer: garbage in; garbage out. If you seek and recognize truth, unaberrated, the brain will take that and submit a result which also is truth. Truth in; truth out.

I think this may be a good time to sidetrack for a moment for another statement about truth. Again and again, I have written about truth and the fullness of its meaning. I believe it is so. I have recently advised you to always feed truth to your brain. However, the idea of truth in its fullest meaning is not always practical.

There is so much to think about all the time that it would be an unwise goal to insist on complete truth (or even close) as being necessary for all problem solving. How much truth is necessary to decide on what brand of paper toweling to buy? Remember the time-telling story?

If you maintain Goal and Truth as a way of life, you will find that your identification of truth in practical matters is enough for valid decisions. And the process will get progressively easier. As time goes on you will become more and more a truth-thinking person and will make better decisions with less effort. The more you seek truth, the easier it will be to find.

With Goal and Truth as a way of life, it will also become easier to determine what goals will lead you to greater happiness. A search for happiness is valid as long as Truth and Conscience (Goal) are maintained.

The ambition for happiness without Truth and Conscience can be most antisocial. Long ago, before I started organizing my own personal philosophy, I read the following thought that had a great impression on me. It was penned by W. H. Davies.

"I had ambition, by which sin
The angels fell;
I rose and, step by step (O Lord),
Ascended into hell."

8

Money

MONEY IS. AS I UNDERSTAND a need for practicality in a personal phi-losophy, I do not ignore the goal of money. Money is the means of trade in our society. Money is necessary to satisfy both our needs and our desires.

Money is the normal reward society gives us in exchange for our pro-ductivity. That is not to say that society always carefully values our input and gives just exchange. Inequities abound all over the place. (The greater the movement toward Goal for society as a whole, the fewer inequities there will be.) This money is the commodity we must have in order to acquire things.

There are other rewards to be obtained from our society, such as fame and power, but fewer people are allowed those things. There are also degrees of fame and power, just as there are almost infinite measures of monies obtained.

Maybe our social order is wrong. Maybe money should not be the re-ward. Maybe we shouldn't use money at all. Many suggested "utopias" deny the need for money. Perhaps money does not exist in the world of Truth and Goal. But money is what our society uses, and we must recognize it and live with it. Money is.

It would be pleasant to feel that people are productive and make contri-butions to society because they "should." Perhaps in Goal, it will so be. But we are not there. You and I are not perfect. Society is not perfect. We need money; we want money; inner rewards are not sufficient. People do want rewards for their contribution, and the normal reward now is money.

I am not suggesting that everything that people do is done for money and money alone. Our emotions stimulate a great part of our behavior and demand different rewards. But in the general area of social living and productivity, we expect a monetary compensation.

Societal rewards have stimulated much of the growth of our society. I often see society as a huge silhouette. The reaching out of individuals rise up from the broad base like fingers pointing upward, like stalagmites from a cavern floor. These fingers represent human aspirations. Society, in general, grows by filling in between those fingers, gradually rising. Society does not grow as a broad bottom band expanding upward in one huge movement. Society grows by accepting the efforts of individuals and learning to utilize them.

Those reaching persons who are the fingers of our growth should be rewarded. I see nothing wrong in that. It will stimulate them to more reaching, more growth. Of course society may offer substitute rewards, honor, fame, etc., but in most instances money is the normal payment. Here, as in all levels, society is not necessarily equitable in the rewards it gives; there is over-rewarding and under-rewarding.

This remuneration system results in, as should be, preconceived inequalities in society. Those who contribute more (usually) get more, have more. But the reward system is necessary to stimulate human aspiration, societal growth. Society is the broad bottom band. Societal needs must stimulate those fingers to reach up.

Money is. It is necessary to have money to exchange for those things which will satisfy our needs and desires. Therefore, in a sense, money is not a goal unto itself but a sub goal. Money is a means to provide for the goal to satisfy the needs of existence and one of the means toward the goal of happiness.

Money is not happiness. It is only one of the means to it. To have more money than our happiness requires suggests that we have wasted efforts in obtaining that money that we cannot use. Truth tells us we should understand our goal of happiness, determine what monies are necessary, and seek only those monies needed to satisfy that goal. Happiness involves much more than money can buy for us. We should be traveling those other paths to happiness at the same time we make an effort to get the monies needed.

"My cup runneth over" sounds nice, but the part that ran over is surely a waste of whatever is in the cup.

Money is, but it isn't everything.

_____

_____

_____

_____

_____

_____

_____

_____

_____

_____

9

Government

GOVERNMENT IS. OUR GOVERNMENT IS. Our government is what it is. I accept that. It doesn't mean that I am perfectly happy with our government and do not want to see any changes. It does mean that I don't want to radically change it. I don't believe radical changes are necessary.

The government of the United States is a democratic republic. I think that is most satisfactory. I like it better than any other type. There is no other government that I know that I think I would like better. The United States has afforded me (and everyone else living here) many, many benefits, more than any other government affords its people. (Note that I did not say affords its CITIZENS: the United States succors all who live within its domain.) Although not a flag-waving zealot, I am always happy and usually proud to be an American.

Government is essential in order for large masses of people to live together, even under the most ideal conditions. Government is that framework wherein we provide for the common needs of humankind. Good government does that. Good government must also provide the environment to stimulate its people to reach up and out and raise our societal quality of life.

Laws, to be just, must do the most good. It is not enough to merely comply with the wishes of the majority; the majority can be only self-seeking and wrong.

This places our lawmakers into a difficult role. They must, at the same time, try to gain the desires of their particular constituents but also to acknowledge (in some way) Truth and Goal so they can make an effort to gain the greater common good for all people.

As the electorate, we must understand that we should not be electing only those people who satisfy our desires but designers and caretakers of a just society. We, too, must acknowledge Truth and Goal. We must make a good and proper effort to elect the right legislators. We, if we maintain some integrity to Truth and Goal, will not be led astray by political hacks who offer us gains for ourselves alone regardless of the effect on others and on our society as a whole. If ever we need the courage to seek Truth, it is here.

All people cannot and should not share equally in all the fruits of society, and laws should not force it. People should be stimulated to achieve, to make contributions to society, and be justly rewarded for them. If people can share equally without any necessity for effort, there will be a retardation of effort. Effort demands reward and should be rewarded.

Government has the task of stimulating achievement by all its people. To do this, we must provide a healthy environment, education, opportunity, and reward.

Government should also provide for those unable to achieve, mentally or physically, young or old.

Government should not do for us what we can do for ourselves.

The usurping (by government) of individual responsibilities is one of the greatest flaws in our government today. In doing so it deemphasizes the individual, the greatest of all that was created, denies the reaching up and out, the fingers of progress and growth, and offers instead a common-ness amid the broad band at the bottom of our societal silhouette.

Government should afford justice in a healthy life-environment, justice in education, justice in opportunity, and justice in reward. Having been granted these justices we can grow. We can grow together as responsible individuals together.

None of us can achieve anything by giving the responsibility for the achievement to someone else, or to government. When we rely on someone else or something else to do for us that which we could do for ourselves, we become slaves to that someone or something. We are always subservient to the provider.

(I hope no one has considered references in the above to be in any way related to an idea of using machines to do chores or a similar idea. We are talking about government, about moral responsibility.)

If we would relieve government of the myriad of responsibilities that we ourselves can achieve, we would then have a government that could achieve the rest for us. We don't. We give more and more of our responsibility to government, and we become less and less able to care for ourselves, which results in government getting still more responsibility for us.

The individual human is the most capable being on this earth. There is virtually nothing that humans cannot accomplish. Effort does bring success. Success stimulates more effort (new goals) and on and on. The greatness of humankind is in the individual, the unique person, not in our common-ness.

The bigger government becomes, the less we become as individuals. The more responsibility we give to government, the more rights and freedoms and privileges we will lose, now or eventually. When we give up responsibility to government, we as individuals become weakened. The only thing that grows is government. The only way government can address the problems of what should be our individual responsibilities, as well as government's proper ones, is to exercise more and more control over us.

I choose big individuals over big government. I have the deepest regard and faith in the individual. I would rather work WITH YOU than FOR GOVERNMENT.

My final thoughts about government concern how to change it.

There are injustices among our laws. There are proper areas of government responsibility that are not being adequately attended to. Education and opportunity are the ones that come most quickly to mind. There are changes that should be made. What is our obligation in this process?

First, we must ascertain if our own thinking includes enough truth and conscience to make us correct in our judgment. How important is this change? How sure are we of the proper change to make? Without this truth, we should not pursue our aim.

Next, we must respect that we do have a good system of government. We don't want to change the whole system, just a part of it. Nor do we want to destroy the many good things in our system in order to attain a different good. To take one step forward and fall back two is not a gain.

Work within the system to make the change. Work within the law. It may be difficult, but it is proper. Do not violate the law. Lawlessness breeds lawlessness. Your reason may be noble, but if you establish a propriety in law-breaking, those who come after you may accept the privilege of breaking the law without having all your nobility of purpose.

Violation of the law is antisocial, unless the government itself is anti-social; our government is not antisocial. Individuals do not have the right to determine for themselves which laws they will obey and which need not be obeyed. Our society, our government affords many ways to expose and change injustices in the law. Defying law is denial of society.

If a law is truly unjust, you will be able to find many cohorts in your goal of changing it. If only you (or very few of you) feel it is unjust, then there may be some doubts about your opinions.

Good government is available to us. It should be one of our goals. With truth, we can assess what good government ought to be. Working together, we can accomplish any goal.

10

How to Develop Your Own Personal Philosophy

Having come to this point you

1. Have been exposed to some of MY philosophy and

2. Have commented on that philosophy vis-à-vis your notes indicating approval, disapproval, omission.

You have already come a long way toward establishing your own personal philosophy.

Now take a fresh sheet of paper and write on it as many simple statements of your beliefs as come easily to mind. Please note, I said SIMPLE STATEMENTS; it is not necessary now to expound on them in any way. You may want to make statements about GOD, TRUTH (or Truth or truth), some specific moral values (your own thou shalts and thou shalt nots), or ideas regarding society or law or government or money.

It is not important that you give these statements a great deal of thought. Just write what you believe (or think you believe).

_____

_____

_____

_____

_____

_____

_____

_____

_____

_____

_____

Put the paper aside until tomorrow (or Thursday or next week), enough time that you have stopped thinking about them for a while. Then pick up that sheet of paper, and review what you have written.

Inspect each statement individually. Do you still believe them? If not, make any changes you feel necessary to make the statements truer to your real beliefs.

Go back to the chapter on CONCEPTS. You made notes there about "Thou shalt not kill" and the treatment of people who commit antisocial acts. Review those statements and add your beliefs about them to your sheet of paper.

If you have made a number of changes, you may want to set aside your notes again for another period of time and make one more review and revision. Be satisfied that your declarations, as revised, properly express your beliefs and/or opinions.

Reread them all. Read them a third time, this time looking to see if any one of your beliefs is in any way contradictory to another.

For example, you might have written as one statement that it is wrong to take a human life. Another statement might have been that abortion is the prerogative of the mother. And a third that when a brain has ceased to function that it is right to "pull the (life sustaining) plug."

Can these statements stand together without contradiction? They may, and they may not, depending on how you view the factors involved.

What you should thus be doing is resolving in your set of statements any inconsistencies of thought. "If I believe this, can I really also believe that?" This may result in your altering, or even removing one or more of your statements. The process may take minutes, or hours, or even days, depending on the variety of thoughts you have expressed, your own natural cohesiveness, and the extent to which you demand your own verification.

The paper containing the revised statements is the BASIS of YOUR OWN PERSONAL PHILOSOPHY. Keep it with you, or at least handy, at all times.

Each day, review your list, adding statements. You may choose to review more or less often than daily depending upon the combination of your desire to expand the list and the convenience of doing it. These statements may come to mind from discussions with other people in the normal course of living and regarding ordinary ideas (not of great import), or from what you read or see in the media, or anything that happens to you or you think about.

As you get more and more involved in this process, you will find that you find you will want to make statements about many things.

Each time you add or make a new statement, review your previously made ones. Is there a consistency of thought? Are there any disagreements? Rethink. Amend. Delete. Do what must be done so that all your thoughts are in harmony.

Let me interject here some balm to what may be frustration. YOU DON'T HAVE TO BE PERFECT. You may find an inconsistency that you cannot resolve, and you still feel strongly about each item. You may also run into ideas about which you may want to make a statement but are not sure what statement you can make; you don't know, for sure, what you believe.

Do not become disconcerted. Prepare another paper describing these complications. In time, and as you continue going through the process, the resolutions may come to you. And, besides, the knowledge of the problem is, in itself, beneficial. It is all part of the process of expanding your personal philosophy, of expanding yourself.

Look back now on what you have already accomplished. You have a reasonable group of statements, fully consistent with each other, that reflect some of your views on life and living. You have already done much more than most people. The joys of the new strength you find in your own ideas are now propelling you to become an even bigger and better person. You have more confidence in what you say. You have more conviction in your ideas.

How far you go is now up to you. You can organize your statements into themes or thought categories. That way, when you enter a new thought and want to challenge it, you can more easily find the "related" thoughts and not have to review everything all the time.

You will want to reread, periodically, ALL your statements. It will be both a good review and will help to further ferret out any inconsistencies.

After a while you may find that you "automatically" challenge new thoughts as they arise even before you think about marking them down.

Excellent. But before you take away from yourself the discipline of the writing, remember these two things. Constant challenging is difficult to maintain. It takes years to really develop that as a habit. Also, one of the pluses of continuing to write is the creation of a continuous and growing GUIDE TO YOUR IDEAS. That little extra that comes of writing your statements is well worth the effort.

Congratulations. You have achieved much more than the vast majority of people. Look at yourself now. Look back on what you were without your own PERSONAL PHILOSOPHY. There are greater achievements available for you, and you will achieve them.

Now, you are on the road to becoming you.

About the Author

The following is Alvin Chester's résumé as written by him postretirement.

THAT YOU CAN KNOW ALVIN L. CHESTER

An Essay Résumé (1988)

(An Autobiography in Miniature)

PREFACE: I have read many résumés in my years in business, as well as application forms (which are the same but in the format of the interviewer). For the reader, they are a convenient way of sifting through acceptance or rejection, quickly establishing which ones are worth of following up on. Only rarely do they give an opportunity to understand the individual making the presentation.

The purpose of this "essay résumé" (my own newly coined term) is to let you know WHO I AM from a variety of perspectives.

GENERAL DATA

Born June 5, 1927, Chicago, Illinois

Currently living in Deerfield, Illinois

> Previously lived in Olympia Fields, Illinois, (for nineteen years), and   before that, in Chicago, Illinois

Height: 5'8"

Build: stocky (with constant diet)

Appearance: presentable

Health is good in all aspects. Never any serious illnesses.

1945, hospitalized for an appendectomy

1985, shattered elbow radial: accident on tennis court

Married Rita Barbara Segal in 1950

>Three children, all professionally educated, all still married to first spouses, and each with at least two children

EDUCATION

All of my primary and high school education was received in the Chicago public school system: Bryn Mawr grammar school and South Shore and Hyde Park high schools. There was no real incentive to learn, and I graduated high school barely in the upper third of the class.

In June of 1944, I enrolled at the University of Illinois in Urbana, specifically, the School of Liberal Arts and Sciences. No career, no future was in my mind; I had planned no real course of study. I graduated in 1949 (my studies had been interrupted by an enlistment in the army) just about in the upper ten percent of the class. The degree was in DSSWV (Division of Special Studies for War Veterans). Actually, I was lucky I qualified for that degree as I had no major course of study (and didn't want one). By this time, most of my courses were in theater and radio with a smattering of other subjects I thought might have some particular interest.

I believe the really important discussion about my education is that throughout it all, I, in retrospect, find that only four classes were truly valuable. They include two high school courses, plain and solid geometry; a course in reasoning with the philosophy department; and one in argumentation and debate with the speech department. This last course was not in itself one of great importance, but it introduced me to the instructor, a woman of tremendous intellect, who influenced me a great deal. Our subsequent friendship lasted for about thirty years, until her death. She taught me to see through the superfluousness of discussion and to arrive at the essence.

You must have recognized by now that what I considered important in my education was learning how to REASON—not the reasoning that leads to good debate techniques but that of being able to separate the TRUTH from the ARGUMENT. I learned the idea of truth before I went into the army, and it was, in fact, part of the reason I enlisted.

In addition to the previously mentioned schooling, I also studied at Northwestern University (summer of 1948; world history), at Tolentino College (evenings during ~1976; sociology), and at Governors State University (evenings during ~1968; economics).

Military Experience

To become a part of the military was not necessary. By the time I was seventeen, the war in Europe was coming to an end. I did attempt to enlist then (we were all "patriots" in those days), but I was rejected due to a cyst on my spine. By the time I had it corrected and cleared up (and also went through an appendectomy), all the fighting was over with. Why should I enlist in 1946?

I was nineteen then and was set to graduate from university the following year. One of the things I learned as part of my "reasoning" education was that I was totally unprepared to become a meaningful, positive part of society. I needed time to put myself together. In 1946, one did not tell one's parents that one wanted to "bum around" for a while. (It is certainly more reasonable today and probably should be.) The draft act was still in effect, and I was able to convince my parents that if I did not enlist, I might be drafted and that the drafting might come at an inopportune time.

During the basic-training period, I utilized my free time to wander the camp and talk things over with a friend of mine from school (who was also there). We discussed many things and then started challenging some of what we were expounding by making sure our ideas were compatible with other things we had proffered. Sometimes they were; sometimes they were not. When we recognized conflicting ideas, we would review them. Determining that we could not believe both things at the same time, we would find that single truth in both we could accept.

This practice became the commencement of a kind of personal philosophy that I continued to develop through the years and that I maintain until this very day.

Basically, it established the individual as the center of his universe and imposes the obligation of seeking the ultimate truth. Virtues are concepts that are revealed by truth. The potential of any individual is almost infinite and limited only by time. (There is more, but this must suffice for now.)

This philosophy makes for continuous testing of oneself and also all ideas and people encountered. It is neither easy for the philosopher nor for those who become involved with him. The demands are great; the potentials, however, are increased abilities.

The army served me in many other ways. My first three months in Japan and Korea (army of occupation) were spent touring on the USO (army shows) circuit as a lead actor in a company of mixed stateside professionals and army personnel. Then I served for nine months as the director of advertising and public relations for the army educational program. In August of 1947, I was made an advisor to the Japanese International Trade Commission, which prepared representatives of the one hundred leading Japanese firms for the reinstitution of trade between Japan and the United States. (My expertise was advertising—at least so the government deemed it.)

I left the army only a corporal, but in command of my life.

My Life In the World of Business

The early years, high school, university, and the immediate period after graduation were spent in scattered efforts in the field of entertainment. They were not significant.

In mid-1949, I commenced working for the B. L. Marder Company, a small manufacturing and distributing firm in the after-production shoe market. My father also worked there and even had a very small interest in the firm. I spent eight years as a commissioned salesman (and in part-time management). In 1957, I purchased my own shares of stock and was completely involved in management. In 1967, I became the sole owner and remained as chief executive until I sold the business in 1985.

During these years, I revised or developed anew every aspect of the company, personally designing all the facets of our operations, including (toward the end) the design and programming of a complete computer system that involved every part of the business except accounting and payroll. Help was received in "how-to-program" but none in the design.

I was always involved in hiring new management, looking to the future and potential growth. During this time, I learned the basic difference in managers. There are countless people who could be employed (if properly trained and controlled) as "maintenance management" (again, my own term)…but "creative management" is very hard to come by.

My best and most significant employees were always those whom I trained personally. I found that people with an integrity of desire could achieve the most, regardless of what their previous education and experience were.

ALVIN CHESTER TODAY

At the moment of my retirement, I made the decision that I would take at least a year and do nothing. This was designed to allow me to change the "pace" of my life so I would not rush to fill my new life with the same tonality as my previous one. I wanted to get to a point where I could have a fresh perspective.

At the same time, I wanted to make sure that my wife received her benefits from my retirement. We spent a lot of time together, learning the rewards and hazards thereof, moved from a far southern suburb to a far northern one (which allows us to live centered among our children and grandchildren), and did a great deal of traveling.

The time has come to once again become a vital, productive force in society. To fulfill my obligation as a living human (and to appease my ego), I must do something that has substance. But what?

I looked for a "need" in society, for that niche that we have not fulfilled. I believe that I have found it.

To pursue in this essay just what it is and how I shall attempt to make my addition to society is much beyond our purpose. Let it be that it is there and the Alvin Chester you have been given in-depth insight to is again working toward a positive goal.

Afterword by the Editor

THIS GUIDE HAS HELPED SERVE me, and I hope it does the same for you. My grandfather is a person who inspires me and, from what I have read, is similar to Benjamin Franklin. They were always striving for the betterment of society and of themselves.

I believe that everyone on this earth, from Nelson Mandela to Mahatma Gandhi to Al Capone to Martin Luther King Jr. to Hillary Clinton to Donald Trump, believes that they are good people. We all go about making the world a better place in our own way.

There is much disagreement about what is good, just, and right. If we all agreed on what was "right" and "good," life would be much easier. The first step in coming to agreement is to agree on facts. If we can agree on facts, then at least we can agree to disagree. But if we disagree on what is true and not true (facts), then we are discussing different ideas.

It is difficult to have conversations about beliefs without becoming emotionally involved. We must learn to have these conversations in a reasonable way and understand that we all do want better for everyone. We are a good people. We feel bad when we do wrong to others. Much of this is learned from the society we have been raised in. We must continue to strive to do better ourselves and for those around us. This is difficult and requires concentrated effort.

It is difficult to get better at anything without practice…and this is probably not different. We (most) do not exercise so that we can exercise harder but so that we can be more useful when needed. We do not lift weights to be able to lift more weights but so that we can use that strength toward other activities (rarely do people lift weights in order to lift more weights). We study math not so that we understand more math (usually) but so that we train our brains to be able to do more complex thinking. We will get slightly better at basketball by playing, but we will improve much more by studying basketball, practicing various features (particularly our weaknesses), and playing. It is through all three that we improve the most. Chess may be the best example of this. It is difficult to improve at chess without study…and with study, one will improve greatly.

Benjamin Franklin recognized that with dedicated effort, he would improve his life, and he listed thirteen "virtues" he aimed to improve within himself. Rather than attempting to focus on all thirteen, he dedicated one week to each virtue (practice). His thought was that with concentrated effort, he would naturally come to adopt the virtue at all other times. He repeated the thirteen practice weeks four times per year for most of his life. The thirteen virtues he focused on were the following:

1. Temperance. Eat not to dullness; drink not to elevation.

2. Silence. Speak not but what may benefit others or yourself; avoid trifling conversation.

3. Order. Let all your things have their places; let each part of your business have its time.

4. Resolution. Resolve to perform what you ought; perform without fail what you resolve.

5. Frugality. Make no expense but to do well to others or yourself. (i.e., waste nothing).

6. Industry. Lose no time; be always employed in something useful; cut off all unnecessary actions.

7. Sincerity. Use no hurtful deceit; think innocently and justly, and, if you speak, speak accordingly.

8. Justice. Wrong none by doing injuries, or omitting the benefits that are your duty.

9. Moderation. Avoid extremes; forbear resenting injuries so much as you think they deserve.

10. Cleanliness. Tolerate no uncleanliness in body, clothes, or habitation.

11. Tranquility. Be not disturbed at trifles, or at accidents common or unavoidable.

12. Chastity. Rarely use venery but for health or offspring, never to dullness, weakness, or the injury of your own or another's peace of reputation.

13. Humility. Imitate Jesus and Socrates.

I am not saying that these are the thirteen virtues that you should focus on. I'm trying to illuminate another person's philosophy on how to become a better person—with practice. In addition, remember that times must and always do change.

Many people "wish" for themselves. I am no different. I wish for everyone (myself included), everywhere, to be happy...now and forever.

I leave you with this: choice is your greatest power; use it wisely.

Notes

Chapter 1: Introduction

1. J. Hirby, "What You Can Legally Do When You're 18," The Law Dictionary, accessed January 9, 2018, https://thelawdictionary.org/article/what-you-can-legally-do-when-youre-18/.

2. John A. Byrne, "$143K Average Total Pay for Emory's 2016 MBAs," Poets&Quants, 2016, accessed January 9, 2018, https://poetsandquants.com/2016/10/24/average-pay-package-143k-emorys-2016-mbas/.

3. Peter Daisyme, "9 Billionaires Who Didn't Graduate High School," Entrepreneur, accessed January 9, 2018, https://www.entrepreneur.com/article/253724.

4. "Biography: Helen Keller," A&E Television Networks, last modified July 7, 2017, accessed January 9, 2018, https://www.biography.com/people/helen-keller-9361967.

5. Stephen Hawking, "The Official Website, Home," accessed January 9, 2018, http://www.hawking.org.uk/.

6. Michelle Fox, "Here's How a Janitor Amassed an $8M Fortune," CNBC, last modified February 10, 2015, accessed January 9, 2018, https://www.cnbc.com/2015/02/09/heres-how-a-janitor-amassed-an-8m-fortune.html.

7. "Anna Karenina principle," Wikipedia, accessed January 9, 2018, https://en.wikipedia.org/wiki/Anna_Karenina_principle.

8. "Finance: How Do We Fund Our Schools?" WLIW New York (PBS), 2008, accessed January 9, 2018, http://www.pbs.org/wnet/wherewestand/blog/finance-how-do-we-fund-our-schools/197/.

Chapter 2: Money

1. Evan Tarver, "What Impact Does Inflation Have on the Time Value of Money?" Investopedia, accessed February 13, 2018, https://www.investopedia.com/ask/answers/042415/what-impact-does-inflation-have-time-value-money.asp.

2. Actual Consumer Price Index (CPI, an inflation index) and S&P 500 geometric means were 3.1 percent and 10 percent respectively, per year, based on years 1913–2017. Data gathered from the following sources:

    •   Robert J. Shiller, Irrational Exuberance (Princeton, NJ: Princeton University Press, 2005).

    •   "Online Data Robert Shiller", Yale University Economics Department, accessed February 15, 2018, http://www.econ.yale.edu/~shiller/data.htm.

    •   "Daily Treasury Yield Curve Rates," US Department of the Treasury, accessed February 15, 2018, https://www.treasury.gov/resource-center/data-chart-center/interest-rates/Pages/TextView.aspx?data=yield.

    •   "Historical Consumer Price Index for All Urban Consumer (CPI-U): US City Average, All Items," US Bureau of Labor Statistics, 2017, accessed February 15, 2018, https://www.bls.gov/cpi/tables/historical-cpi-u-201711.pdf.

3. John T. Harvey, "What Actually Causes Inflation (and Who Benefits from It)," Forbes, 2011, accessed January 8, 2018, https://www.forbes.com/sites/johntharvey/2011/05/30/what-actually-causes-inflation/2/.

4. Gold data accessed and verified through two sources:

    •   CMI Gold and Silver Inc., "Historical Gold Prices," accessed February 13, 2018, http://onlygold.com/Info/Historical-Gold-Prices.asp.

    •   USAGOLD, "Daily Gold Price History," accessed February13,2018, http://www.usagold.com/reference/prices/goldhistory.php.

5. "US Department of the Treasury, 10-Year High Quality Market (HQM) Corporate Bond Spot Rate [HQMCB10YR]," retrieved from FRED, Federal Reserve Bank of St. Louis, accessed February 15, 2018, https://fred.stlouisfed.org/series/HQMCB10YR.

6. I largely used a crowd-sourced method (reddit.com/r/personalfinance/wiki) to answer this question. Reddit.com/r/personalfinance is an excellent source of information for the most common money advice. Peruse that website and find a plethora of information, including many specifics not offered in this chapter.

7. Charles Munger, "Berkshire Hathaway Annual Letter to Shareholders 2014," Berkshire Hathaway Inc., accessed February 15, 2018, http://www.berkshire-hathaway.com/letters/2014ltr.pdf

8. Morgan Housel, Twitter post, November 28, 2016, https://twitter.com/morganhousel/status/803228111525543936.

9. Warren Buffet, "Berkshire Hathaway Annual Letter to Shareholders 2016," Berkshire Hathaway Inc., accessed February 15,2018, http://www.berkshirehathaway.com/letters/2016ltr.pdf.

CHAPTER 3: COLLEGE (OR NOT COLLEGE)

1. "How Long Do Parents' Legal Obligations to Their Children Continue?" FindLaw, accessed January 9, 2018, family.findlaw.com/emancipation-of-minors/how-long-do-parents-legal-obligations-to-their-children-continue.html.

2. "Join the Military," United States of America, last modified August 4, 2017, accessed January 9, 2018, https://www.usa.gov/join-military.

3. E. A. Locke, "Setting Goals for Life and Happiness," in Oxford Handbook of Positive Psychology, edited by S. J. Lopez and C. R. Snyder (NY: Oxford University Press, 2002), 299–312.

4. Napoleon Hill, Think and Grow Rich (Connecticut: The Ralston Society, 1937), 76.

5. Hill, Think and Grow Rich, 76–80.

6. Catherine Seraphin, "Getting Education Requirements: What's the Point?" College Express, 2013, accessed January 9, 2018, https://www.collegexpress.com/articles-and-advice/majors-and-academics/articles/college-academics/general-education-requirements-whats-point/.

7. "Average Undergraduate Tuition and Fees and Room and Board Rates Charged for Full-Time Students in Degree-Granting Institutions, by Type and Control of Institution: 1964–65 through 2006–07," National Center for Education Statistics, accessed January 12, 2018, https://nces.ed.gov/programs/digest/d07/tables/dt07_320.asp.

8. "What's the Price Tag for a College Education?" National Association for College Admission Counseling, accessed November 22, 2017, https://www.collegedata.com/cs/content/content_payarticle_tmpl.jhtml?articleId=10064.

9. "Average Undergraduate Tuition," National Center for Education Statistics.

10. "What's the Price Tag," National Association for College Admission Counseling.

11. "What Happened in 1967," The People History, accessed January 12, 2018, http://www.thepeoplehistory.com/1967.html.

12. Kelsey Mays, "Here's What the Average New Car Costs," Cars.com, 2017, accessed January 12, 2018, https://www.cars.com/articles/heres-what-the-average-new-car-costs-1420694975814/.

13. "What Happened in 1967," The People History, accessed January 12, 2018, http://www.thepeoplehistory.com/1967.html.

14. "Median and Average Sales Prices of New Homes Sold in United States, United States Census Bureau," 2017, accessed November 22, 2017, https://www.census.gov/construction/nrs/pdf/uspricemon.pdf.

15. "1967 Income: Consumer Income," United States Census Bureau, 1968, accessed January 12, 2018, https://www2.census.gov/prod2/popscan/p60-062.pdf.

16. "Income: Income and Poverty in the United States: 2016," United States Census Bureau, 2017, accessed January 12, 2018, https://www.census.gov/data/tables/2017/demo/income-poverty/p60-259.html.

17. "Educational Attainment—People 25 Years Old and Over, by Total Money Earnings, Work Experience, Age, Race, Hispanic Origin, and Sex," United States Census Bureau, 2017, accessed January 12, 2018, https://www.census.gov/data/tables/time-series/demo/income-poverty/cps-pinc/pinc-03.html.

18. Jennifer Ma and Sandy Baum, "Trends in Community Colleges: Enrollment, Prices, Student Debt, and Completion," The College Board, 2016, accessed January 9, 2018, https://trends.collegeboard.org/sites/default/files/trends-in-community-colleges-research-brief.pdf.

19. "What's the Price Tag for a College Education?" 2017, accessed 07/12/2018 https://www.collegedata.com/cs/content/content_payarticle_tmpl.jhtml?articleId=10064

Chapter 4: Jobs

1. C. Goetz and M. Axelrod, *The Great Entrepreneurial Divide* (Atlanta, GA: Rathskeller Press LLC, 2011), 12.

2. Dan Froomkin, "Members of Congress Get Abnormally High Returns from Their Stocks," Huffington Post, 2011, accessed February 15, 2018, https://www.huffingtonpost.com/2011/05/24/members-of-congress-get-a_n_866387.html.

3. Theo Anderson, "The Second-Mover Advantage," Kellogg School of Management, Northwestern University, 2013, accessed February 15, 2018, https://insight.kellogg.northwestern.edu/article/the_second_mover_advantage.

Chapter 5: Credit and Large Purchases

1. Tim McMahon, "Inflation Adjusted Housing Prices," Capital Professional Services, LLC, 2018, accessed February 15, 2018, https://inflationdata.com/articles/inflation-adjusted-prices/inflation-adjusted-housing-prices/;

   • "S&P Dow Jones Indices LLC, S&P/Case-Shiller US National Home Price Index [CSUSHPINSA]," retrieved from FRED, Federal Reserve Bank of St. Louis, accessed February 15, 2018, https://fred.stlouisfed.org/series/CSUSHPINSA.

2. "Credit Score," Investopedia, https://www.investopedia.com/terms/c/credit_score.asp.

3. "How to Get a Good Deal on Tires," WikiHow, accessed February 15, 2018, https://www.wikihow.com/Get-a-Good-Deal-on-Tires.

4. Thomas Lee, "Buy These 12 Cars Used, Not New Based on Study of 14 Million Cars," iSeeCars.com, 2018, accessed February 15,2018,https://www.iseecars.com/used-car-finder#section=studies&study=cars-to-buy-used.

Chapter 6: Taxes

1. "Tax Scams/Consumer Alerts," Internal Revenue Service, last modified January 17, 2018, https://www.irs.gov/newsroom/tax-scams-consumer-alerts.

2. "The Federal Budget in 2016: An Infographic," Congressional Budget Office, 2017, accessed February 15, 2018, https://www.cbo.gov/publication/52408.

3. "State and Local Expenditures," Urban Institute, 2016, accessed February 15, 2018, https://www.urban.org/policy-centers/cross-center-initiatives/state-local-finance-initiative/projects/state-and-local-backgrounders/state-and-local-expenditures.

Chapter 8: Sex

1. Hui Liu, Linda Waite, Shannon Shen, and Donna Wang, "Is Sex Good for Your Health? A National Study on Partnered Sexuality and Cardiovascular Risk Among Older Men and Women," Journal of Health and Social Behavior. 57, issue 3 (September 2016): 276–296, doi: 10.1177/0022146516661597 https://

www.ncbi.nlm.nih.gov/pmc/articles/PMC5052677/.

2. "Genital HPV Infection—Fact Sheet," US Department of Health and Human Services, accessed January 15, 2018, https://www.cdc.gov/std/hpv/stdfact-hpv.htm.

3. H. W. Chesson, E. F. Dunne, S. Hariri, and L. E. Markowitz, "The Estimated Lifetime Probability of Acquiring Human Papillomavirus in the United States," Sexually Transmitted Diseases 41 (November 2014): 660–664, accessed February 7, 2018, as found at http://www.ashasexualhealth.org/stdsstis/statistics/.

4. H. Bradley, L. E. Markowitz, T. Gibson, and G. M. McQuillan, "Seroprevalence of Herpes Simplex Virus Types 1 and 2—United States, 1999–2010," Journal of Infectious Diseases 209, issue 3 (February 2014): 325–333, accessed February 7, 2018, as found at http://www.ashasexualhealth.org/stdsstis/statistics/.

5. A. Satcher Johnson, R. Song, H. I. Hall, "Estimated HIV Incidence, Prevalence, and Undiagnosed Infections in US States and Washington, DC, 2010–2014," Journal of Acquired Immune Deficiency Syndromes 76, issue 2 (October 1, 2017): 116–122, accessed February 7, 2018, as found athttps://www.ncbi.nlm.nih.gov/pubmed/28700407,doi:10.1097/QAI.0000000000001495.

6. "Urinary Tract Infections (UTIs)," NHS Choices (Government of the United Kingdom), 2017, accessed February 7, 2018, https://www.nhs.uk/conditions/urinary-tract-infections-utis/.

7. Al Vernacchio, "What Teens Really Want to Know about Sex," TED Conferences, 2014, ideas.ted.com/what-teens-really-want-to-know-about-sex/.

8. "What Consent Looks Like," Rape Abuse and Incest National Network, accessed January 15, 2018, https://www.rainn.org/articles/what-is-consent.

9. "Is Sex Painful the First Time?" NHS Choices (Government of the United Kingdom), last modified March 30, 2015, accessed January 15, 2018, https://www.nhs.uk/chq/pages/3047.aspx?categoryid=118.

10. Tamekia Reece, "10 Ways He Can Have Better Baby-Making Sperm," Meredith Corporation, accessed February 7, 2018, https://www.parents.com/getting-pregnant/trying-to-conceive/tips/better-babymaking-sperm-healthy/.

11. "Making Love in the First Trimester of Pregnancy: What Is Safe, What Is Not," Mykids Ventures Private Limited, accessed February 7, 2018, https://www.beingtheparent.com/making-love-in-the-first-trimester-of-pregnancy-what-is-safe-what-is-not/.

12. "Can You Get Pregnant on Your Period?" American Pregnancy Association, 2016, accessed February 7, 2018, http://americanpregnancy.org/getting-preg-

nant/can-get-pregnant-period/.

13. "All about Birth Control," Planned Parenthood Federation of America, accessed February 7, 2018, https://www.plannedparenthood.org/learn/birth-control.

14. "STDs and Infertility," Centers for Disease Control and Prevention, accessed February 7, 2018, https://www.cdc.gov/std/infertility/default.htm.

15. "Reported STDs in the United States, 2016," Centers for Disease Control and Prevention, 2016, accessed February 7, 2018, https://www.cdc.gov/nchhstp/newsroom/docs/factsheets/std-trends-508.pdf.

16. "Sexually Transmitted Diseases," Centers for Disease Control and Prevention, accessed February 7, 2018, https://www.cdc.gov/std/general/default.htm.

CHAPTER 9: PARENTING

1. Association for Psychological Science, "Copycat Behavior in Children Is Universal and May Help Promote Human Culture," ScienceDaily, accessed February 14, 2018, https://www.sciencedaily.com/releases/2010/05/100503135705.htm.

CHAPTER 12: THE BILL OF RIGHTS APPLIED

1. Suzanne Ito, "Protecting Outrageous, Offensive Speech," American Civil Liberties Union, 2010, https://www.aclu.org/blog/free-speech/protecting-outrageous-offensive-speech.

2. "What Does Free Speech Mean?" Administrative Office of the US Courts on behalf of the Federal Judiciary, accessed February 12, 2018, http://www.uscourts.gov/about-federal-courts/educational-resources/about-educational-outreach/activity-resources/what-does.

3. Ullmann v. United States, 350 US 422, 426 (1956).

CHAPTER 14: POLITICS

1. "What Affects Voter Turnout Rates," Fairvote.org, accessed February 16, 2018, http://www.fairvote.org/what_affects_voter_turnout_rates.

2. "Lesson Plan: Off-Year Elections and Why Down Ballot Voting Matters," NewsHour Productions, 2016, accessed February 16, 2018, http://www.pbs.org/newshour/extra/lessons-plans/down-ballot-voting-lesson-plan/.

3. Stephen J. Dubner, "The True Story of the Gender Pay Gap," Freakonomics Ra-

dio podcast, January 7, 2016, http://freakonomics.com/podcast/the-true-story-of-the-gender-pay-gap-a-new-freakonomics-radio-podcast/.

4. Senator Dan Coats and Representative Kevin Brady, "An Economic History of Federal Spending and Debt," Joint Economic Committee, 2015, accessed February 16, 2018, https://www.jec.senate.gov/public/_cache/files/c90da849-986a-41d3-ab20-77f38a393d85/20150910-jec-spendingstudy.pdf.

5. Patrick Caddell, "An Independent Can't Be President; Here's the Real Reason Why," Capitol Hill Publishing Corp., 2016, accessed February 16, 2018, http://thehill.com/blogs/congress-blog/presidential-campaign/280045-an-independent-cant-be-president-heres-the-real.

6. David Himmelstein, Deborah Thorne, Elizabeth Warren, Steffie Woolhandler, "Medical Bankruptcy in the United States, 2007: Results of a National Study," The American Journal of Medicine volume 122, issue 8 (2009): 741–746.

7. Barack Obama, "United States Health Care Reform Progress to Date and Next Steps," Jama 316.5 (2016): 525–532, accessed February 16, 2018.

CHAPTER 15: DRUGS

1. A.C. Parrott, "Does Cigarette Smoking Cause Stress?" American Psychology 54, issue 10 (October 1999): 817–820, accessed February 9, 2018, at https://www.ncbi.nlm.nih.gov/pubmed/10540594.

2. A.Hajnal, G. P. Smith, and R. Norgren, "Oral Sucrose Stimulation Increases Accumbens Dopamine in the Rat," American Journal of Physiology: Regulatory, Integrative, and Comparative Physiology 286, issue 1 (2004): R31–7;

   - K. Boutelle, C. E. Wierenga, A. Bischoff-Grethe, A. J. Melrose, E. Grenesko-Stevens, M. P. Paulus, W. H. Kaye, "Increased Brain Response to Appetitive Tastes in the Insula and Amygdala in Obese Compared to Healthy Weight Children When Sated," International Journal of Obesity, 2014, doi: 10.1038/ijo.2014.206;

   - Donald B. Katz and Brian F. Sadacca, Neurobiology of Sensation and Reward, ed. Jay Gottfried (Boca Raton, FL: CRC Press Taylor & Francis Group, 2011), Chapter 6.

3. "What Are the Long-Term Effects of Cocaine Use?" National Institute on Drug Abuse, accessed February 9, 2018, https://www.drugabuse.gov/publications/research-reports/cocaine/what-are-long-term-effects-cocaine-use.

4. Suprabha Pulipparacharuvil et al., "Cocaine Regulates MEF2 to Control Synaptic

and Behavioral Plasticity," *Neuron* Volume 59, issue 4 (August 2008): 621–633.

5. Richard Rosenquist, "The Truth about Your Painkillers: 6 Biggest Myths Debunked," Cleveland Clinic, accessed February 9, 2018, https://health.clevelandclinic.org/2016/04/6-myths-about-painkillers/.

6. "Drug Use Changes Brain over Time," University of Utah, accessed February 9, 2018, http://learn.genetics.utah.edu/content/addiction/brainchange/.

7. Thomas J. Gould, "Addiction and Cognition," Addiction Science and Clinical Practice 5, issue 2 (December 2010): 4–14, as accessed on February 9, 2018, at https://www.ncbi.nlm.nih.gov/pmc/articles/PMC3120118/;

   • Madeline H. Meier, Avshalom Caspi, Antony Ambler, HonaLee Harrington, Renate Houts, Richard S. E. Keefe, Kay McDonald, Aimee Ward, Richie Poulton, and Terrie E. Moffitt, "Cannabis Use and Neuropsychological Decline," Proceedings of the National Academy of Sciences, August 2012, 201206820, DOI:10.1073/pnas.1206820109;

   • M. P. Becker, P. F. Collins, K. O. Lim, R. L. Muetzel, M. Luciana, "Longitudinal Changes in White Matter Microstructure after Heavy Cannabis Use," Developmental Cognitive Neuroscience 16 (December 2015): 23–35, doi: 10.1016/j.dcn.2015.10.004;

   • B. M. Lopes, P. D. Gonçalves, M. Ometto, B. Dos Santos, M. Cavallet, T. M. Chaim-Avancini, M. H. Serpa, S. Nicastri, A. Malbergier, G. F. Busatto, A. G. de Andrade, P. J. Cunha, "Distinct Cognitive Performance and Patterns of Drug Use among Early and Late Onset Cocaine Users," Addictive Behavior 73 (October 2017): 41–47, doi: 10.1016/j.addbeh.2017.04.013.

8. "2015 National Survey on Drug Use and Health (NSDUH). Table 2.41B—Alcohol Use in Lifetime, Past Year, and Past Month among Persons Aged 12 or Older, by Demographic Characteristics: Percentages, 2014 and 2015," Substance Abuse and Mental Health Services Administration (SAMHSA), accessed January 18, 2017 at https://www.samhsa.gov/data/sites/default/files/NSDUH-DetTabs-2015/NSDUH-DetTabs-2015/NSDUH-DetTabs-2015.htm#tab2-41b.

9. Richard Saitz and Stephanie O'Malley, "Pharmacotherapies for Alcohol Abuse: Withdrawal and Treatment," *Medical Clinics of North America* Volume 81 Number 4, (July 1997):881-907

10. J. M. Berning, K. J. Adams, B. A. Stamford, "Anabolic Steroid Usage in Athletics: Facts, Fiction, and Public Relations," Journal of Strength and Conditioning Research 18, issue 4 (November 2004):908–917.

11. P. C. Gupta, and S. Warnakulasuriya, "Global Epidemiology of Areca Nut Usage," *Addiction Biology* vol. 7, (2002):77–83.

12. Marcus A. Bachhuber, MD, MSHP; Sean Hennessy, PharmD, PhD; Chinazo O. Cunningham, MD, MS; and Joanna L. Starrels, MD, MSAm, "Increasing Benzodiazepine Prescriptions and Overdose Mortality in the United States," Journal of Public Health 106, issue 4 (April 2016): 686–688, published online April 2016, doi: 10.2105/AJPH.2016.303061, PMCID: PMC4816010;

   - "National Survey on Drug Use and Health (NSDUH) 2012 and 2013," Substance Abuse and Mental Health Services Administration, 2013, accessed February 10, 2018, https://www.samhsa.gov/data/sites/default/files/NSDUH-DetTabsPDFWHTML2013/Web/HTML/NSDUH-DetTabsSect1peTabs47to92-2013.htm.

13. Bryan Bordeaux, Harris Lieberman, David Seres, Daniel Sullivan, "Benefits and Risks of Caffeine and Caffeinated Beverages," UpToDate Inc., 2018, accessed February 11, 2018, https://www.uptodate.com/contents/benefits-and-risks-of-caffeine-and-caffeinated-beverages.

14. "Key Substance Use and Mental Health Indicators in the United States: Results from the 2015 National Survey on Drug Use and Health," Center for Behavioral Health Statistics and Quality, 2016, HHS Publication no. SMA 16-4984, NSDUH Series H-51, accessed on February 11, 2018, https://www.samhsa.gov/data/sites/default/files/NSDUH-FFR1-2015/NSDUH-FFR1-2015/NSDUH-FFR1-2015.pdf.

15. T. P. Freeman and A. R. Winstock, "Examining the Profile of High-Potency Cannabis and Its Association with Severity of Cannabis Dependence," *Psychological Medicine* volume 45, issue 15 (November 2015):3181–3189, doi: 10.1017/S0033291715001178.

16. "Key Substance Use and Mental Health Indicators in the United States," Center for Behavioral Health Statistics and Quality.

17. "Key Substance Use and Mental Health Indicators in the United States," Center for Behavioral Health Statistics and Quality.

18. "Heroin: Statistics and Trends," National Institute on Drug Abuse, 2016, accessed February 11, 2018, https://www.drugabuse.gov/drugs-abuse/heroin.

19. "Key Substance Use and Mental Health Indicators in the United States," Center for Behavioral Health Statistics and Quality.

20. Teri S Krebsa and Pål-Ørjan Johansen, "Over 30 million psychedelic users in the United States," F1000 Research 2: 98. Published online 2013 Mar 28. As accessed 02/11/2018 https://www.ncbi.nlm.nih.gov/pmc/articles/PMC3917651/#ref-4

21. "Key Substance Use and Mental Health Indicators in the United States," Center for Behavioral Health Statistics and Quality.

22. "Key Substance Use and Mental Health Indicators in the United States," Center for Behavioral Health Statistics and Quality.

23. Drew Griffin, Neil Black, and Patricia DiCarlo, "9 Things Everyone Should Know about the Drug Molly," CNN, 2016, accessed February 11, 2018, https://www.cnn.com/2013/11/22/health/9-things-molly-drug/index.html.

24. "Key Substance Use and Mental Health Indicators in the United States," Center for Behavioral Health Statistics and Quality.

25. "Key Substance Use and Mental Health Indicators in the United States," Center for Behavioral Health Statistics and Quality.

26. L. A. Pratt, D. J. Brody, Q. Gu, "Antidepressant Use among Persons Aged 12 and over: United States, 2011–2014. NCHS Data Brief, No. 283," National Center for Health Statistics, 2017, accessed February 11, 2018, https://www.cdc.gov/nchs/products/databriefs/db283.htm.

27. J. Jones, W. Mosher, K. Daniels, "Current Contraceptive Use in the United States, 2006–2010, and Changes in Patterns of Use Since 1995. National Health Statistics Reports; No. 60," National Center for Health Statistics, 2012.

28. Teri S. Krebs and Pål-Ørjan Johansen, "Psychedelics and Mental Health: A Population Study," PLoS One 8, issue 8 (2013): e63972, doi: 10.1371/journal.pone.0063972. PMCID: PMC3747247.

29. Robin L Carhart-Harris, Leor Roseman, Mark Bolstridge, Lysia Demetriou, J. Nienke Pannekoek, Matthew B. Wall, Mark Tanner, Mendel Kaelen, John McGonigle, Kevin Murphy, Robert Leech, H. Valerie Curran, and David J, Nutt, "Psilocybin for Treatment-Resistant Depression: fMRI-Measured Brain Mechanisms," Scientific Reports volume 7, article 13187(2017), accessed February 11, 2018, https://www.nature.com/articles/s41598-017-13282-7, doi:10.1038/s41598-017-13282-7.

CHAPTER 16: HEALTH

1. Neil Mehta and Mikko Myrskyl, "The Population Health Benefits of a Healthy Lifestyle: Life Expectancy Increased and Onset of Disability Delayed," Health Affairs, 2017, 10.1377/hlthaff.2016.1569 DOI: 10.1377/hlthaff.2016.1569;

   - Christopher Labos, MD, "Lifestyle Interventions: The Best Medicine You're Not Using," WebMD, 2015, accessed February 15, 2018, https://www.medscape.com/viewarticle/843028.

2. Mayo Clinic Staff, "Weight Training: Do's and Don'ts of Proper Technique," Mayo Foundation for Medical Education and Research, 2018, accessed February 15, 2018, https://www.mayoclinic.org/healthy-lifestyle/fitness/in-depth/weight-training/art-20045842.

3. Mayo Clinic Staff, "Stretching Essentials," Mayo Foundation for Medical Education and Research, 2018, accessed February 15, 2018, https://www.mayoclinic.org/healthy-lifestyle/fitness/in-depth/stretching/art-20047931?pg=2;

   - "Stretching before Exercise 'Is Counter-Productive,'" *Telegraph*, 2010, accessed February 15, 2018, https://www.telegraph.co.uk/active/7594484/Stretching-before-exercise-is-counter-productive.html; Sonya Collins, "The Truth about Stretching: Find Out the Best Ways to Stretch and the Best Times to Do It," WebMD, accessed February 15, 2018, https://www.webmd.com/fitness-exercise/features/how-to-stretch#1.

4. C. Drake, T. Roehrs, J. Shambroom, T. Roth, "Caffeine Effects on Sleep Taken 0, 3, or 6 Hours before Going to Bed," *Journal of Clinical Sleep Medicine* 9, 11 (2013): 1195–1200.

5. S. D. Youngstedt and C. E. Kline, "Epidemiology of Exercise and Sleep," *Sleep and Biological Rhythms* 4 (2006): 215–221, doi:10.1111/j.1479-8425.2006.00235.x.

6. Heather Hatfield, "Power Down for Better Sleep," WebMD, 2018, accessed February 15, 2018, https://www.webmd.com/sleep-disorders/features/power-down-better-sleep#1.

7. "Four Key Ways Meditation Cures Sleeplessness, Insomnia, and Sleep Problems," EOC Institute, 2018, accessed February 15, 2018, https://eocinstitute.org/meditation/meditation-for-insomnia-and-better-sleep/.

8. R. Ackerley, G. Badre, H. Olausson, "Positive Effects of a Weighted Blanket on Insomnia," *Journal of Sleep Medicine and Disorders* 2(3) (2015): 1022.

9. "Sleep and Health," Division of Sleep Medicine at Harvard Medical School, 2018, accessed February 15, 2018, http://healthysleep.med.harvard.edu/need-sleep/whats-in-it-for-you/health.

10. "It's True: Frequent Sex Is Healthy Sex," WebMD, 2018, accessed February 15, 2018, https://www.webmd.com/sex-relationships/features/sex-use-it-or-lose-it;

    • University of Maryland, "Use It or Lose It: Stopping Exercise Decreases Brain Blood Flow," ScienceDaily, accessed February 15, 2018, https://www.sciencedaily.com/releases/2016/08/160829140440.htm.

11. "Overweight and Obesity Statistics," US Department of Health and Human Services, 2014, accessed February 15, 2018, https://www.niddk.nih.gov/health-information/health-statistics/overweight-obesity.

12. Mayo Clinic Staff, "Counting Calories: Get back to Weight-Loss Basics," Mayo Foundation for Medical Education and Research, 2018, accessed February 15, 2018, https://www.mayoclinic.org/healthy-lifestyle/weight-loss/in-depth/calories/art-20048065.

13. Peter S. Eriksson, Ekaterina Perfilieva, Thomas Bjork-Eriksson, Ann-Marie Alborn, Claes Nordborg, et al., "Neurogenesis in the Adult Human Hippocampus," Nature Medicine, 1998.

14. Sandrine Thuret, "You Can Grow New Brain Cells. Here's How," TED@BCG London, accessed February 15, 2018, https://www.ted.com/talks/sandrine_thuret_you_can_grow_new_brain_cells_here_s_how.

15. Eileen Luders, Arthur Toga, Natasha Lepore, Christian Gaser, "The Underlying Anatomical Correlates of Long-Term Meditation: Larger Hippocampal and Frontal Volumes of Gray Matter," *NeuroImage*, vol. 45, issue 3 (2009): 672–678.

16. "How Stress Affects Your Health," American Psychological Association, 2017, accessed February 15, 2018, http://www.apa.org/helpcenter/stress.aspx.

17. University of Bonn, "Anxiety Linked to Blood Clots: Fear That Freezes the Blood in Your Veins," *ScienceDaily*, accessed February 16, 2018, https://www.sciencedaily.com/releases/2008/03/080325111800.htm.

Index

CPSIA information can be obtained
at www.ICGtesting.com
Printed in the USA
LVHW03s0753130818
586654LV00003B/3/P

9 781732 237513